I0128444

THE VALUE
OF COMPARISON

THE LEWIS HENRY MORGAN LECTURES /

A SERIES EDITED BY ROBERT J. FOSTER AND DANIEL R. REICHMAN

PETER VAN DER VEER / THE VALUE OF COMPARISON

With a Foreword by Thomas Gibson

Duke University Press   Durham and London   2016

© 2016 DUKE UNIVERSITY PRESS. All rights reserved

Designed by Courtney Leigh Baker
Typeset in Trade Gothic and Arno Pro by Westchester Publishing Services

Library of Congress Cataloging-in-Publication Data
Names: Veer, Peter van der, [date] author. | Gibson, Th omas, [date] writer of foreword.
Title: Th e value of comparison / Peter van der Veer; with a foreword by Th omas G ibson.
Other titles: Lewis Henry Morgan lectures.
Description: Durham : Duke University Press, 2016. | Series: TheL ewis Henry Morgan lectures | Includes bibliographical references and index.
Identifiers: LCCN 2015043613
ISBN 9780822361398 (hardcover)
ISBN 9780822361589 (pbk.)
ISBN 9780822374220 (e-book)
Subjects: LCSH: Anthropology—China—Comparative method. | Ethnology—China—Comparative method. | Sociology—China—Comparative method. | Anthropology—India—Comparative method. | Ethnology—India—Comparative method. | Sociology—India—Comparative method.
Classifi cation: LCC GN34.3.C58 V447 2016 | DDC 305.80095
LC record available at http://lccn.loc.gov/2015043613

COVER ART: Wang Jinsong, *One Hundred Signs of Demolition*, 1900–1999 (detail). Photographs. Courtesy of the artist.

CONTENTS

A founder of modern cultural anthropology, Lewis Henry Morgan was one of the city of Rochester's most famous intellectual figures. He was also a patron of the University of Rochester and left a substantial bequest to the University for the founding of a women's college. The lectures named in his honor have now been presented annually for over fifty years and constitute the longest running such series in North America. Each lecture is intended to result in the publication of a monograph that embodies some aspect of the current state of anthropological thought.

This book is based on the Lewis Henry Morgan Lecture that Professor Peter van der Veer delivered at the University of Rochester on November 13, 2013. The lecture was followed by a daylong workshop in which members of the Department of Anthropology and a group of invited guests discussed the entire manuscript. We had to cast our net particularly wide in this case because of the ambitious nature of the topic, the value of anthropological comparison, and the wide range of ethnographic examples that were discussed. The formal discussants included Joanne Waghorne and Bethany Lacina on South Asia; Magnus Fiskesjö and Thomas Gibson on Southeast Asia; and Gareth Fisher and John Osburg on East Asia.

In this book, Professor van der Veer argues that many recent attempts at comparison in anthropology have been based on a misplaced quest for generality. This quest may be based on pan-human psychic universals, whether those that, like rational action theory, privilege the Mind, or those that, like cognitive science, privilege the brain; on the mathematical manipulation of sets of "big data" that ignore the relevant conceptual schemes that governed the activities that generated the data in the first place; or on the uncritical extension of Western cultural categories, such as "religion," to social and historical contexts to which they either do not apply or in which they possess very different relationships to other institutions such as the state or the economy.

But while rejecting generalizing forms of comparison, Professor van der Veer insists first that "there is no escape from comparison when we deal with 'other societies'... since we are always already translating into Western languages what we find elsewhere." Second, when we do encounter concepts in other societies that are similar to Western concepts, this is often because they were spread by Western imperialism. But even in this case, the concepts have acquired new meanings as local actors have reinterpreted them under different conditions. It is therefore pointless to try to craft universal definitions of concepts like religion and to assume that we are dealing with the same kind of practice in different situations, even when the practices have the same name. Such practices do not refer to universal attributes of human beings but to historical processes of universalization and particularization that are subject to a balance of forces on a world scale.

In place of the generalism that strives to make statements that are valid for whole societies, nations, or even civilizations, van der Veer advocates the intensive study of fragments of social life like caste, race, or gift exchange. The meaning of these fragments are determined in each case by their relationship to other fragments of social life with which they are intertwined in particular times and places. As this sort of inductive comparison proceeds, it will inevitably lead us to rethink the meaning of the concepts with which we started, and to ask new questions about the way they function in our own society.

The central part of the book consists in a series of comparative analyses of the different places occupied by social fragments such as money, markets, Muslim minorities, iconoclastic movements, mountain tribes, and public sanitation in different parts of Europe, India, Southeast Asia, and China. Professor van der Veer does not approach these regions as coherent "civilizations" defined by simple, unchanging essences. Each region is composed of complex sets of traditions that are engaged in endless internal debates with one another and are endlessly borrowing and translating concepts and practices from other regions around the world.

Given Professor van der Veer's insistence on the need to stay focused on particular ethnographic examples, the best way to characterize his argument as a whole is to provide a brief sketch of the topics he takes on. In chapter 2, he shows that the capitalist financial markets of New York and Hong Kong are as subject to as much "hysteria, panic, and mystery" as the gambling dens of Las Vegas and Macao. In chapter 3, he shows that the Muslim has come to be regarded as the quintessential stranger in China, India, and Europe, but in very different ways and for very different reasons. In chapter 4, he shows that the rise of nationalism in Europe, India, and China targeted certain material symbols of the religious past for iconoclastic destruction. But as long as the religious communities that created these structures in the first place persisted, these movements inevitably failed to achieve the aim of purifying the nation. In chapter 5, he shows that all attempts by authors such as Leach, Friedman, and Scott to explain life in the mountains separating India from China in terms of simple structural models fail because they do not take account of the complex and fragmentary nature of the actual history of this region. In chapter 6, he compares the way middle-class attitudes toward the descendants of slaves in the United States and of peasants in China shifted in such a way that the state came to take responsibility for the public hygiene of all citizens. By contrast, the persistence of hierarchical attitudes toward the descendants of "untouchable" bonded laborers in India has prevented the state from instituting effective public hygiene measures in the slums that surround middle-class housing.

Professor van der Veer makes a sustained argument for tempering the thirst for generality with the rigorous analysis of particular ethnographic situations, and for using those analyses to critique our own traditions of thought for the errors of ethnocentrism and essentialism. This book thus constitutes a spirited defense of the continuing relevance of the comparative project of anthropology for both the humanistic and the quantitative social sciences. It also serves as a reminder of the ethical responsibility of all those who study the human condition to subject their own categories and practices to continuous critique.

—THOMAS GIBSON
Editor (2007–2013),
Lewis Henry Morgan Lecture Series

ACKNOWLEDGMENTS

The Lewis Henry Morgan Lectures of 2013 were given just a few weeks before the birth of my twins, Linh and Koos, and are thus indelibly connected in my mind to that joyful event. I deeply appreciate the opportunity to organize my thoughts on the importance of comparison in anthropology and on the unique contribution of anthropology to the social sciences. Tom Gibson extended the original invitation to give the lectures on comparison, and he, Robert Foster, and the rest of the Anthropology Department at the University of Rochester have been extremely welcoming and supportive. Magnus Fiskesjö from Cornell University and Joanne Waghorne and Gareth Fisher from Syracuse University were among the specialists invited to comment on my presentations. Graduate students from the University of Rochester, Columbia University, Cornell University, and the University of Chicago also participated in the discussion. I have greatly benefited from their contributions.

Parts of the book have also been presented to audiences at Minzu University in Beijing, Yunnan Academy of Social Sciences in Kunming, the University of Cambridge, the University of Chicago, the National University of Singapore, Boston University, and the New School for Social Research in New York. I want to thank the participants in these discussions for their comments. An earlier version of chapter 2 appeared in *Social Compass* 59, no. 2 (June 2012). A special thanks goes to Professor Wu Da, at Minzu University, who has been my host and guide on a number of occasions. I have been involved in a number of larger comparative projects, one of which is the comparative study of religion in Asian cities (Mumbai, Singapore,

Shanghai, and Seoul), which was partly supported by a grant from the Korean Academy.

I have been fortunate to have had many conversations on the topic of the book with the extraordinary group of scholars that is collected at the Max Planck Institute for the Study of Religious and Ethnic Diversity in Göttingen. I want to single out Nate Roberts for his generous, scholarly, and always extremely helpful advice. Also I want to thank Steve Vertovec, my codirector at the Max Planck Institute, whose collegial presence has in many ways enabled me to do my work. In Göttingen and elsewhere (Singapore, Xiamen), Kenneth Dean has given me the benefit of his immense scholarship and equally valuable friendship. Chris Fuller, an old friend, has gone over the text and has pointed out several deficiencies and problems. I am very grateful for the time he spent on it, although I have not been able to answer everything satisfactorily.

At Duke University Press the book was read by two anonymous reviewers who have given me extremely helpful and generous comments. Ken Wissoker steered the process in a very friendly and efficient manner. The final production of the book was helped by my secretaries, Jie Zhang and Julia Müller.

This book could not have been written without my wife, Tam Ngo, who has introduced me to many aspects of social life in Southeast and East Asia that I reflect on in this book. I am deeply grateful for her presence in my life.

As is well known, Lewis Henry Morgan contributed substantially to the study of kinship and of social evolution. Today Morgan is still a household name among Chinese anthropologists, thanks to the influence he had on Marx and Engels. It is an irony of history that the ghost of Morgan, a brilliant capitalist, still haunts the academic institutions of Communist China. Morgan's thought has become part of Marxist orthodoxy and thus fundamental for the Communist Party's approach to minorities in China. The Han majority was seen in evolutionary terms as more advanced than the minorities, a theory well suited to earlier civilizational perspectives. Superior in its material civilization (agriculture) the Han had the historical task of leading the minorities to higher development. Fei Xiaotong, one of the fathers of Chinese anthropology, still asserted this theory in the 1980s, and it continues to be one of the pillars of Chinese policy toward nationalities.[1] Fei argues in his Tanner Lectures that an ethnic group, first known as Hua Xia and later as Han, who lived in the Yellow River area in Central China, expanded from this area by absorbing other groups. This became the nucleus of "the Chinese people." The name *Han* came from the Han dynasty, but only after the ethnicity had already been formed. Fei thus proposes a theory of gradual absorption, partly by expansion by the Han and partly by absorption of non-Han peoples who had conquered Han areas but adopted Han names. Fei's explanation of this successful expansion and absorption is the following: "What, then, has made the Hans a nucleus with such centripetal force? The main factor, in my view, has been their agricultural economy. Once a nomadic tribe made its entry into the plains and found itself in the midst of the careful, orderly society of farmers, most of the nomads would eventually throw themselves all too voluntarily into the embrace of the Hans." When Fei moves from his historical exposé to contemporary ethnic policy (that he helped to develop) he argues that "the policy is for the better-developed groups to help the underdeveloped ones by furnishing economic and cultural aid." His entirely apolitical view of the processes involved is best illustrated by the following comment on the last page of his lectures: "The Tibetans, for example, who are used to living and working at high altitudes, can play a major role in the effort to develop the economy on the highlands, while cooperating and exchanging with other ethnic groups for the ultimate purpose of general prosperity."[2]

Outside of China, evolutionary comparisons of contemporary societies have become widely discredited, at least in academic discourse, although, as I will show, evolutionary perspectives in relation to cognitive science have again come into vogue. This rejection of evolutionism should, however, not lead to a rejection of comparison. The main purpose of this book is to show the value of anthropological comparisons that are not grounded in evolutionary theory, through essays on topics as varied as iconoclasm, urban poverty, social exclusion, and mountain people. The case material for the comparative essays presented here is taken from work done in India and China. That material is only partly ethnographic. Much of it provides an anthropological lens on historical material. The connection laid between anthropology and history is certainly not new. It has its ancestral roots in the work of the French school, including Marcel Mauss, Marcel Granet, Georges Dumézil, and later Louis Dumont. This is the basis of Marcel Detienne's passionate plea for comparison between contemporary and past societies and for connecting anthropology and history.[3] Such a plea, though with a somewhat different genealogy and execution, is also made in the journal *Comparative Studies in Society and History*, and for India in the work of Bernard Cohn.[4] It has inspired my comparative work on Britain and India as well as that on India and China. In this book the focus is on the problematic notion of civilization that informs issues like social inequality, ethnicity and nationalism, representation, and religion.

One of the previous Morgan lecturers, Ward Goodenough, who recently passed away and who was in the late eighties my (very senior) colleague at the University of Pennsylvania, delivered the Lewis Henry Morgan Lectures in 1968 on the topic "Description and Comparison in Cultural Anthropology." Goodenough argued that the description of the basic emic categories, primarily those of kinship, that one's informants used could be used to reconstruct their culture, as if it was a language. This reconstruction then could be the basis of comparison in the service of generalized knowledge. Description is a means to the end of generalization by way of comparison. This research program came under heavy critique in the 1980s. Generalization from fieldwork seemed no longer feasible, and the main task of anthropology became description. As Ladislav Holy observes, "the word *comparison* itself has completely disappeared from the vocabulary of methodological discourse."[5] In Holy's view, "the high value ascribed to non-comparative analytical description reflects the redefinition of anthropology as an interpretative humanity concerned with cultural specificity and cultural diversity, rather than as a generalizing science."[6] What Holy sees as the remaining possibility of a comparative approach in a humanistic interpretative anthropology that emphasizes description of specificity is to search for formal principles of human cognition. This is a move that was fundamental to structuralism, but it has been highly stimulated over the last two decades by advances in cognitive psychology and brain research. Some of those who developed symbolic anthropology under the influence of structuralism, like Dan Sperber and Maurice Bloch, have come more and more under the influence of cognitive science. Others, like Marshal Sahlins, though equally influenced by structuralism, have rejected the sociobiology that underlies much of the combination of anthropology and cognitive science. Again others, like Harvey Whitehouse, have embraced sociobiology by arguing that "anthropology should be to the cognitive sciences what fieldwork is to experimental primatology."[7] Since Whitehouse seems to represent an extreme case of enthusiasm for cognitive sciences among anthropologists, we may have a look at some of his ideas. In a recent article, Whitehouse and Cohen want to show the importance of anthropology to the study of cognitive evolution by focusing on group synchronous activity (like singing or dancing) in explaining human cooperation. While the idea that anthropology should play a role in the development of a multidisciplinary study of human cognition is correct, the focus on singing and dancing might fall short in explaining human cooperation. The authors propose to reduce the various forms of human cohesion to two types, "the one small-scale uniting face-to-face communities and the other large-scale uniting 'imagined communities,'" and argue that "these divergent patterns of group formation are a consequence of the frequency and emotionality of ritual performances."[8] This proposal most certainly does not help in providing an explanation of human cooperation. Using the Human Relations Area Files and coding 644 rituals from seventy-four language groups, Whitehouse and Cohen come to the astonishing conclusion that "groups with high frequency/low-arousal rituals tend to be much larger than groups with low frequency/dysphoric rituals." What could this possibly mean? One could perhaps say that this finding seems to be confirmed, for instance, by the ethnographic descriptions of the small-scale society of the Marind-Anim, where initiation rituals in New Guinea are anxiety producing and intense and happen only when a group of youngsters comes of age.[9] And, in contrast, by the fact that the Catholic Mass is happening every Sunday and appears to be less intense, although one does remember that in Europe pogroms often happened after the celebration of Easter (but once a year and thus low frequency, although not entirely dysphoric). But what about Hindu death rituals or Daoist possession cults, or Korean shamanistic performances? In fact, we have such a wide variety of practices that we put in the container category "ritual," and indeed such a wide variety of societal forms, that the attempt by Whitehouse and Cohen to reduce them to two types that are correlated with two types of societies seems absurd. More than of the precise linguistic descriptions of Ward Goodenough, it reminds one of the sweeping materialist evolutionism of Marvin Harris but this time with a focus on mental processes and emotions (thanks to the cognitive sciences) instead of material conditions.[10] There is a seemingly indomitable desire for generalization in the name of theory that has revived an interest in large data-sets, such as the Human Relations Area Files, that were started by Murdoch in the 1950s but became unconvincing after the rise of Geertzian interpretive anthropology. Geertz's critique of "common-denominators of culture" is that it should demand "that the universals proposed be substantial ones and not empty categories; (2) that they be specifically grounded in particular, psychological, or sociological processes, not just vaguely associated with 'underlying realities'; and (3) that they can convincingly be defended as core elements in a definition of humanity in comparison with which the much more numerous cultural particularities are of clearly secondary importance. On all three of these counts it seems to me that the *consentium gentum* approach fails; rather than moving toward the essentials of the human situation, it moves away from them."[11] This critique is still fully valid and does not imply that anthropology is not scientific in its pursuit of detailed particularities. However, it does imply that the rise of the cognitive sciences, largely enabled by new (less intrusive) observational techniques, while of great importance, cannot be expected to answer many of the important questions that are asked in anthropology (not yet, and maybe never). Both Freud and Lévi-Strauss believed that a science of society and of the mind would ultimately rest on an understanding of the brain, and there are good reasons for believing that, but as of now there is hardly a productive way brain research can be connected to the interpretation of ethnographic materials. Our human nature is shared, but our languages, beliefs, practices are immensely diverse.

On the other hand, there is also no reason to essentialize cultural differences, as is done in the recent assumption of radical ontologies. Philippe Descola, for instance, comes up with a fourfold taxonomy of ontologies, differentiated in their assumptions of physicality (what is believed about bodies) and interiority (feelings and beliefs both inside oneself and in relation to other intentional beings).[12] The problem with this kind of taxonomy is that it captures only part of what is clearly in most societies a debate about relations between humans and things that is constantly changing, and not a characterization of an entire culture's way of thinking. For example, Buddhism's emphasis on ahimsa (not killing, not harming) emerges in the context of a radical critique of Brahman sacrifice but never comes to dominate the debate entirely, so that several ontological options remain available. There is certainly no sense that the participants in such debates cannot understand each other because of the radical differences in their ontologies. In fact, structuralist approaches have never shown much interest in the historical and fragmented debates that characterize society.

Surely there is a coherence in cultural debate, and there are great and sometimes fundamental differences between the kinds of debates that are going on, for example, among the ancient Greeks and the ancient Chinese. As the classicist G. E. R. Lloyd, who tries to compare these two worldviews, helpfully puts it: where the Greeks would have seen things, the Chinese would have seen events.[13] This quite substantial philosophical difference does not prevent us, however, from understanding both points of view and even choosing between them. At the same time one needs to recognize that Lloyd may overstretch his point, as not all Greeks see "things" instead of "events," since the processual nature of things is also emphasized by some Greeks as in the famous *panta rhei*, everything flows. While these are internal debates in civilizations, it is the characteristic of our common age that we are more than ever interacting with different worldviews in shared spaces. While there is quite a scope for misunderstanding and error, this does not seem to be an obstacle to many forms of communication, such as travel and trade. Philosophical arguments within civilizations like China or Greece should not be taken to characterize the entirety of these civilizations, since they are often only held by some social actors and always subject to debate.

Surely, the sinologist Edward Slingerland is right in arguing that the early Chinese did not lack concepts of body-mind dualism but wrong in thinking that he has found anything significant.[14] His entire debunking of the way leading sinologists have assumed a radical difference between Western (dualist) and Chinese (holistic) thought by showing evidence that dualism also existed in China is based on the premise that one can reduce complex arguments to simple oppositions. What is understood as "mind" or "body" has been subject to much too complex arguments in both the West and in China to be simply captured under the terms *holism* or *dualism*. It cannot be a surprise to anyone that Chinese make a difference between the living and the dead and that Confucius, cited by Slingerland, thinks that the dead have lost something that is basic (*ben*本). That this implies that Confucius made a sharp distinction between body and mind is an altogether unsupported claim by Slingerland and can only be argued by a deep hermeneutical engagement with the Confucian corpus. Slingerland, however, has opted for a radically different approach, namely to get rid of possible bias in selecting our textual evidence by "a keyword-focused random sampling of passages from the pre-Qin corpus."[15]

To me this describes the problem of abstract generalization in a nutshell. Slingerland seems to think that one can get at the meaning of a textual corpus by selecting one term (in this case, "heart," 心) and mechanically coding it in its relation to, say, the body. If this would get us at the development of early Chinese thinking it would be great, but in fact it only gets us at a corroboration of Slingerland's theory of mind, which indicates a universal human propensity that ascribes intentionality to mind-possessing agents and mindless things. In short, the Chinese also have a Mind. This does away with the intricate arguments in philosophical texts in the West and in China about "intentionality" that are unresolved and thus still engage us,[16] not to mention the anthropological complications in interpreting ritual practices in both the West and China.

This book makes the claim that it is fruitful to continue the comparative approach initiated a century ago by Mauss and Weber without striving for unified theories.[17] It resists the growing tendency to define science as a method of model making based on variables and quantitative samples and to portray ethnography and historical sociology as "unscientific" since they do not strive for generality. Many of these battles have been fought before, but the ascendancy of model making in sociology and of cognitive evolutionism in anthropology make them again inevitable. My own work over the last decades on nationalism and religion raises the issue of "generality" also at another level, since both nationalism and religion are totalizing ideologies.[18] The difficulties are both at the level of the object of study and at the level of method and theoretical representation. For instance, Partha Chatterjee has eloquently shown the contradictory fragments that constitute anticolonial nationalism in Bengal, but his neat division of spiritual and material domains in nationalist imaginations again ends up reifying structural oppositions.[19] In the face of such ideologies, one needs to make an extra effort to capture how removed they are from the much more fragmented and contradictory realities people inhabit. Obviously, this is in itself a general claim and, just as obviously, one constantly makes general claims. This, however, is different from the demand that a case study of, say, a particular region of China should be generalizable to all of China if it is to be of any value. It might be more important to show the region's specific differences from other parts of China. To give an ethnographic example, the sinologist Kenneth Dean has in a number of important publications on his fieldwork in Putian, a region in Fujian (Southwest China), shown the existence of a regional system of ritual alliances that seems to have connected the region more with Southeast Asia than with Central China.[20] This evidence goes against the grain in Chinese studies toward showing a Confucian civilization that unifies all of China. It is not that such regions are entirely separated from the rest of the Mainland, but the point is that they are in conversation with the rest without being assimilated or entirely unified. In one of the rituals that Dean shows in a recent documentary, a Confucian master is incorporated in local ritual instead of local ritual being incorporated in the Confucian worldview.[21] Often such diversity is only recognized in the case of ethnic minorities, but the Putianese are so-called Han, although they speak a language that is entirely unintelligible for Mandarin-speakers or Minnanhua-speakers who live in adjacent regions. Again, one can see the power of ideologies of unity that are replicated in scholarly work.

Assumptions of civilizational unity are also found in the study of India. The caste system has been often understood as a "system" that integrates a wide variety of peoples with different languages and practices. Again, a number of historical studies have shown that while there are castes everywhere in India, it is hard to see it as an integrated system that organizes Indian society as a whole.[22] There is not such a system, and principles of kinship and value intersect with structures of opportunity and mobility to produce "castes" like Rajputs and Brahmans. Today's India shows a highly diversified picture in which caste, class, regional identity, and transnational mobility are combined with Hindu nationalism to reproduce inequality in education, health, social services, and, ultimately, politics. Similarly, the idea that Sanskrit civilization provides unity has been argued, for instance by M. N. Srinivas, but has also shown to be highly ideological and "a view from above" that discounts the great differences in Sanskrit traditions that have developed in different parts of India.

My own work has focused on India for a long time but has over the last few years developed a comparative perspective on India and China. This kind of work is "secondary," in the sense that it tries to make sense of a wide variety of arguments by historians and anthropologists without going into the interpretation of primary sources and fieldwork data, unless one's own fieldwork or historical research contributes significantly to the problem selected. The growth of specialist knowledge on these societies has grown exponentially since Weber wrote his studies in the early twentieth century, and the Weberian comparative enterprise to discover the unique features of Western historical developments has been replaced by a noncomparative urge to make sense of national societies on their own. The marginalization of comparative analysis is particularly glaring in history, the national discipline par excellence.[23] However, it has also become glaring in anthropology, which was supposed to be comparative from its beginning. As I will argue at some length later in the book, there is no escape from comparison when we deal with "other societies" as historical sociologists or anthropologists, since we are always already translating into Western languages what we find elsewhere, using concepts that are derived from Western historical experience to interpret other societies and other histories. It is therefore necessary to engage one's implicit comparison and make it more explicit. At another level, comparison should highlight certain aspects of a society that are not given enough attention by specialists and are highlighted by the study of another society. India and China are huge agrarian societies with deep civilizational histories that go through similar transformations in the interaction with modern Western imperialisms. The pathways and solutions chosen by actors in these societies are very different, and their comparison helps us to understand them better, namely as historical options rather than the inevitable outcomes of their cultures. My work seeks to help develop a historical sociology that applies an anthropological perspective and is based on historical materials as well as fieldwork that raises new questions and highlights differential patterns and their causes.

At this point let me summarize briefly what is in my view the comparative advantage of anthropology in the pursuit of cultural comparisons, which I will seek to demonstrate and illustrate in the rest of the book:

—Anthropology is primarily an engagement with "difference" and "diversity" and focuses on problems of cultural translation. As such it offers a critique of the universalization of Western models and provides thus a basis for a comparative historical sociology. Ethnographical data derived from fieldwork form a big part of anthropology, but the study of other kinds of material, historical, textual, and visual, also benefits from an anthropological perspective.

—A necessarily fragmentary approach to social life, in which the intensive study of a fragment is used to gain a perspective on a larger whole, offers a greater potential for social science than the analysis of large data, undergirded by game theory and rational choice theory. In chapter 2 I will seek to substantiate this claim, and in the rest of the book I will illustrate it with a number of examples. One should not confuse this attention to "the micro" with any form of methodological individualism that assumes that "the macro" emerges from the actions and motivations of individual actors. The study of a fragment cannot be generalized to the level of "society as a whole" or to Weberian "ideal-types." The construction of the individual as a rational actor in order to be able to make large-scale generalizations is part of a modern ideology of individualism and the very opposite of a comparative approach as proposed here.

—What I will call *generalism*, namely the assumption of the integration of nations and civilizations or the assumption of society as an integrated whole is different from anthropological *holism*, which implies the drawing of larger inferences from the intensive study of fragments of social life. The latter approach derives from Durkheim's emphasis of studying "social facts," which he conceived to be different from other facts, and especially from Mauss's focus on the "total social fact," which is simultaneously legal, economic, religious, and political. Mauss's famous example of such a "total social fact" is "gift-exchange," a phenomenon that he used to elucidate important aspects of social life by comparing a number of very different societies. The other major inspiration is Weber, who tried to understand the specificity of historical developments through comparison.

—Anthropology has always taken the body (its symbolism, its functions, its gender) as a focal point of the study of society. However, from Durkheim onward, the anthropological contribution to the study of embodied practice emphasizes the social and provides a critique of sociobiological determinism by showing how it is full of modern Euro-American prejudice. An anthropological emphasis on "the body" and its disciplining requires an attention to configurations of power that cannot be replaced by psychological experiments or tests.

From a methodological point of view, the intensive study of a slice of human reality in relation to what Durkheim calls "the representation" of that slice allows one to question many assumptions that come out of the preoccupations of Western common sense. For instance, as Webb Keane demonstrates, the conceptualization of the relation between humans and material objects in Sumba, Indonesia, is so radically different from how Calvinist missionaries understand this relation that the conversion process is one of constant miscommunication and translation.[24] If that slice can capture immediate attention of a general audience (say, Chinese gamblers in Macao and their notions of "good fortune" and speculation), anthropology approximates investigative journalism in observation and description, but the difference lies in anthropology's conceptual contribution to deeper interpretations of risk and uncertainty as aspects of larger cultural wholes. Some contemporary work, like the sociologist Eric Klinenberg's writing on a heat wave in Chicago or on Hurricane Sandy in New York, is good journalism, but what makes it also good sociology is that it proposes some theoretical understandings of the social responses to climate challenges.[25] Comparative sociology comes in when one goes beyond the analysis of American responses to climate challenges and compares it to, say, responses to earthquakes in Turkey, Iran, or China. What I would see as the anthropological contribution is the analysis of grief, pain, and lament as part of a holistic interpretation of what is, variably, seen as the divide between nature and society and between human agency and "acts of God" in different societies. A good ethnographic example is Eric Mueggler's work on the ways a Yi community in Southwest China deals with a history of violent state formation, focusing on "rotating headman-ship," a major political aspect of Yi society. Mueggler is able to show the poetics of local memory that summons up and exorcises the terror of the past.[26] Obviously, nobody would claim that this picture would be generalizable to China as a whole or even the Yi as a whole. That is clearly not the purpose of this kind of work, which nevertheless provides the reader with a penetrating account of a local understanding of historical events like the Great Cultural Revolution. What larger problem is addressed through one's study depends on the fragment one focuses on and the research questions one asks. For example, Jonathan Parry's excellent ethnography of Hindu death rituals cannot be used to explain the rise of Hindu nationalism, but it gives us an important picture of ideas of death and regeneration of life in India that are comparable with ideas and practices elsewhere.[27]

Comparison is, in my view, in the first place a question not of the right research design, the correct choice of cases to be compared (the "what" and "how" to compare), although this is obviously important, but of an awareness of the conceptual difficulties in entering "other" life worlds. That "otherness" should not be exaggerated, since everyone is in some way interacting and communicating with everyone else. Moreover, anthropology is highly equipped to engage problems of translation and of bridging different semantic universes. Its contribution is therefore not to utter always the qualifier *but* when social scientists are generalizing, but rather to contribute to radically new and open ways of understanding reality. This is an uphill struggle and against the spirit of the time (Zeitgeist), which is deeply convinced of universality and generalizability and the ultimate genetic basis of all and everything. Nevertheless, it is a struggle worth pursuing.

What would be an example of a "fragmentary approach" that allows us to ask questions about a larger whole? It might be helpful for the reader if I give a concrete example. I am inspired here by Sydney Mintz's brilliant exposé of the story of sugar, which connects a seemingly marginal commodity (a fragment of social reality) to the emergence of world capitalism, including the production of sugar in plantations across the world and the increasing use of sugar in Britain. Given my interest in the comparative analysis of India and China, it would be tea and opium that could provide such an example.

When I came to North India in the early 1970s I drank a lot of tea. Tea was available everywhere. It was cooked with milk and sugar and thus pretty nutritious. In fact, in my fieldwork it was the breakfast that my host served me every morning at 6 a.m. and the only thing I would get till 11 or 12 a.m., when the first meal (of two) was served. Alcohol was not available in the Hindu pilgrimage center where I did my fieldwork.[28] More in general, drinking alcohol was a thing for men in secluded booths or at private parties and mostly not social, but to get drunk. It was also seen as a foreign thing. In my first passport I had a license to buy alcohol in the dry (alcohol-free) state of Tamil Nadu, mentioning that I as a foreigner needed alcohol. For the rest, drinking country liquor (and smoking *beedi*) was for the lowest castes, and my Brahman hosts in North India frowned on it. They would see it as habits that belonged to lower natures and would reproduce lower natures. So tea was the drink, and it was safe, because it was cooked. Only once in a while *sharbat* would be served, a sweet rosewater drink, or some fizzy soft drink like Limca. Coca-Cola was banned in the 1970s, as it is again in some Indian states today. Since tea was the only available real universal social drink (coffee was only served in elite coffeehouses for men in cities), I took it for granted that it had been in India forever. Moreover, I was aware that tea was produced in Assam, Darjeeling, and Ceylon, since we drank tea with those names in Holland. I never wondered why Indians mostly used the relatively cheap British tea brand Lipton.

These days of naiveté are over. I now realize that the tea with sugar that I drank at home in Holland had only become popular in the eighteenth century and that the quintessential British ritual of afternoon tea is of similar recent vintage. Tea plantations in India were started by the East India Company in the 1820s to break the monopoly of the Chinese and to produce tea for British consumption. Only in postcolonial India did tea become the widespread drink that I found in the 1970s. Today, 70 percent of India's huge tea production is consumed in India itself; it is hard to imagine India without tea. But it is even harder to imagine that it is such a recent phenomenon.

China's tea is a whole other story. Tea is made from the young leaves of what were originally trees that were for production reasons reduced to shrubs. There are all kinds of speculation about the origins and development of tea ("bitter drink," called *tu* or *ming*). The historian Barend ter Haar argues that in the eighth century tea became a replacement for alcohol in the context of the rise of Buddhism (propagating *bujiu* 不酒, do not drink, alongside *busha* 捕杀, do not kill) and of the emergence of the imperial exams, where one needed to keep oneself awake.[29] Tea's popularity grew to the extent that it became a major part of the tributary system. That tea is a useful alternative to alcohol is clear to anyone who has visited China, but how successful an alternative it is seems less clear. I have not participated in a banquet in which tea has replaced alcohol, although women are allowed to stick to tea, and my recollection of visiting several Yi groups in Sichuan is blurred and soaked in alcohol. Men can hardly refuse to drink alcohol if they want to show themselves to be masculine and trustworthy partners in an exchange, while women have an easier time.

Anyway, this is the baked cha that we know as tea today, and obviously besides smoothening social relations it has all kinds of medicinal purpose and effects (different teas, different effects). Whatever the case may be, tea is a Chinese commodity that became highly sought after by Western seafaring nations in the seventeenth and eighteenth centuries and most prominently by the British after they had defeated Dutch sea power at the end of the eighteenth century. Before that, the Dutch had been the most important tea traders, and tea is still an important drink in Holland. After that, Britannia ruled the waves and the tea. Tea was the most important item in the China trade, and since the Chinese did not need much from Britain in exchange, it was paid for with silver. Sidney Mintz observes that tea, coffee, and chocolate were all introduced in the third quarter of the seventeenth century, but the British contribution was to add sugar to these bitter substances.[30] He suggests that tea absorbed sugar more readily than coffee and that was the reason that the sugar planters promoted tea. It is indeed striking how much tea came to define British drinking habits much more than it did Continental ones. The Germans, French, and Italians prefer to drink coffee. Tea in Britain was at first expensive and only drunk by the elite, but gradually in the eighteenth century the working classes, who had beer as their regular beverage and source of nutrition, also became hooked. The government levied taxes on tea, and this became a major source of income. In Britain tea became a substantial part of the economy (much less so in China). Tea was 80 percent of the British East India Company's turnover. Mintz shows how dramatically sugar and tea changed the drinking and food habits of the British, but also how crucial these imports from the tropics were in the transformation of Britain's economy. At the same time he shows the rise of an entirely new labor regime, built on slavery, to produce sugar. Consumption and production go hand and hand. Here is a powerful quote from William Ukers, a historian of tea and coffee, about the British East India Company:

> Its early adventures in the Far East brought it to China, whose tea was destined later to furnish the means of governing India. During the heyday of its prosperity John Company maintained a monopoly of the tea trade with China, controlled the supply, limited the quantity imported into England, and thus fixed the price. It constituted not only the world's greatest tea monopoly but also the source of inspiration for the first English propaganda on behalf of a beverage. It was so powerful that it precipitated dietetic revolution in England, changing the British people from a nation of potential coffee drinkers to a nation of tea drinkers, and all within the space of a few years. It was a formidable rival of states and empires, with power to acquire territory, coin money, command fortresses and troops, form alliances, make war and peace, and exercise both civil and criminal jurisdiction.[31]

The trade imbalance between Britain and China was, obviously, something the British tried to change, especially with the exponential growth of the tea trade. The solution was opium, which was grown in India after it had come more and more under the control of the British, who had defeated the French. The Qing government had forbidden the sale of opium and tried to stop British illegal trade. The 20,283 boxes of opium that the Qing official Lin Zexu ordered to be thrown into the ocean in 1839 (the cause of the First Opium War) had an estimated value of $9 million. After the opium wars, importation increased, for example, to sixty thousand boxes in 1860. Already between 1830 and 1860 the value of the opium exported to China was larger than the value of the tea and silk imported from China.[32] In 1833 the British government took over the opium monopoly from John Company.

Famously, the Qing government did not think that China needed any imports from outside China, as illustrated in the following quotation from a letter sent by Emperor Qianlong to King George III: "Our heavenly Kingdom has everything that it needs in abundance and there is no lack of any products within its boundaries. Therefore there is no need to import goods from Barbarians in exchange for our goods."[33] It is less clear and a subject of considerable debate among economic historians how much the Qing economy needed silver from Britain. Whatever may have been the case, the flow of silver to China came to an end with the growing exchange of opium for tea.

British trade and imperial expansion went hand in hand. The First Opium War was planned by the trader William Jardine of the opium importing firm Jardine, Matheson, and Company. Jardine directly advised Palmerston in 1839–40 how to conduct the war. On the Chinese side, trading guilds (Hong) were active but less able to influence state policies. While in Britain the tax on tea was a considerable part of the state's income, such tax was very marginal in China. The Daoguang emperor blocked the use of a harbor in Fujian, where most of the tea came from, although that would have made costs ten times lower, and therefore everything was shipped via Kanton until the First Opium War. The purpose of that war was to force the Chinese to open more harbors close to the places of production. At the same time, the British developed plans to circumvent the Chinese monopoly on growing tea by starting plantations in Assam. They used indentured labor under penal sanction, which Hugh Tinker has called "a new system of slavery" and, which after the abolition of slavery, came to characterize not only plantations in Assam but plantations all over the British Empire.[34] The Indian populations one finds today in Mauritius, Fiji, the Guyanas, Trinidad, Kenya, Uganda, and South Africa are largely descendants of these indentured laborers. This was totally different from the small family businesses that grew tea in China. It was therefore the British imperial system that led to plantations and the conditions of slavery, not the cash crop itself.[35] In general, small farmers remained dominant in China until the twentieth century, as is still observable in the tea-growing area of Anxi in Fujian.

Despite the creation of tea plantations in India and Ceylon, the British still needed increasing imports of tea from China and wanted to pay for it with opium from India. Opium was produced in Bengal and Bihar (called Patna opium) and in West India (called Malwa opium). Besides raw cotton and later cotton yarn, it was the most important export item to China. Since the trade in opium was forbidden by the Qing government, both Indian and British private traders played a significant role. The Indian ports were Calcutta and Bombay. The Indian traders were mostly Parsis, Jains, and Hindu Marwaris, as well as some Baghdadi Jews, like David Sassoon and his sons, who were to play a significant role in the rise not only of colonial Bombay but also of Shanghai. The first Bombay traders to go to China were the Jivanjis, who adopted the surname Readymoney. Many of the big merchant families of today's Bombay, like the Wadias and the Tatas, built their fortune in the China trade. In Bombay, the Parsi merchant Jamsethjee Jeejeebhoy had a special relation with the aforementioned William Jardine, the architect of the First Opium War. Jamsethjee built a fleet of cargo ships to serve the trade, and in 1842 he was knighted for his leadership in business and philanthropy.[36]

As argued before, Indians did not drink tea but slowly got hooked on it during the nineteenth century and became the world's largest tea producers. Indians did know opium, but I have never come across any research showing that opium was a big problem in India. When I did my fieldwork, there was opium available in government-run shops, as was hashish. The anthropologist McKim Marriott has a hilarious account of the Holi (spring) festival that is Bakhtinian in nature; he was given *bhang* (milk laced with hashish) and consequently was unable to write any field notes.[37] Despite this widespread use of intoxicants, I have never encountered a widespread problem with it. The great addiction is alcohol. General consensus has it that opium addiction was a huge problem for the Chinese and that it was created by the British to solve their trade imbalance with China. However, in Frank Dikötter's engaging inaugural lecture at the School of Oriental and African Studies in London, he calls China "Patient Zero" of opium addiction and then goes on to bust the myth of China's opium addiction.[38]

In nineteenth-century England opium and laudanum were used against pain. It was not seen as causing widespread addiction, and in fact people could use it in regular quantities throughout life without creating addiction. This was also the case in China, as Dikötter argues: "Men and women would smoke a pipe or two at festivals and ceremonies several times a year without ever becoming regular users. R. A. Jamieson, a doctor in Shanghai, noted at the end of the nineteenth century that if those who smoked a few pipes on the occasion of a festival such as a marriage were to be counted, few adult males could be excluded, although regular consumers were very rare. A British consul based in Hainan also reported that "although nearly everyone uses it . . . one never meets the opium-skeleton so vividly depicted in philanthropic works, rather the reverse—a hardy peasantry, healthy and energetic."[39]

Dikötter argues that the wide spread of opium (鸦片, *yapian*) in China from the eighteenth century depended on smoking. Tobacco, found in America and introduced in China in the late sixteenth century, became the

ideal companion of tea (烟茶, *yancha*). Opium was for a time laced with tobacco, but this combination was dropped later. To smoke pure Patna opium
from expensive pipes became a sign of high status and wealth. Smoking was
a social experience, and opium houses, like teahouses, were sites of male
sociability. The other reason to use opium was medicinal, as in England,
against fever and especially diarrhea. If it was so harmless, why did it
become the object of narcophobia? For this Dikötter suggests a Foucauld-
ian theory, pointing at the rise of the medical profession, which wanted to
monopolize opium, and the emergence of anti-imperial nationalism with
its discourse of enslavement and physical weakness. In the 1940s, however,
the Communists in Yan'an still used the opium production and trade to
finance its struggle against the Kuomintang, but once they gained power in
1949, they stamped it out in three years. Cigarette smoking, however, was
stimulated. Not by chance, therefore, China is now the world's leading tobacco producer and consumer. Dikötter's debunking story of narcophobia
is entertaining and partly persuasive, but he underestimates the ravaging
effects of opiates on some parts of the population.[40] It is difficult to produce
a seamless narrative of the pathways of opium.

What to make of these stories of tea and opium? A political economy
narrative seems the most convincing and rather obvious. Sidney Mintz is
the pioneer of such a narrative, which focuses on sugar and world capitalism. The commodity shapes the nature of production and consumption
and connects worlds that were hitherto unconnected. The meanings given
to such a commodity are secondary to the force of capital. Whatever disputes about details there may be, this is a compelling narrative, but it does
not satisfy, for it gives us no access to the ways people shaped their understanding of these world historical processes. This is precisely Marshall
Sahlins's critique of the "mode of production" approach in Eric Wolf's celebrated *Europe and the People without History*.[41] Sahlins examines the indeed
quite fascinating refusal of the Qing emperors to be impressed or interested
in the products of the British, thus only accepting silver in exchange for
tea.[42]

As is typical of Sahlins's approach to intercultural encounters, he emphasizes worldviews and thus focuses on the Qing understanding of Lord
Macartney's visit to the Chinese emperor. According to Sahlins, the emperor had indeed everything in his *yuanmingyuan* (圆明园, gardens of perfect brightness) at the old summer palace, which was partly destroyed in
1860 during the Second Opium War. This was a huge curiosities cabinet like

the ones princes had in Europe, but much bigger. This was the collection of tributes that signified the sovereign power over the world that was enjoyed by the emperor. As Sahlins sees it, "by setting China apart while at the same time making it the central source of world order, this theory of civilization lends itself equally to projects of imperial expansion and cultural withdrawal, to hegemonic inclusions or xenophobic exclusions, according to the contingencies of the situation."[43] It was not that the Qing were "self-sufficient" but that they found the barbarians too far away and thus too difficult to control.

What we have here in Sahlins's analysis are different cosmologies that clash. In work done by James Hevia and others, this cosmological analysis is complemented by an interpretation of ritual performance, centering on the question whether Lord Macartney had performed the *koutou* (kowtow). Hevia focuses on the "guest ritual" (宾礼, *binli*), which itself is the basis of power, as in Geertz's beautiful summation of Balinese politics: "Power serves pomp, not pomp power."[44] Where Sahlins puts the emphasis on cosmology, Hevia puts the emphasis on ritual (*li*), but, as both authors would probably agree, these two belong to each other. In the cultural theorist Lydia Liu's interpretation of the Treaty of Tianjin after the Second Opium War in 1858, the emphasis is on the translation of the word *yi* (夷), which the British insisted referred to barbarians, while the Chinese insisted that it only referred to non-Han people.[45] This can help us to see that what we have here are not just incommensurable ontologies, but in fact communications, negotiations, and trading commodities, while trading insults. It all has to do with notions of hierarchy and precedence, but these notions are not independent of power relations. On both the Qing and the British sides, "honor" and hierarchy played an important role, but they were part of political economy, not separate from it. To me it makes little sense to think that the Qing and the British did not understand each other. However, it is clear that they had very different objectives and interests. The Qing did not want to enter into the Age of Commerce on British terms, but that does not mean that they were not interested in trade. Moreover, at many levels it was of course not the Beijing or the Westminster courts that were central to actual trade but local traders and local officials and, very importantly, illegal traders. In conclusion, one might suggest that following the pathways of commodities is a very useful heuristic device, but it is not sufficient if one wants to understand the changes of political economy. These commodities are embedded in social relations and ideas of sociability. The fact that opium is produced in India but does not define international relations or political economy in the way it seems to have done in China shows already that it is not the commodity itself that provides us with a full explanation. That opium cannot have been the sole reason for "the opium wars" seems clear from the fact that it was really after the successful establishment of tea plantations in India that the British felt impelled to force the Chinese to open their economy and society.

This excursion into the interpretation of two fragments of the world of trade in commodities, tea and opium, should not be taken to imply that commodities and their pathways are the only or even privileged examples of a study of the fragment, nor that the world system of capitalism is necessarily "the whole" where the analysis should lead us. In the rest of the book I shall give a number of examples from a range of topics in which the study of the fragment leads us to ask larger questions without coming to generalizations.

In part I (chapters 1 and 2) this book offers a theoretical critique of increasingly mainstream generalizing methods and theories in the social sciences, specifically quantitative methodologies in sociology and political science, as well as rational choice theory on the one hand and cognitive evolutionism in psychological anthropology on the other, as well as a critique of unreflexive uses of the concept of "civilization" to signify unity or essentialized ontological difference, which is the other side of the same coin. On the positive side, this book wants to argue that societies are historically evolving: that one can discern historical pathways in their development, but that these developments are also open to a considerable extent. Anthropology studies specific social configurations that are in specific interaction with outside forces. To understand these interactions anthropology focuses continuous double reflection on one's concepts and on the ways the history of interaction has affected the social configurations one studies. The comparative analysis that I propose here critically engages and carries forward programs developed by Marcel Mauss and Max Weber. This implies both appreciation and critique of the ways those programs have been carried forward by the Maussian Louis Dumont and the Weberian Shmuel Eisenstadt and Charles Taylor. The general themes I explore here show the relative advantage of anthropological comparison in relation to forms of sociological "generalism," and especially approaches based on "rational choice" theory, the concept of civilization and its comparative consequences, and the comparison of forms of social exclusion.

Chapter 1 explores the advantage that particular forms of anthropology have for comparative analysis and seeks to ground the study of the fragment theoretically. Anthropology is the only social science that reflects on Western ethnocentrism and takes the problem of translation seriously. The chapter gives a detailed critique of quantitative analysis of nationalism, of evolutionary cognitive understandings of religion, and shows the superiority of a more interpretive anthropology in the study of nationalism and religion. It thus gives not only a critique of some existing approaches but also a demonstration of preferable perspectives.

Chapter 2 argues that market theories of religion that are based on the notion of "rational choice" do not contribute to our understanding of the transcendental value of money and markets in our social life. Such theories not only depend on a too narrow interpretation of "rationality" but also neglect the importance of enchantment in financial transactions, consumption patterns, and religious life. The chapter addresses studies of religion in China and South Asia to illustrate its theoretical points.

Part II (chapters 3 and 4) provides positive examples of the proposed approach, focusing on the exclusionary use of the notion of civilization. Chapter 3 goes into the problem of civilization and who belongs to it. Like culture, civilization is a complex and highly contested concept, since it operates at the level of not only scholarly discourse but also common-sense understandings of hierarchy and difference. The focus in this chapter is on the exclusion of Muslim minorities in Europe, India, and China and the civilizational legitimation of that exclusion. The chapter highlights the similarities and differences in these patterns of exclusion.

Chapter 4 goes to the heart of civilization practice, namely the religious worship of images in India and China and especially the recurrent campaigns to destroy them. It examines the variegated histories of iconoclasm in India and China and the problem of sovereignty that is central to them. The chapter moves on to discuss the extent to which modern urban planning can be understood as a form of iconoclasm.

Part III goes on to develop the comparison of exclusionary practices that are inherent in the notion of civilization. Chapter 5 focuses on those who live in the mountainous margins of civilizational heartlands and, today, in the border areas of modern nation-states. These peoples have been the typical subjects of anthropological research, because of their remote, relatively isolated, location, the small scale of their societies, and their cultural differences from the civilizations that are adjacent to them in the plains. The chapter critiques forms of romanticization of those who live in the mountain areas that connect India and China and attempts to give a contextualized picture of anthropological thinking about hill people in this area.

Chapter 6 discusses why Indian middle classes seem to have no compelling interest in improving sanitation for the poor, despite the fact that their own health is affected due to their close proximity to the poor. It examines some cultural theories of attitudes toward "the dirty outside world" and argues that these theories ignore the importance of caste and especially untouchability. It further argues that one cannot expect the poor themselves to improve their condition through participatory development, considering their internal fragmentation and the conditions of slavery under which many of them live. It compares the Indian situation with some theories about what happened in Europe with sanitation (and the well-understood self-interest in the common good) and in the United States with the abolishment of slavery. It ends with the revolutionary transformation of China in dealing with the life conditions of the poor.

Finally, the conclusion takes up the problem of methodological nationalism in much of social science and the way out that the comparative method in anthropology offers.

PART I / THE FRAGMENT AND THE WHOLE

1 / THE COMPARATIVE
ADVANTAGE OF ANTHROPOLOGY

Despite general agreement that there is a variety of materials (film, video, audiotapes, music, sermons, documents) that anthropologists are working with and a variety of methods applied to these materials, the empirical part of anthropology continues to be primarily based on the ethnographic method, which consists of a long stay "in the field," a familiarization with the "way of life" of the people one studies, and thus in many cases a long linguistic preparation to acquaint oneself with the local language. The rather vague term *way of life* suggests a "holistic" approach in which a society is examined in its entirety. As one knows, it is practically not possible to have such a total vision, unless one fantasizes societies as outside history and outside a larger world of interaction. In the early stages of the development of anthropology, students of small-scale societies may have been tempted to isolate their fieldwork sites, but no student of an Indian or a Chinese village would have been able to sustain such a fantasy (despite the questionable focus on the "village" as a self-contained unit in the 1950s and 1960s). What ethnographers do claim, however, is that their study of everyday life in a small setting allows them to interpret a larger entity (local, regional, national, or even global) and that that knowledge cannot be gained through the deployment of large-scale surveys. The claim here is that through close study of a fragment one is able to comment on a larger whole and that an understanding of the larger whole allows one to interpret the fragment (whatever that particular whole or fragment may be). It is the choice of a particular fragment of social life that determines what its relevant context is or what the larger question is that one wants to address. While this resembles the hermeneutic circle of textual interpretation, one needs to recognize that social life is not a "social text" and certainly not a closed text and that the openness of social change is multidirectional. Similarly, one needs to steer clear of a universalizing approach that first defines some kind of essence, like "ritual" or "prayer," and then studies it comparatively across cultures.[1]

At this point it is important to emphasize that what I am suggesting is not to be misunderstood as a process of generalization from the particular. The purpose is not to come to some general truth but to highlight something that is not general, something specific without any pretense to general truth, but definitely of broader significance. What is general is often banal, and while anthropologists deal with ordinary life, they strive to say something about it that is not banal. This is also the reason why anthropologists, however much they are prepared when going on fieldwork, generally have to change the questions they ask and the general direction of their fieldwork while confronted with the real-life situations in the field. Moreover, these situations are in fact processes and can only be grasped in dynamic terms. They change during and after the fieldwork, and this process implies that the findings are often difficult to replicate in later fieldwork by other fieldworkers. This problem is compounded by the fact that ethnographers do not ask the same questions and thus come up with different pictures of the societies they study. There is a significant difference not only between ethnographers who continue to study a particular society for most of their professional lives (for example, Kenneth Dean on Fujianese society or Chris Fuller on South India) and those ethnographers who spend a fieldwork period in one site after the other (the prime example is Fredrik Barth on the Pathan, on Oman, on New Guinea, on Bali, on Bhutan), but also in the kinds of questions asked.[2] Anthropologists study historically evolving, open configurations, and the anthropologists themselves are part of them.

The emphasis on fieldwork should not be taken as a far-reaching empiricism in which it suffices that the minutiae of social life are recorded in exasperating detail. As Marilyn Strathern wrote in 1998, "if at the end of the twentieth century one were inventing a method of enquiry by which to grasp the complexity of social life, one might wish to invent something like the social anthropologist's ethnographic practice."[3] Such a purpose cannot be sustained by precision of observation and description (extended case study or situational analysis) alone or by claims to producing a representative sample. The perspective I offer is obviously close to that of Clifford Geertz in his famous essay on "thick description," where he argues that the ethnographer seeks to give an interpretation of "what our informants are up to, or think they are up to."[4] Geertz also offers an enticing example of what comparison can offer in his essayistic comparison of Islam in Morocco and Indonesia.[5] What I do not agree with, however, is the Geertzian penchant for generalization, as in his definition of religion as a universal entity (as a "cultural system"), a definition that fails to reflect on the nature of the global Western political expansion that enabled the universalization of this concept as a way to explain and govern practices all over the world, or in what in his work on Indonesia he calls "the general Javanese religious system."[6]

The move from fragment to larger insight is a conceptual and theoretical one and not a form of generalization. It does not come from mere observation but is theory-laden. Theory should here be taken in its original sense of observing and contemplating. This is not theory as generalization, as in "a general theory of action" (Parsons) or a "theory of practice" (Bourdieu).[7] Therefore, I take the concept of "holism" to refer not to a form of generalization or to the ethnographical method per se but to anthropology as a conceptual engagement with a fragment that allows us to interpret another conceptual universe, in which translation plays a central role. Some observational methods in microsociology, urban geography, and actor-oriented political science resemble the ethnographic method but do not share this radical theoretical orientation of anthropology.

Anthropology's starting point is to question the universality of what in modern society is taken to constitute the separate domains of the "economy" of "politics," of "law," and of "religion," as well as the dichotomy between state and society or between the individual and society, or even between "inner feelings" and "outward appearance." In fact, these pervasive dichotomous conceptualizations have a particular history in modern Western societies and languages. The "holistic" perspective of anthropology allows us to "bracket" Western assumptions and investigate how people outside "the modern West" are conceptualizing their social life without presuming the universality of Western understandings.

My approach raises two related issues. First of all, nobody today is totally outside "the modern West," because in fact we are all "becoming modern" (Latour) and because Western modernity is one among many modernities (Eisenstadt).[8] Moreover, there is a history of a century or longer of Western hegemony in the world. This makes it impossible to assume that there is a "pure outside" that can be investigated. Instead, what we study are various forms of interaction between different cultural worlds, forms that are in some cases of very long duration and in some cases have a nineteenth-century origin.[9] In the latter cases we deal with imperial interactions that engender modern transformations. We find interactions also *within* societies, such as, for example, India's "split public," divided between the English-speaking public in India and the much larger vernacular public, or the oppositions of ethnic majority versus ethnic minorities in contemporary Europe.[10] In fact, there is such a great variety of cultural exchanges and interactions that it is not possible to think of society as an integrated whole, despite politicians' emphasis on integration and social cohesion and the fear of society "falling apart."

Second, by acknowledging this history of interactions we turn a critical eye on universal pretensions of models that are solely based on a putatively isolated Western historical experience. The pervasiveness of ethnocentrism in the social sciences is astonishing, ranging from discussions of democracy, the public sphere, and civil society to discussions of religion, secularism, class, and the family. One of the greatest flaws in the development of a comparative perspective seems to be the almost universal comparison of any existing society with an ideal-typical and totally self-sufficient Euro-American modernity.

Comparison should be conceived not primarily in terms of comparing societies or events, or institutional arrangements across societies, although this is important, but as a reflection on our conceptual framework as well as on the history of interactions that have constituted our object of study. One may, for instance, want to study church-state relations in India and China, but one has to bring to that study a critical reflection on why one would suppose the centrality of church-like organizations as well as the centrality of Western secular state formation in an analysis of developments in India and China. That critical reflection often shows that Western concepts do not fit the social reality one wants to investigate and, in turn, may lead to the exaggerated claim that societies outside the West should be understood in their own terms and cannot be understood in Western terms. However, one cannot escape the fact that in today's world "native" terms have to be interpreted and translated in relation to Western scholarship. Moreover, such translation and interpretation is part of a long history of interactions with the West that became dominant in the nineteenth century. For example, in the Indian case it is good to realize that English, despite its foreign origins, has over the centuries become an Indian vernacular. In the case of China it is good to realize that communism, despite the prevailing notion that everything has an ancient Chinese origin, in fact did not originate in the Song dynasty but is a Western invention. Any attempt to make a sharp (often nationalist) demarcation of inside and outside is spurious in contemporary society. Comparison is thus not a relatively simple juxtaposition and comparison of two or more different societies but a complex reflection on the network of concepts that underlie our study of society as well as the formation of those societies themselves. It is always a double act of reflection.[11]

This is not to say that Western ideas and models are not powerful. Again, what needs to be studied are forms of interaction, since no one can deny, for example, the significance and power of universal models in economics for economic policy everywhere. Such models function both as "models of" and "models for," since global institutions like the IMF and the World Bank impose their models on societies (with sometimes disastrous effects, as in the "Asian Crisis").[12] These models' power derives not from the fact that they are universally applicable (on the basis of the assumption that we all are in the same world and are all human beings) but from the fact that they are *universalized* and thus have a universal impact to the extent that they are backed by global power. What anthropological discussions of the "informal economy" and of "corruption" have taught us is that the Western ideas and models are partly uncovering reality and partly covering it up and that that is their universal characteristic.

The anthropological lens enables a critique of universal modeling and is, as a consequence, outside the mainstream of the development of social science. The orientation toward comparative sociology in the era of empire has shifted since World War II to a focus on differences within national societies in the West.[13] The dominant trend in sociology is to study one's own society, and thus American sociology studies the United States, the world's dominant society. The silent assumption of those who think that sociology is a form of universal science is that what is true for the United States is true everywhere. Much of sociology and political science today is macro-oriented, depends on large data sets, and is geared to constructing universally applicable models. Quantitative analysis is certainly an important and necessary way in economics and demography to increase our knowledge about longitudinal trends and patterns in society, as Thomas Piketty's recent book on capitalism and increasing wealth inequality shows.[14] However, students of societies like India and China tend to have doubts about the validity of surveys and data sets in these societies. As the

Nobel Prize–winning economist Paul Krugman put it recently in a characteristically scathing opinion piece, "all economic data are best viewed as a peculiarly boring genre of science fiction, but Chinese data are even more fictional than most."[15]

To stay with the example of the so-called informal economy, statistics based on the "formal economy" in many societies are clearly partial, and in India and China they miss a large chunk of reality, although we cannot say for sure how large, for the reasons just outlined. In my own field, the study of religion, statistics gathered on the growth of Christianity in China, for instance, have to be regarded with as much suspicion as, for example, statistics on sexual behavior in any country (see chapter 2). More generally, one needs to examine survey data with great methodological care, since nonresponse is often extremely high and responses can be socially acceptable ones that have little to do with reality. Despite the enormous importance and investment in electoral research the outcome of elections is very hard to predict. This should not lead to the lament that the social sciences are not quite "science" as yet, since sciences like geology and meteorology cannot predict earthquakes or the weather over a longer period than a few days either. Similarly, brain research is making progress thanks to new observational technologies, but despite huge claims by neuroscientists we still know very little about the brain. The one social science that is sometimes elevated to the status of "science" because of its use of mathematical modeling is economics, but we are reminded daily of the unpredictability of the economy.

One should perhaps acknowledge that instead of the great divide between science and social science (and the humanities) we are dealing with a great number of different pursuits of knowledge and evidentiary practices and arenas of argumentation that are methodologically and theoretically wide apart without the possibility of making one successful research paradigm the model for others.[16]

Comparisons in political science based on large data sets have great and perhaps unsolvable problems. An example is the work done by the comparativists Ronald Inglehart (Michigan) and Pippa Norris (Harvard) that has resulted in the Survey of World Values.[17] It strikes the anthropologist immediately that their categorization of China, Korea, and Japan as "Confucian" is to mistake a history of cultural exchanges for a shared system of values. Similar mistakes are made by leading political scientists, for example, the late Samuel Huntington in his concept of the "clash of civilizations" or by Peter Katzenstein in recent work on East Asia.[18] There is a serious lack of historical understanding at work when one thinks that Confucianism is a coherent system of values and that a core value like "filial piety" does not change when family arrangements change as a result of government interventions (antifeudalism campaigns by the Chinese Communists as well as the one-child policy in China) or demographic changes (dramatic in Japan, Korea, and Taiwan). Finally, the notion that these societies are characterized by Confucianism ignores the impact of other value orientations, such as Buddhism, Daoism, Shintoism, Christianity, and, last but not least, Communism.

While these are conceptual misunderstandings, they can be combined with tendentious opinion making, as in the Pew Foundation's recent report "Faith on the Move," which divides migrants into seven categories that are not problematized (Christians, Muslims, Hindus, Buddhists, Jews, Others [mostly Chinese religions], and Unaffiliated). The picture that emerges from the report is that poor religious fellows are flooding the secular-religious parts of the world. As it is put in the preface of the study, "in Western Europe, a more recent influx of Muslim immigrants is producing political tensions along with greater cultural diversity."[19] That these tensions are produced in a political process twenty or thirty years after the immigration of laborers from Muslim-majority countries and have only recently focused on religion cannot be captured by the Pew Report's reliance on surveys and mere statistics. These reports are highly quotable by news media and instrumental in producing deeply simplified political views of the world, backed by so-called science.

What happens in these large comparative data sets is a totally different form of "holism" from the anthropological one and should be distinguished from it by calling it "generalism." It does not research the various ways people think that parts make up a whole but starts with the assumption of a society as a unified whole. This allows for the typecasting of societies and religions in a particular unifying way. One could call it the macro-sociological form of ethnic profiling. This continues a long discredited tradition in American anthropology that aimed at determining the *culture and personality* of an entire society (Benedict, Linton, Kardiner, Hsu).[20] The desire to do this has both disciplinary and political origins and consequences. The social sciences take the nation-form as the object of their study, and as a consequence we have sociologies of national societies that lend themselves to comparison.

Social science disciplines emerged with the rise of the nation-state in western Europe and take it as the natural object of inquiry. After World War II many new "nations" were formed and were also studied as if all of a sudden by an act of sheer political will they had become nations. Their interactions and comparative developments came to be studied in international relations, a subfield of political science. This form of methodological nationalism has been critiqued by those who study transnational migrants and border-crossing environmental problems. However, the more serious conceptual problem is that what is taken as the object of study, the nation-state, is a highly contested, historically changing set of institutions and practices that cannot be seen as occupying the entire social field one might want to study. The forms it takes are also highly variable, for example, the democratic state in India and the Communist state in China. To compare these two states as typological opposites, democratic versus undemocratic, for example, begs a number of important questions about the nature of power in these societies. This is not to say that one cannot compare nation-states as well as nation-forms but to suggest that one should not impose a strictly typological definition on the various forms that nations and states take. Similarly, to take class as the basis of comparisons of stratification leads one to insurmountable problems with Indian caste as well as with forms of familism that we find in China today.

The foregoing should not at all be taken as an argument against comparison. In fact, the point I want to make is that social and cultural analysis always takes place within a comparative frame. Some of us are acutely aware of this; others less so. In general there is inadequate consideration of the extent to which our approaches depend on arguing and comparing with the already existing literature on a topic, on the use of terms that have emerged in entirely different historical situations and thus convey implicit comparison (such as "middle class" or "bourgeoisie," or "religion"), and on the ways the people we study are constantly themselves comparing the present with the past or their situation with that of others. To therefore claim that one is a Sinologist or Indologist or Africanist and believe that specialization in a region and subject, given sufficient linguistic and cultural competence, is enough to claim mastery over that subject, as if one is not standing constantly in a reflexive relation to both discipline and subject, gives perhaps a certain confidence, but is untenable.

It is in the light of the importance of comparative analysis that Jack Goody urges anthropology to interact with other social science disciplines.[21] However, the question remains whether anthropology should only function as critique, as correcting overgeneralizations made by these other disciplines, from the margins. I would propose that there is a more positive role to play for anthropology as a producer of valid knowledge in its own right through comparison. Anthropology can go beyond methodological and theoretical nationalism, not only by examining the marginal, the transient, the betwixt and between, but also by comparing concepts of personhood, of nation, and of civilization. In that sense anthropology may offer an alternative to research that takes these concepts as unproblematic, empirical objects.

While the ethnographic method sensitizes us to the importance of the fragment in relation to anthropological holism, brings us closer to popular experiences of the "everyday state," and allows us to better analyze what "seeing like a state" (James Scott) implies for actors in a society,[22] anthropological holism is, as I suggested earlier, a theoretical perspective that goes beyond the ethnographic method. Most fruitfully, anthropological holism addresses the conceptual issues that have concerned comparative sociology from its French, German, and British beginnings. In the rest of this chapter I will explore anthropology's comparative advantage in the study of three major topics that are of crucial importance in contemporary, complex society: social inequality, nationalism, and religion. In this exploration I will oppose holism to "generalism," interpretation to coding, and finally cultural analysis to sociobiology.

SOCIAL INEQUALITY

One of the most important subjects in the social sciences is the comparative understanding of social inequality. A recurrent element of social transformation is the rejection of "old" forms of inequality accompanied by the introduction of "new" forms of inequality. Most common is the transition from premodern hierarchy to modern inequality that characterizes, for example, capitalist or communist regimes. The conceptual question is to what extent the social sciences are able to critically distance themselves from the norms and values that are dominant in the societies in which the social sciences themselves are produced. This is also an ethical question, since that distancing can be accompanied by a relativism that is objectionable in the face of oppression and exploitation. A convincing position in this particular matter has been developed by Clifford Geertz in his distinguished 1984 American Association of Anthropology lecture "Anti-Anti-Relativism," in which he argues that it is neither necessary nor desirable to reject relativism on the basis of universal morality or knowledge. His point is that one can hardly find relativism as a serious pursuit anywhere in the social sciences. He compares relativism accusations with Communism accusations in the McCarthy period in which people who were not Communist at all were attacked as such.[23] More urgent than moral grandstanding is how to understand societies that are radically different from that of the interpreter.

Louis Dumont has argued that traditional India was characterized by a hierarchical value system and that it was very difficult for social scientists who had been socialized in an egalitarian value system to really understand India.[24] His comparative perspective allowed him to ask penetrating questions about the differences between caste, class, and race, about the position of "the individual" as a normative subject in Indian society, and about the relation between religious status and temporal power. His work has been foundational for the modern anthropology of India, but many of his answers to these questions have been successfully challenged in subsequent empirical work. The fundamental problem with Dumont's perspective is that he uses anthropological holism to ask fundamental questions but ends up positing an Indian "whole" as distinct from a Western "whole," creating artificial unities over time and space. While we have to reject this "generalism," Dumont nevertheless asks the important question whether modern categories of time and space can be indiscriminately applied to conceptualizations of them that are fundamentally different. Dumont has rightly argued in regard to these categories that the Sanskritic conceptualization of "history" is radically different from the modern, Western one (and, one might add, from the Islamic one that one also finds in India) and that this creates particular problems for the historical study of Indian society. He does not argue that we cannot give a historical account of Indian society but that the historicity of the textual material we use to produce historical accounts devalues history in the modern Western sense. At the same time, it has to be acknowledged that by focusing on "Sanskrit history" Dumont has effectively disregarded not only the historical impact of Islamic power and British colonial power but also the existence of vernacular sources that allow for a much more nuanced history of parts of India. The historians Narayana Rao, Sanjay Subrahmanyam, and David Shulman have recently argued against Dumont's position by showing that South Indian literary genres in fact offer a wealth of historical information, but they fail to systematically address the question of what one might call "regimes of historicity," ways the past is represented, as distinct from the modern historian's craft of reading against the grain.[25] Dumont's strategic isolations of parts of history to construct a "traditional India" are useful for constructing Weberian ideal-types but hinder the understanding of a history of interactions.

The anthropology of India has somewhat moved away from the study of caste since the publication of Arjun Appadurai's critique of caste studies and the general rise of cultural studies focusing on youth culture, film studies, and the study of various forms of nationalism.[26] This shift in anthropological attention does not imply, however, that the social phenomenon has become less important. Caste continues to be a major component of Indian politics and society. Caste tends to be crucial in social competition for scarce resources, distributed by political authorities, and especially in reservation policies. Caste is also crucial in the social exclusion of a major part (between 15 and 20 percent and if one also adds the scheduled tribes around a fourth) of the Indian population, the so-called untouchables or Dalits. Urbanization shows this continuing pattern of exclusion very clearly, since a large part of the slum population is Dalit (see chapter 6).

In sociological terms caste is a special case of the principles of status order. The latest attempt to throw light on these principles from the viewpoint of a general sociological theory is Murray Milner's analysis of what he calls "resource structuralism" in his book *Status and Sacredness: A General Theory of Status Relations and an Analysis of Indian Culture*, published in 1994.[27] Milner, like Weber before him, observes that status in India is not simply dependent on wealth or political power. He argues that status is a resource that is relatively inalienable and inexpansive (not expanding) in India. This explains in sociological terms why in India conformity to norms and control of associations with outsiders is so strong. While Milner's observations are not wrong, it remains unclear how they further our understanding of Indian society. It seems to me that what he does in formulating his theory (and we can see this also more generally in sociological theory) is the building of a conceptual apparatus and a translation in a more generalized and abstracted language of what is empirically known through ethnography. This is in principle a necessary operation in efforts to systematize our knowledge, but in the end for it to be of use it needs to offer us new perspectives and insights.

In contrast, I do think that Dumont's general theory has been able to offer an important insight on the differences between "caste" and "race" by using a comparative approach. He argues that Indian caste is different from

American race, since caste depends on a hierarchical ideology, while race depends on an egalitarian ideology. These are two systems of inequality that resemble each other but are fundamentally different, since they are related to opposite value systems. Let us examine this argument a bit further. Obviously, there are significant differences between the systems at the level of observation, such as the proliferation of castes in the Indian case and the existence of two castes (black and white) in the American case. Moreover, Dumont's assumption that India's hierarchical ideology is a *shared* all-encompassing system of values is deeply problematic. That would only be true if untouchables would accept the values of the caste system, but, as Berreman has already shown on the basis of his fieldwork in North India, they do not.[28] Deliège takes a middle position on the basis of his fieldwork in South India and has suggested that untouchables are "both the victims and the agents of the caste system, its defenders and its enemies."[29] This can perhaps be seen as a general feature of a functioning hierarchical system as explained in Hegel's master-slave dialectic. It can be safely said, however, that whatever may have been the case in the past, at least at the political level today untouchables see themselves as "oppressed," which is indicated by their adopting the name *Dalits* (oppressed) and rejecting the term Gandhi coined for them, *Harijans* (children of God). The ethnographic finding of reproduction of hierarchical values among Dalits does not mean that they are unaware of being oppressed. As many anthropologists have been arguing, the category of "resistance" is too simple to capture a wide variety of relations to power. It is the comparison of race and caste that allows for examining some of these subtleties without reducing them to the opposition of hierarchy and egalitarianism.[30]

While there are myriad caste distinctions in India that make one think of caste as a unique social system, the divide between people who have caste and those who are outcast resembles the black-white opposition in the American South before the 1960s. In both cases one can observe important class and ethnic divisions among the dominant population but a more definite cleavage between white and black, or between caste people and outcasts. The extent to which this cleavage is reproduced even under changing political conditions, in which one has a black president in the United States and an untouchable one in India, is an intriguing question. In the United States it is the stunning incarceration rate among black men that shows the persistence of a deep inequality; in India the fact that the majority of so-called slum-dwellers are Dalit demonstrates a similar persistence

of the old discrimination. Similar, however, is not the same. The comparative approach makes it productive to inquire why race expresses itself in
the United States through criminalization and violence, whereas in India it
expresses itself through the denial of basic state services.

What makes the comparison between racial discrimination in the United
States and untouchability in India even more productive is that they are
both rooted in systems of slavery. The patterns of abolishment of slavery are
connected to the emergence of new labor conditions that produces a black
underclass and an untouchable footloose labor force. The memory of slavery
and the representation of suffering in performative traditions are powerful
elements in the unification of these underclasses. In both the United States
and India these classes have produced new religious forms of organization
and ritual representation. It is especially the role of missionary Christianity
in India and of the black churches in the United States that invites comparative work.[31] It is evident that Christian churches play an outsized role in the
organization of social life in the slums and ghettos, but at the same time
Christianity is part of the ideological core of American nationalism, while it
is seen as "foreign" in India. It is much easier for dominant society in India
to delegitimize Christian churches than for dominant society to do so in
the United States, although one needs to keep in mind that radical black
Christianity is not part of mainstream Christianity, as Barack Obama found
out when his pastor, Jeremiah Wright, got some intense media attention for
what were seen as anti-American and anti-white positions.

The question whether it is productive to think of caste in terms of race
is not a purely academic or scientific one. This emerged clearly at the UN
World Conference Against Racism, Racial Discrimination, Xenophobia
and Related Intolerance held in South Africa in September 2001. The NGO
conference that preceded the official meeting of government representa-
tives had a 160-member Dalit caucus, representing untouchables in not only
South Asia but also Japan and Senegal. The government of India, however, strongly rejected the claim that caste discrimination against the Dalit
population should be regarded as racial discrimination and succeeded in
preventing its inclusion in the concluding document of the conference.[32]

The remarkable thing is not so much that the Indian government, after
many decades of claiming the higher moral ground of anti-imperialism and
nonalignment, rejected outside condemnation of a basic feature of Indian
society. For my discussion, the interesting element is that they were supported in their position by leading Indian anthropologists André Béteille

and Dipankar Gupta.[33] Béteille argued correctly that there had been attempts in the colonial period to find a racial basis to caste but that such attempts had failed. He concluded therefore that on scientific grounds one needed to reject the claim that caste was based on race. What Béteille misses entirely is that what caste and race share is that they are social rather than biological facts. While there might be some physical aspect (like skin color; in India fair is higher than dark) it is the fact that caste and race are both based on descent and on the cultural understanding of that descent that connects both. It is the pattern of discrimination against a descent group that requires attention. Similarly, Dipankar Gupta's discussion of the immense diversity of castes and caste relations in India completely bypasses the important point that all over India there is a systematic pattern of discrimination against untouchables. His observation that many members of untouchable castes have left the ritually polluting professions they had been associated with in the past further ignores the fact that in general they have moved into the category of poor, footloose, seasonal labor, replacing an earlier form of deep-seated discrimination with another. Obviously, the discrimination against American blacks has taken different forms from that against untouchables, but there are strong similarities between their positions in past society, as there are in contemporary society.

My conclusion is that the comparative anthropological (and historical) interpretation of these forms of inequality in their cultural and institutional context has great social science value and helps us to ask better questions than are allowed by the construction of taxonomies of social inequality, in which class, caste, and race are conceptualized as ideal-types or by the construction of Western and non-Western social systems that are characterized by totalizing ideologies.

NATIONALISM

A second area of inquiry in the social sciences where the anthropological perspective has a comparative advantage is that of nationalism. Nationalism was already a major concern for Durkheim in the years leading up to World War I. In the 1980s both Ernest Gellner and Benedict Anderson made important theoretical contributions to the study of nationalism using comparative perspectives on culture based on historical anthropology.

Today, quantitative sociologists attempt to take this research forward, giving us an opportunity to assess the use of quantitative modeling in a field in which anthropology is particularly strong. I take as a telling example (an extended case) of this quantitative approach a recent work by the award-winning sociologist Andreas Wimmer: *Waves of War: Nationalism, State Formation, and Ethnic Exclusion in the Modern World*.[34]

Ernest Gellner has famously argued that the shift from agricultural to industrial society brings about nationalism and eventually the nation-state.[35] Wimmer tests this by coding the length of railway tracks per one thousand square kilometer. He shows that there is no significant correlation between the length of railway tracks and nation-state creation. However, the assumption that the length of railway tracks is a good indicator of industrialization can be easily falsified by pointing at the Indian example, in which the British developed the largest railway system in the world while at the same time deindustrializing India to make it a producer of raw products for industry in England. Gellner's modernization theory has been subjected to a whole literature of critique (including my own) showing that his functional "generalism" has the advantage of clarity but therefore also lends itself to relatively easy refutation.[36] Nevertheless, Gellner's functionalist narrative of nationalism provides us with much more insight than Wimmer's quantitative testing.

Benedict Anderson has famously argued that the imagination of a national community is made possible by the emergence of print capitalism and a reading public.[37] Wimmer translates this argument in the following hypothesis: an increase in the literacy rate in vernacular language should make nationalism, nation building, and ultimately the transition to the nation-state more likely. Wimmer finds that his data set refutes Anderson's argument: "The relationship between mass literacy and nationalism might therefore be less straightforward than Anderson's account suggests." The problem here is that Anderson's argument, in fact, is not about mass literacy but about the emergence of a reading public (enabled by "print capitalism") and about the new imagination of community in "creole nations outside of Europe" that is not based on the old hierarchies of Europe. Moreover, as Wimmer himself acknowledges, there are huge empirical problems in estimating literacy rates before the development of systematic censuses.[38] Again, as in the case of Gellner, we see a complex argument being reduced and substantially transformed to a formulaic hypothesis. In Anderson's work it is really his creative interpretation of a fragment, such as the significance of the first nationalist novel in the Philippines or the importance of the colonial map of Indonesia in imagining new nations, that has furthered our understanding.

The conclusion about quantitative work in this area is that it says very little but what it says is being said with great precision and unfortunate banality. The intellectual labor goes into the development of data sets and modeling, while making use of rational choice and game theory assumptions about human actors that make their actions quantifiable. The great gap that has developed in the social sciences between sociology and anthropology can largely be blamed on the desire of the sociologists to develop a science of society and the desire of the anthropologists to become novelists describing a rich life world. Often this gap is understood as one between quantitative methods and qualitative methods, but that is a wrong understanding.

Talal Asad has pointed out that "experience" in ethnography as the legitimate base of knowledge is inevitably subjective and hard to replicate and thus questionable, but that quantitative research also does not provide certainty of knowledge.[39] In the case of statistics, certainty is not aspired to but probability. The issue is not the relative certainty of qualitative and quantitative methods but the fact that statistics is connected to administrative practices. All of this, however, depends on the state's ability to collect reliable data about its population. As Asad astutely observes, governmental statistics are not meant merely to represent but also to regulate and transform. Statistics allows comparison in "converting the question of incommensurable cultures into one of commensurable social arrangements without rendering them homogenous."[40]

In the study of nationalism, statistics and large data sets seem desirable, since nationalism is largely a "politics of numbers." Does a particular course of action express the will of the people? That is a question that is asked both by a politician in a democratic polity and by a Communist politician who cannot ignore popular sentiment. How is "the will of the people" expressed, created, listened to?

My own interest in the question of nationalism arose during my fieldwork in Ayodhya, a North Indian pilgrimage center.[41] There was a mosque in the center of town that was supposedly built in the sixteenth century by the Mughal emperor Babar on the spot where the god Rama was born. In 1949, after Partition, an image of Rama had "appeared" in the mosque (put there in the night by a Hindu nationalist monk), and since then the site had been closed off for both Hindus and Muslims. In 1984, thirty-five years after that event, suddenly a movement "to liberate Rama's birthplace" started and in 1992 was successful in destroying the mosque, though not (yet) in building a temple on the spot. My ethnography shows that the locals did not have any interest in starting this campaign, although they did believe or at least paid lip service to the idea that the mosque was in fact a Hindu place that had been usurped by Muslims. The campaign was started by a nationwide political movement to make Hindu nationalism the core of political action. The symbolism of purifying Hindu soil from the signs of Muslim oppression was so successful that the Bharatiya Janata Party (Indian People's Party) suddenly shot to power and defeated the Congress Party. The Bharatiya Janata Party and its predecessor, the Jan Sangh, had never been able to gain much votes since independence, but this campaign allowed them to formulate an issue that could mobilize people all over the country. Much has been written about this, but the point I want to make is that one needs to understand the successful rise of Hindu nationalism in the 1980s in terms both of clever engineering by a political party (as well as the failure of other parties to respond adequately) and of the historical formation of a Hindu anti-Muslim mentality (mass sentiments). To privilege one above the other makes it into a chicken-or-egg problem without perceiving the dynamic character of the phenomenon, which is now already less extreme than it was in the 1990s, although politically very successful and pervasive in its effects on Indian culture. When trying to understand the waxing and waning of nationalist sentiments and their employment in political campaigns the devil is in details that cannot be captured in static models.

RELIGION

Finally, from Durkheim and Weber onward the emphasis in the social science study of religion has been on the social. This emphasis does not exclude the body but sees "the individual" and "experience" as a social construction that is different from one culture to another. It thus focuses on the social disciplining of the body as part of social transformation. This has been brilliantly explored by Marcel Mauss in his essay "Techniques of the Body," in which he developed a theory of "habitus" or "acquired ability," which emphasizes acquisition by learning and then embodied practice.[42] In reference to Taoist body techniques, he states: "I believe precisely that at the bottom of all our mystical states there are body techniques which we have not studied, but which were studied fully in China and India, even in very remote periods. This socio-psycho-biological study should be made. I think that there are necessarily biological means of entering into 'communion with

God.' "[43] Mauss's use of the Latin term *habitus* was adopted by Pierre Bourdieu (without Bourdieu's acknowledgment) in his development of a "theory of practice," and in Bourdieu's theory the social remains the dominant perspective.[44]

Today, however, there is a strong movement in anthropology that moves away from the social. At first glance it seems to continue this focus on the body and on learning (sometimes with reference to Mauss), but it does so from an evolutionist perspective that privileges cognitive and biological aspects above the social. This research direction universalizes its findings on the basis of the idea that we all have a body and especially a brain.

A century after Durkheim's rejection of psychology's attempts to understand society, we see the successful expansion of psychological perspectives that are cloaked in the authority of evolutionary cognitive science, enabled by new techniques of brain research. Evolution has never been far removed from anthropology, and in some departments in the United States one finds therefore a four-field approach in which archeology, linguistics, social-cultural anthropology, and physical anthropology are combined. The Max Planck Society in Germany, of which I am a member, boasts a highly successful Institute for Evolutionary Anthropology at Leipzig. Generally speaking the guiding notion is that the human body (including obviously the brain) is universal and that humans have evolved out of humanoid predecessors. Again we have a comparative enterprise here. The task for evolutionary anthropology is to find through crosscultural comparison explanations for variations in culture, given the universality of the human body. The principles are the same as in evolutionary biology: searching for patterns of adaptation to the environment in terms of the "survival of the fittest."

Biologists have been successful in showing some continuity in the behavior of the great apes and humans in simple forms of bodily gesture and response but have been unable to resolve opposite observations on morality and forms of cooperation in comparisons of primates and young children that have been made by Michael Tomasello at Max Planck and Frans de Waal at Emory University, both leading researchers in this field.[45] If one reflects for a moment on the conceptual difficulties in connecting empathy (German *Einfühlung*) to moral decision-making in humans, then one can appreciate the problems in judging animal behavior.[46] Despite these inconclusive debates, there is widespread enthusiasm for the use of evolutionary biology in the interpretation of human society. The London School of Economics anthropologist Maurice Bloch explains his own enthusiasm by the fact that "it is clear that all human beings are, in many respects, very similar."[47] He does not seem to grasp that the observation of human similarity does not automatically lead to assumptions about "the selfish gene" (Dawkins). It is amusing to see how Bloch has exchanged his earlier Marxist reductionism for a biological reductionism. Marshall Sahlins has usefully shown how these arguments are rooted in Western philosophical preoccupations: "Since the seventeenth century we seem to have been caught up in this vicious cycle, alternately applying the model of capitalist society to the animal kingdom, then reapplying this bourgeoisfied [sic] animal kingdom to the interpretation of human society."[48]

The most important uncharted territory is that of the higher functions of the brain, as manifested in human language and religion. However, despite considerable attempts in the area of language, there is no convincing account of the evolution of language. In addition, all attempts to teach apes language have failed.[49] These failures and the considerable controversies about relatively simple issues like sharing and cooperation among evolutionary anthropologists seem not to deter them from exploring one of the most complex fields of human behavior: religion. The anthropologist Pascal Boyer, a prominent proponent of the evolutionary perspective on religion, has (together with the psychologist Brian Bergstrom) helpfully reviewed the state of the art in this field. In Darwinian terms, one of the questions is whether and in what measure religious thought and behavior result in fitness to survive. Another question is to what extent religion is a by-product of cognitive systems that are not exclusive to it. This kind of work is crucially dependent on crosscultural comparisons (as Boyer observes).[50] An important first step is to establish general features of human evolutionary biology and then see how religion fits in it. Boyer discusses in this context what he calls "the costly signal hypothesis." The example he gives is the following: "Gazelles advertise their strength and dexterity by high-jumping in front of a predator." Is religion perhaps a form of costly signaling? Of course, religion is costly, and of course it is a form of communication, so it is also signaling. However, have we made any step forward by translating social communication in evolutionary terms as "costly signal adaptation"? As Boyer himself observes, "one must specify to what extent 'religion' is actually costly and signaling, in the precise sense required by biological modeling."

All this does not sound very promising, but Boyer advocates what he calls the "standard cognitive model of religion" as the basis for research. He suggests that there are "domain-specific learning processes" and that the central feature of religion is "a set of beliefs about nonphysical agents." One may note here that this is not different from Tylor's definition of religion as the belief in spiritual beings, as well as that, as Rodney Needham already pointed out long ago, this definition is problematic since the concept of "belief" is in fact absent from many traditions.[51] Jumping from here to the proposition that "concepts of religious agency can be described as derived from (and a possible by-product of) evolved dispositions to represent physical objects and intentional agents" allows Boyer to introduce without any further reflection the idea that these are all anthropomorphous projections and dependent on a distinction between true understandings of the behavior of natural objects and false illusions. However "new" this evolutionary perspective presents itself to be, it has not evolved beyond its nineteenth-century prejudices, exemplified by the following propositions put forward by Boyer: (1) People's beliefs about morality are ex post facto rationalizations of commitment and solidarity mechanisms. (2) Rituals are derived from precautionary concerns about invisible danger.[52] (3) Religious institutions illustrate cognitive adaptations that predate their historical development. These late nineteenth-century prejudices are supplemented by late twentieth-century American prejudices about rational choice in religious markets: "Differences in doctrine may be seen as a consequence of the specific markets and commodities involved."[53]

Evolutionary cognitive anthropologists give special attention to rituals or, as Liénard and Boyer insist, "ritualized behavior."[54] Their description of a ritual performed by the Turkana of Kenya confirms Roy Rappaport's listing of the "obvious" features of ritual: no obvious empirical goals; compulsion; literalism and rigidity; repetition, reiteration, redundancy, order and boundaries, specific concerns like pollution and cleansing. From this rather standard description of ritualized behavior Liénart and Boyer move on to the evolutionary perspective. They propose a neurocognitive model of ritualized behavior in child development and pathology, as based on the activation of a specific hazard-precaution system specialized in the detection of and response to potential threats. The idea is that rituals activate the individual neurocognitive hazard precaution system. The big elephant in the room of this theory (a true hazard in itself) is the assumption that rituals are about avoiding danger, for which assumption no clear evidence is shown. The analogies that are sought for ritual are in children's rituals and in obsessive-compulsive disorder, recalling in an uncanny way Freud's understanding of religion as a collective form of neurotic obsession, for which Liénard and Boyer try to find evolutionary causes.

Emerging out of these prejudices or, positively formulated, assumptions comes an interest in measuring the skills that people acquire to "hear God." Tanya Luhrmann (together with Howard Nusbaum and Ronald Thisted) has recently examined "absorption" in experience of God.[55] Luhrmann is a distinguished university professor at Stanford University, whose anthropological work is able to reach a larger audience. Her latest book was featured in the *New Yorker*, and she writes regularly invited op-eds in the *New York Times*. Her starting point is evolutionary: "Beliefs in invisible intentional beings are so widespread because they are a byproduct of intuitive human reasoning (and) the biases in these intuitions evolved to enable us to survive." She quotes with approval Stewart Guthrie (1993), who argues that we see faces in the clouds because it was adaptive for our ancestors to interpret ambiguous sounds as potential threats.[56] Despite these rhetorical nods to evolutionary theory, the article does not engage evolution but deals with an interesting ethnographic puzzle, namely the fact that some people are more able to experience God than others. Luhrmann cites approvingly the work of Marcel Mauss, Talal Asad, and Asad's student Charles Hirschkind, all of whom have emphasized the importance of the body as the site of "learning apt performance" and "acquiring certain abilities." Luhrmann points out that the ability to experience God has to do with frequency of prayer and thus with a process of learning. I do not find that surprising, since in my Protestant youth it was already said by my elders that I should pray harder if I wanted to believe in God. What is more interesting is to find out why some are better at it than others, the question of talents or individual difference, similar to what Paul Radin called the conundrum of the "primitive man as philosopher."[57]

According to Luhrmann, the intense experiences of God that she considers are "technically hallucinations." She puts religious experiences together on a scale developed by psychologists, from light forms of self-absorption to psychotic hallucinations. However, she does not explain the difference in talent for experiencing God, nor does she explain how training creates experience in a systematic way, although this is the stated (and interesting) aim of her research. The argument basically reiterates the generally accepted fact that cultural behavior has to be learned, but cloaks this in a quasi-scientific, experimental language that uses an existing hypnosis-hallucination scale for measuring people's "proclivity" to experience God.

Luhrmann seems to be primarily interested in hallucinations, sensory experiences without a material source, for example, hearing the "voice of God." She interprets these as "mistakes." In her view they are similar to but different from psychoses, because they do not cause substantial impairment and seem to come from cultural expectations. Again, the focus is here on learning to experience, but since this goes for all experience and not only for learning to hallucinate, as it were, it is unclear whether what she argues is anything more than the old anthropological adage "culture is learned behavior" (Kroeber).[58]

Evolutionary and experimental psychology is not going to be of a great help in understanding religion if it remains tied to Western nineteenth-century prejudices and to exclusive research on Western populations. Henrich, Heine, and Norenzayan conclude on the basis of extensive research on data banks that "behavioral scientists routinely publish broad claims about human psychology and behavior in the world's top journals based on samples drawn entirely from Western, educated, industrialized, rich, and democratic (WEIRD) societies. Researchers—often implicitly—assume that either there is little variation across human populations or that these "standard subjects are as representative of the species as of any other population."[59]

CONCLUSION

The arguments I have presented here constitute an *apologia pro anthropologia*. This is necessary in the light of the marginalization of cultural anthropology in the social and behavioral sciences by quantitative and experimental methodologies, as well as by an evolutionary mind-set. In spite of the increasing economic integration of the world, there is a continuing Western ethnocentrism in research. Theoretically and methodologically, this is characterized by generalization inherent in quantitative sociological models, universalism inherent in psychological models, and the essentialization of society. Practically, it is characterized by the overwhelming number of empirical studies on the West and the relative dearth of such studies in the Rest. Given the social power of abstract models in policy-making it is essential for the social sciences to have a counterforce in anthropology.

This is also evident in the recurring issue of the relation between globalization and area studies. There was a period at the end of the 1990s when at least in American academia this issue was heavily debated and focused on the significance of globalization (especially of new media), with some in the United States arguing from a more or less Marxist point of view that the workings of global capital had to be focused on rather than the idiosyncrasies of local (or national) cultures. These discussions tended to overdraw the opposition between the local and the global and have gradually subsided in the 2000s. Communication technologies are indeed globally produced and consumed, and they do change the world everywhere, but at the same time they do so differently in different places. To understand what they exactly do in a particular historical setting still depends on our interpretation of the relevant content and context. One of the striking elements of the spread of television and other media technologies in Asia is vernacularization, and one needs local (including linguistic and cultural) knowledge to be able to access the vernacular.

A related but more enduring attempt to go beyond area studies (and again especially in the United States) has been the almost total separation of social science disciplines (except for anthropology and history) from area study content. Disciplines like sociology and political science have developed models and approaches that claim not to require area specificity. Moreover, the growth of cognitive science and its increasing reach into the social sciences have deepened the gap between a claimed universalism and the so-called particularism of area studies. This institutionalized opposition has continued the Europe-America centrism of the social sciences and has thus gravely undermined our capacity to understand what goes on in the larger part of the world. It seems to me that any attempt to understand contemporary social reality needs to have a historical awareness of at least the period of the emergence of the nation-state that is in fact part of an entire spectrum of interactions between the national and the transnational. Such a historical awareness will immediately show that what we call the "nation-state" has very different shapes and trajectories in different parts of the world, a fact that has, for example, led some political scientists to speak about "civilizational state" in the case of China. In short, the false opposition between the local and the global belongs to a series of misleading oppositions, for example, the secular and the religious, state and society, the city and the rural, that all attempt to indicate a break with the past and a heralding of the modern. This is why the older social science project of comparison has to be revitalized—because it shows so clearly how much such oppositions are part of a particular European historical understanding of modernity.

2 / MARKET AND MONEY
A CRITIQUE OF RATIONAL CHOICE THEORY

Survey methods are used in opinion polls and market research. In economic research they are combined with assumptions about the maximizing, rational actor. Especially under the influence of the work of the economist Gary Becker, these methods and assumptions have increasingly been adopted in studying aspects of social life that did not used to be considered part of the "market."[1] In the sociology of religion we find a remarkable interest in using economic models for explaining religious growth and decline. Such market theories of religion have originated in the United States and have been exported to the rest of the world.[2] They have now become popular in China among sociologists for the simple reason that, since the economic opening up of China in 1978, religion has not been as repressed as before and is thus both more visible and gaining in popularity. This makes religion a social force that is watched carefully by the Communist Party. Survey data and market theories to interpret them are tools that are appreciated by party technocrats who want to further economic growth without political change. Christianity especially is considered a threat because of not only its "foreign" origins and affiliations, but also its potential to replace Communism as a unifying ideology of development and progress. It is interesting to note that in India, in contrast to China, adherents of the market theory of religion can hardly be found among those who study religion. This is not to say that there is no work on the ways gurus attract followers or on missionary activity by Hindus, Muslims, or Christians, but it is telling that the notion of "rational choice," underlying market theory, does not seem convincing as an explanatory model in India.[3]

Since I grew up in the Netherlands I am wary of market theories of religion. The majority of the Dutch population was affiliated to some religious denomination in the 1950s and 1960s. Those who were not religious were still affiliated in very similar ways to communities devoted to socialism, liberalism, or other secular ideologies. Religious or ideological affiliation organized social life. Political parties, labor unions, even welfare services, as well as where one went to shop or for leisure activities, was determined by this kind of communal divide. This societal form was a product of modernization processes that included mobilization of religious groups in the nineteenth century. It has been called pillarization or "consociational democracy" in the literature.[4] Therefore, it flies in the face of classical secularization theories that predict a progressive decline of religion with modernization. But market theories also do not fit, because these communities were very stable over a century and hardly ever converted people to cross over to other communities. Boundaries were so strict that intermarriage between religious communities hardly occurred. Market theories also cannot explain why this system collapsed in the 1960s and why the Netherlands has become one of the most secularized countries in the world within the last fifty years.

Dutch religious history certainly provides a cautionary tale when one follows the Popperian axiom of falsification in assessing the truth value of market theories of religion. The more interesting point, however, is that it shows that one has to be historically specific if one wants to explain religious developments in a society. To have a universal model of religious change is therefore unfeasible. That is also why one should situate market theories of religion in their place of origin, the United States. Market theories of religion have developed in the United States for the historical reason that the U.S. Constitution stipulates a wall of separation such that the state is secular, while society is given religious freedom. Historically, proselytizing Protestant groups especially have thrived in the United States, and they have set an example that is followed by other denominations. In that sense there is a "market" for competing faiths in the United States in a way one does not find elsewhere. Which is not to say that "rational choice" theory applies to that market in the United States. As far as secularization theory is concerned, European modernization theorists have often mentioned the United States as an exception to the rule of secularization because of the religious nature of American society, while American market theorists have argued that Europe was the exception to the rule, since established religions (state religions) in Europe monopolized the religious economy and took market incentives away. However, both Poland and Ireland are Catholic monopolies and are at the same time hardly secularized. One can learn from the debate between sociologists of religion that one should not strive for universal models but develop meaningful comparative analysis.[5]

Besides the fact that market theories of religion cannot be applied universally, they have some further theoretical difficulties. Market theories often assume that individuals make a "rational choice" between different options and that they have stable preferences. This assumption allows for generalized description and prediction. The problem, obviously, is how to demarcate rational and irrational choices. To examine this problem I propose to have a closer look at one sophisticated example of market theory developed by the Swiss sociologist of religion Jürgen Stolz.[6] He argues that religious choices that are seen by the majority in a society as irrational can still be considered rational if people have good reasons to believe in their choice, given the information that they have available to them. However, I would object that in such a case the distinction between rational and irrational choices is entirely arbitrary. Moreover, what if people just perform certain religious acts without putting any emphasis on believing or do not in general have the concept of belief central in their religious activities?[7] If we equate rationality with understandability, then we effectively replace the actor's rationality with the sociologist's rationality. The problem that sociologists who follow the economic model of "rational choice" run into is that their definition of rationality is too one-dimensional to be useful for the interpretation of much social behavior. When they realize this and try to expand the principle, the concept loses its value for prediction. These problems are not new. In the 1970s they were the subject of a sophisticated debate among Peter Winch, Steven Lukes, Martin Hollis, Ernest Gellner, and others. This debate was largely inspired by Evans-Pritchard's ethnographic work. In his classical study of witchcraft and magic among the Azande, he showed that magic, as a set of concepts, practices, and techniques, has to be understood within a wider range of moral understandings and cannot be separated from them.[8]

If one applies a Weberian concept of rationality, one ends up making precisely a distinction between the rationality of religious morality (value rationality that can be found in world religions) on the one hand and irrational magic on the other.[9] This is in Weber's case (and in that of modernization theory) connected with an evolutionary view of the disenchantment of the world. It is precisely these assumptions, which are part of ideologies of modernizing elites, that deserve to be studied by sociologists rather than to be adopted as the guiding models for studying religion. As I have shown elsewhere, these assumptions about modernity and backwardness have been foundational to the antisuperstition campaigns of the Chinese state over a century, with devastating effects.

For Weber magic is an irrational way of dealing with uncertainty, but recently social scientists have started to analyze magical practices as an integral and essential part of global capitalism.[10] These practices are premised on a general, absolute, and apparently transcendent faith in the market, which appears both in the daily discourses of traders in the financial markets and in the rhetoric of former U.S. president George W. Bush, for instance, when in response to the decline of credit he spoke about "the faith-based economy."[11] The magical practices that flow from this faith cover a range of terrains, including the manipulations involved in the evolution of the large class of financial products called "derivatives," all of which have in common the sequences of metonym and metaphor identified by Evans-Pritchard as primary properties of magical practices. After the most recent financial crises we are now officially living in a world where faith, risk, and trust have completely redefined their relationship to one another. An important element in this is what Mary Poovey has called "the culture of finance": "the conflation of representation and exchange has also become possible because the primary form of representation used in financial markets, quantification, is an inherently abstracting process: in order to depict an exchange in numbers, one must abstract some features that are considered essential (because they are amenable to quantification) and marginalize others (because they are not quantifiable). Mathematics, of course by operationalizing quantification takes the level of abstraction to a new level."[12] It is striking how Poovey's argument is also applicable to some of the quantification that is de rigueur in the forms of sociological reasoning that I have criticized in chapter 1.

Capitalism itself in the last decades of the twentieth century has been observed to be tied up with numerous forms of hysteria, panic, and mystery. Local entrepreneurs in financial centers from New York to Hong Kong connected new forms of gambling, speculation, and scam to the related languages of salvation and millennial profit. These new forms of reenchanted capitalism have generally been tied to traditions of fetish and phantasm that have frequently surrounded money and its reproduction, giving rise to many brands of casino capitalism, Ponzi schemes, legal and illegal lotteries, and evangelical entrepreneurship.

The U.S.-based sociologist Fenggang Yang has in recent writings been trying to promote market theory in the study of Chinese religions. Obviously, he observes that there is no "free market" with free choices, since in the Chinese case religion is heavily regulated. He argues that this results in a division of the market in a red market that comprises all officially permitted religious organizations, believers, and religious activities, a black market that comprises all officially banned religious organizations, and so on; and a gray market that comprises all religious and spiritual organizations, practitioners, and activities with ambiguous legal status. In the gray market one finds illegal practices of legally existing religious groups and religious and spiritual practices that manifest in culture instead of religion.[13] He further advances the proposition that "increased religious regulation will lead not to reduction of religion per se, but to a triple religious market." Much of this reminds me of the long-standing sociological discussion of the "informal sector" or "informal economy." Sociologists working on so-called developing economies are, at least since the 1970s, aware that official statistics about economic performance do not take large sectors of the economy into account. The scholarship on this could have inspired Yang to have a more dynamic understanding of the relation between the state and the market. The state is not monolithic, and state actors often work in different and sometimes mutually contradictory ways. David Palmer has shown, for instance, the extent to which Qi Gong activities were not repressed but actually supported by the Party at various levels.[14] Qi Gong was therefore during one period part of the "red market" and during another period part of the "gray market" and is now largely part of the "black market." This is a quite dynamic situation that cannot be reduced to a static model. The same is true for Chinese medicine: it is largely state supported, but state actors attempt to disconnect it from its wider religious connotations. Since the liberalization of the economy in China, local, regional, and national authorities have developed divergent attitudes toward religious activity.[15] At the local level religious shrines can be an important economic resource because of tourism. Even the often distrusted Christianity can be allowed to flourish in some regions, such as Wenzhou or Shandon, while the national policy is still more of the repressive kind.[16] Labor sociologists have pointed out how interconnected the formal and the informal are and speak of processes of formalization and informalization.[17] A general point made in these studies is how unreliable statistics are in assessing economic activity. This is *a fortiori* true for the religious market, and this puts quite some doubt on the usefulness of American sociological models that so heavily depend on statistics for the Chinese situation (and actually for a lot of other situations).[18] It is unclear to me how we can trust any surveys on religion in a society like China in which public knowledge of one's religious affiliation can bring considerable risk. More generally, however, one needs to reflect on the conceptual difficulties in distinguishing different sectors of social life through the use of categories like state, market, and religion. We are already aware that the category of religion has a complex genealogy in Western history and has been applied to China (and elsewhere) not to describe but to produce a particular social field in the process of nation-building.[19] Similarly, sociologists working on China after liberalization repeatedly caution for sharp demarcations of the boundaries of the state and the (free) market.[20] What is needed is a more culturally and historically informed understanding of state-market dynamics in China and not a simple use of the term *market* in describing the Chinese situation. More generally, we need a better theoretical understanding of the social embeddedness of finance and money to be able to do comparative sociological analysis of religion and market.

THE TRANSCENDENTAL VALUE OF MONEY

Anthropological interpretations of "traditional" economy may be helpful in formulating theoretical perspectives of "modern" economy. As shown in a classic essay by Appadurai and Breckenridge, we find at the core of the South Indian temple, an institution traditionally of fundamental importance to South Indian society and history, the circulation of "honors," *mariyatai*, that underlies a redistributive process constitutive to both society and the state.[21] In the general, dichotomous way of opposing traditional society to modern society one would be tempted to call the culture centering on the South Indian temple both religious and based on the secrecy of the transcendent, whereas one would be tempted to call the market economy both secular and based on public knowledge of the value of money. However, these dichotomies are notoriously unhelpful. Capitalism does not melt all that is culture into air, and therefore the market and money are culturally situated. The sociology of religion needs to deal with the transcendent and sacred nature of money. I want to argue here that the increasing importance of finance over production in the global economy and the unpredictability of global capital flows does not fit the idea that we live in what Charles Taylor calls "a secular age."[22]

Imagine living in Ireland. Long one of the poorest countries in Europe, it became the Celtic Tiger by being propelled to sudden wealth, thanks to a boom between 1995 and 2007. From 2008 onward the country went from boom to bust, with a GDP contraction of 14 percent in 2010 and a very rapid increase of unemployment. Ten to fifteen years passed in which Ireland's economy resembled a roller coaster. Or imagine living in Iceland, a country with a population equivalent to that of a middle-sized European town, after 2001 in the grip of great banking expansion and then experiencing a collapse in 2008 that reduced it to bankruptcy. These are epic stories of rise and decline within a decade, but if one takes the Asian Crisis of the late 1990s and the regular inflation-devaluation patterns in Latin America in the decades before that into account, it is hard to avoid the impression that to turn to the state or to international governing bodies such as the IMF and the World Bank and expect that they come up with solutions that dispose of these recurrent crises is to misunderstand the relation between states, markets, and money. The metaphysical understanding of the state as an arbiter and regulator of something that is outside the state underpins much of the debate about the "free market" and its regulation. In line with dominant theories of democracy, there is with every financial crisis a call for "transparency." When the Chinese economy (which has survived many of the crises of the last few decades but is not free from its own fictional Great Leaps Forward) is discussed in Western research and journalism today, there is an acute awareness of the interpenetration of state and market, of party officials running big companies and so on, but this interpenetration and lack of transparency is made into a special, deviant (and devious) case, an aberration that should be solved. The reason that Western economies are not subjected to a similar critique is that factual invisibility and secrecy is, paradoxically, covered up by economic and political ideologies of the "open society."

What is relevant for anthropological inquiry in all of this is precisely the metaphysical nature of the state and of money. Money is an ultimate sign of a nation's sovereignty, as the word for the coin ("sovereign") itself indicates and as the portraits and symbols and inscriptions on money signify. Moreover, the state's power depends on its tax base. Indeed the welfare of the nation as well as the effectiveness of the state depends on monetary value. Inflation, devaluation, revaluation, exchange value, the value of one's labor, all are signs of the health of the polity and the trustworthiness of political leaders. The state guarantees the value of its money, and people hold a strong belief in that invisible power of the state when they hold visible coinage in their hands. The state is held accountable for the functioning of the market, and this is in effect more important for people's political judgment than most other fields of political action. Nevertheless, the value of money depends on invisible market forces that are not controlled or only partly controlled by the nation-state. Here, as in espionage, the foreign hand comes in to explain sudden changes in the fortunes of the nation, together with the accusation that that foreign hand is helped by the disloyalty of marginal economic groups, for example, Jews or Lebanese or Indians or Chinese, who connect the local to the global via trade and money lending. Since money signifies exchange and thus the basis of society itself, it attracts moral thought on the possibilities and limits of exchange. Money then is the source of evil, the province of the devil. And indeed much religious thought is focused on banking and interest. Islamic thought on interest and usury is only one instance of this. Through its fetishism and circularity, money transcends purity and opens social life up for corruption. Corruption is often regarded to be that aspect of economic action that takes place behind the scenes, in the dark, but what about the invisible hand of the market itself? This is again a field of great fantasies of conspiracy and great, never-to-be-fulfilled demands of transparency. And it immediately concerns the central institutions of the modern nation-state.

The interplay of what is visible and what remains invisible is important not only for money and the market but also for that other currency, discourse. Not only communication and "openness" are crucial to civil society and the public sphere, as has been most prominently argued by Jürgen Habermas, but also their opposite, secrecy. Reinhart Koselleck has argued that the emergence of the secret societies of Freemasonry has been essential in the development of the Enlightenment critique of the absolutist state.[23] The important point here is that the Masonic lodges in the eighteenth century were able to erect a wall of protection for their debates and rituals against both intrusion from the state and intrusion from the profane world. It is precisely the moving away from state institutions and official politics that enables a fundamental moral critique of power. It should be clear, however, that this critique can take an unpleasant and terrorist form, as it did in the Jacobin theory of the French Revolution. It is this uncomfortable dialectic between secrecy and critique that troubled German theorists like Habermas and Koselleck after World War II. Both in civil society and in the state there is a constant creative tension between what is made visible and what is made invisible. Seeing is believing, but obviously not seeing is also believing.

I have used terms like *metaphysical, transcendent,* and *invisible* in my description of modern society. In Charles Taylor's acclaimed analysis of what he calls "our secular age," the disappearance of the transcendent is seen as a major development, while it seems to me that the transcendence of the state and the metaphysics of the market are foundational to modern society. With Taylor we have a Weberian understanding of a process of *Entzauberung* (demystification), which is fundamentally unhelpful in our understanding of modern society. It is precisely in the heart of society (markets and the state) that *Bezauberung* (mystification) takes place. The term *virtuality* describes best our contemporary moment of societal transformation. We have virtual money, virtual communication. In what sense would that be secular? According to William James, religion is founded on the subjective experience of an invisible presence.[24] We only have access to that subjective experience through the mediation of concrete practices. Crucial in that mediation is the relative invisibility, the abstractness of the supernatural or, perhaps better, its virtuality. Uncertainty is essential to religion but also to markets and money.

Here another element in Weber's sociology might be more useful than his evolutionist notion of *Entzauberung*. His analysis of the Protestant ethic as a source of methodical capitalism turned on his analysis of the Calvinist doctrine of the certainty of salvation in the face of the radical uncertainty about who was already one of God's elect. In his recent interpretation of *The Protestant Ethic*, Arjun Appadurai has suggested that "the calling" in Protestantism has something irrational but is the spirit of modern capitalism. Since one cannot know whether one belongs to "the elect" who are saved by God or not, one gambles on God's grace, and one acts as if one belongs to the elect, although one cannot be certain about that. This is what Appadurai calls a *derivative gamble* or *a gamble on a gamble*.[25] While entrepreneurial activities and financial operations invariably involve risk-taking and, if successful, are narrativized as heroic adventures, social life (markets and the state) involves metaphysical uncertainty. It is uncertainty and virtuality that characterizes both religion and society, making Taylor's notion of a secular age problematic.

Durkheim's sociology of religion might be useful to get at the metaphysics of money and market.[26] The power and attraction of goods that leads us to purchase them does not lie in the goods themselves but in the value we ascribe to them. Purchasing of goods not only positions the buyer in society but in a way produces society itself. This ideational value of goods is to an extent fetishistic, as in Marx's commodity fetishism, which locates value in the production process, but it is also totemic, as in Durkheim's understanding of the power attributed to an object by society. Through the ritual theater of advertising, the passions are produced that make us participate in the acts of market exchange. It is not possession as such that is at issue but imaginative value. Money is a perfect illustration of this, since it is a complete abstraction without any of the concrete characteristics of a good.

While in the art, car, computer, and cellphone markets symbolic value is created by groups of believers, it is especially in the market of gambling and lottery that we get closer to the religious nature of society. The wager may show the metaphysics of society and religion best. As Pascal argued, since God's existence cannot be proven by reason, one might wager that he exists. It is interesting that Pascal's wager underlies decision theory, which is fundamental to economics. One can perhaps say that the mathematical sophistication of decision theory and game theory may have been further developed, but that the fundamental uncertainty that pertains to religious and financial transactions cannot be taken away.

The anthropologist Steven Kemper has described Sri Lankan national lotteries as combining self-interested wager and selfless acts of charity, since the profits of these lotteries are tied to development goals.[27] One can interpret this as a special case of the general phenomenon that citizens are summoned to save or spend or wager as part of their belief in the nation. It is through these acts of citizenship, enforced or encouraged by the state, that the economy works. This was well expressed in the eighteenth century by the saying that public interest derives from private vice. The ways citizens are produced by being identified as consumers has been recently well illustrated by the offer made to the Indian state by the boss of Master Card, Ajay Banga, that his company could help conduct the campaign to give identification numbers to all Indian citizens. Betting and consuming are part of the circulation of money that constitutes society in ways that remind one of the redistribution of "honors" in the South Asian temple. What is most striking is the moral language in which these transactions are couched. This is not a fixed language. The morality of exchange is constantly negotiated, since what is at one point celebrated as entrepreneurial risk-taking is at another point in time vilified as antisocial profiteering.

While it is tempting to see modern capitalism as an all-encompassing break with the past of human society, the virtuality of the circulation of money, the very transcendence and abstraction of money, shows that the ways we break the religious and the sacred apart from the secular and the profane does not help us to provide better understandings of the disjunctures and differences that constitute social life.

It seems to me that a contribution to the understanding of the great abstraction that is "money" continues to be the study of the ways people are drawn into monetary interaction by consuming, betting, saving, participating in the stock market, speculating on house prices, and so on in the context of the lifeworlds that these activities are constituting. Instead of narrowing our understanding by the use of reductive theories of "rational choice" in "religious markets," we may be able to provide richer accounts of the ways transcendental values permeate human interaction.

PART II / CIVILIZATION AND COMPARISON

3 / KEEPING THE MUSLIMS OUT
CONCEPTS OF CIVILIZATION, CIVILITY, AND CIVIL
SOCIETY IN INDIA, CHINA, AND WESTERN EUROPE

Abstractly, this chapter deals with the problem of the stranger in relation to the connected concepts of civilization, civility, and civil society. Concretely, it refers to findings in the social anthropology of India, China, and western Europe. The problematic is the increasing diversity of social interaction in these societies. This is not the diversity within societies and between societies that has always been impressive, but the interaction between different kinds of people as a result of increased migration. The question of how to live with diversity has been important throughout human history, but it is now seen as the most important sociocultural question facing humankind in the twentieth century.[1] Spectacular urbanization in India and China is paralleled by constant flows of immigration into Europe and the United States, Australia, and Canada. Steven Vertovec has established that 40 percent of the inhabitants of Frankfurt (around 700,000 within a metropolitan area of more than 5 million people) have a migration background and that they belong to 170 nationalities. This constitutes what he calls "super-diversity."[2] In Europe this immigration is not only that of large nationalities, say from Turkey or the Maghreb, but is now also from everywhere else in both small and large numbers. While the process of modern urbanization in Europe has taken a century, and urban centers do not grow rapidly anymore, although their populations keep diversifying, the rate of urbanization of India over the last fifty years and especially that of China over the last thirty years is almost unimaginable. This is part of a world historical trend in which 10 percent of the world population was urban in the beginning of the twentieth century, while it is expected that 70 percent will live in cities in 2050, but in Asia the trend is accelerated. Shanghai had 16 million people in 2000 and 23 million people in 2011, of which 9 million are said to be "floating." Mumbai had 17 million in 2001 and 21 million in 2011, with 8 million so-called slum-dwellers.[3]

The obvious difference between migration into Indian and Chinese cities on the one hand and western European cities on the other is that between internal and external migration. The foreign population in Shanghai is only around 100,000, but that number refers to Westerners (*laowai*), while it does not include the vast number of Taiwanese living in Shanghai (approximately half a million). Statistics are hard to come by in the case of Mumbai, but there is not a large Western expat community, although there is a large (partly illegal) immigration from Bangladeshi nationals (indistinguishable from Bengalis but identifiable as Muslims). The rural-urban migration in western Europe does continue today, but it has been going on for a century or more, and the countryside is depopulated, while population growth is low or negative. In terms of diversity, the significant immigration in European cities is from abroad.

Internal and external migrations have features in common. External migration may be as much rural-urban as internal migration. One can move from some rural district in Gujarat to Mumbai or to London. One can move from some county in Wenzhou to Shanghai or to Paris. In both cases chain migration will help the migrant to find his or her place in a new environment. In both cases one can be without a residence permit and not have full citizenship rights. While "internal" and "external" refer to national citizenship and sovereignty, some borders are relatively recent and arbitrary. There is no obvious cultural difference between Indian Bengali and Bangladeshi Muslims, nor is there one between Mainland Chinese and Taiwanese, except for state-defined citizenship. There was a difference in state-defined citizenship between East and West Germans, but that disappeared with the collapse of the German Democratic Republic. What is inside and what is outside is arbitrary, depending on processes of boundary formation and maintenance. In North Indian villages the term *bahar ke log* (people from outside) was equally used for me as foreigner as well as for Indians coming from elsewhere and even for so-called untouchables who belonged to the village but lived outside it.

The problem I want to address is the problematic of "the stranger" in society in relation to concepts of civilization, civility, and civil society. The concept of civilization has to be taken seriously, despite all the conceptual confusion surrounding it. In the discussions on the European constitution, the question of civilization has loomed large. Christian Democrats pointed out that Europe was founded on a Christian civilization, while liberals and socialists pointed at Europe's secular-liberal foundations. Both arguments were also used against the inclusion of Muslim Turkey as a member state of the European Union. The fact that there were already millions of Turks (as well as other Muslims) in Europe seemed to have no bearing on the question whether Europe was Christian or secular-liberal. The fact that Turkey has a secular state and a secularism that most resembles French *laicité* also did not have an impact on the discussion of the inclusion of Muslim Turkey. This civilizational debate shows the extent to which Muslims are defined as strangers in Europe. The Bharatiya Janata Party in India constantly points at Hindu civilization as foundational to India, a sentiment most cogently expressed in the foundational text of Hindu nationalism, written by the nationalist ideologue V. D. Savarkar in 1923, which states: "A Hindu is a person who regards this land of BHARATVARSHA, from the Indus to the seas as his Father-land as well as his Holy-land that is the cradle-land of his religion."[4] The secular Congress Party has a more inclusive but still quite Hindu understanding of Indian civilization, as laid out in Jawaharlal Nehru's *The Discovery of India*.[5] As in Europe, the Muslim in India is the significant stranger, despite the presence of Islam in South Asia for almost as long as Islam has existed. In China the Communists have recently rediscovered Confucianism as the basis of Chinese civilization after having battled it for decades. Following an old pattern of Chinese hegemonic thinking, different religions should submit to the harmonious society (*hexie shehui* 和谐社会) controlled by the Chinese state. Here the most significant strangers are Uyghur Muslims and Christians, routinely seen as "foreign," while Tibetan Buddhists are seen as part of the Chinese civilization who have to be brought to that understanding.

CIVILIZATION

One of the more disturbing recent theoretical applications of the concept of civilization has been Samuel Huntington's book *The Clash of Civilizations and the Remaking of World Order*, in which he argues that global conflict arises out of the clash of civilizations that culturally divide the world. These civilizations are (1) Western, (2) Latin American, (3) Islamic, (4) Sinic (Chinese), (5) Hindu, (6) Orthodox, (7) Japanese, and (8) African. The core of each of these civilizations is formed by religious traditions. If we look at the regions I discuss in this chapter, this theory of international relations does not sound very convincing. Pakistan and Bangladesh were together after Independence because of shared religion but later split because of ethnicity; China and Vietnam had a war in the late 1970s despite their common civilization and common communism; the Irish fight each other as Catholics and Protestants within the same civilization. The only case that seems to fit the civilizational theory is that of al-Qaeda fighting Western civilization. Al-Qaeda itself, however, is a terrorist network, not a civilization. Huntington's theory is only partly about international relations, pleading for peaceful coexistence between civilizations (using the language of Cold War containment policies); it is mainly about the need for civilizational unity in the West (and especially the United States). It is here that the problematic of the stranger who threatens the unity of a civilization comes into the foreground in thinking about civilization. While European intellectuals are worried about Muslim demographics in their societies, Huntington is worried about the Hispanic demographics in the United States.[6] Cultural relativism abroad and cultural homogeneity at home seems to be the message of Huntington's final book: *Who Are We? The Challenges to American Identity*.[7]

From a purely academic point of view Huntington's ideas may not be worth discussing at length, but the attention that has been given to his theory shows that the concept of civilization is very much alive in the study of international relations. One finds a recent example in writing on East Asia by Peter Katzenstein, a leading international relations theorist, who has been arguing that "civilizations are social and operate at the broadest level of cultural identity in world politics. Because they are culturally integrated, civilizations can assume a reified identity when encountering other civilizations." Following the sociologist Randall Collins, Katzenstein sees civilizations as "zones of prestige that have one or several cultural centers." In Katzenstein's view India and China, as well as the United States, are civilizational states. Religious traditions are central to their identities and to their civilizing projects of Indicization, Sinicization, and Americanization.[8]

A major element in thinking about civilization is to search for deep history or even unchangeable essences. Max Weber's brilliant understanding of Western modernity is based on a theory about the rationalization of religion in Europe, which he compares with the rationalization of religion in India and China. It has inspired a group of scholars around the late

S. N. Eisenstadt to suggest a deeper history of civilizational (religious) patterns that lead to differences in their modernities. Eisenstadt argues that a disjunction (but not a split) between the transcendental and the mundane was for the first time made in a number of civilizations in roughly the same period, the first millennium before the Christian era.[9] These civilizations include ancient Israel, ancient Greece, early Christianity, Zoroastrian Iran, early imperial China, and the Hindu and Buddhist civilizations. Sociologically this development assumed the emergence of intellectual elites (e.g., Confucian literati, Brahmins, Buddhist *sangha*) who wanted to shape the world in accordance with their transcendental vision. This revolution in civilizational thought that occurred in all these civilizations in a relatively short time span around 500 BC is called the "Axial Age Breakthroughs," using a concept developed by the philosopher Karl Jaspers, who argued that in this period a shared framework for universal historical self-understanding emerged.[10] The central idea in this theory is that in the Axial Age a new emphasis on the existence of a higher transcendental moral order was developed across civilizations, at the same time as the concomitant emergence of the problem of salvation and immortality. How this problem is addressed differs from civilization to civilization.

Jaspers and Eisenstadt's Axial Age framework is the background to Charles Taylor's work on Western modernity, which he characterizes as a "secular age," without prejudging what might have been the evolution of, for example, Chinese civilization. In this connection Taylor mentions in passing that "one often hears the judgment that Chinese imperial society was already secular," an idea that in his view totally ignores the tremendous role played by the immanent/transcendent split in the Western concept, which has no analogue in China.[11] In Taylor's view the Axial Age dyad of immanent/transcendent (these two belong to each other) was radically split in European thought from the seventeenth century onward, and that split gave rise to the possibility of seeing the immanent as all there is and the transcendent as a human invention. "This-worldly" in the Chinese case, then, does not mean exactly the same as "secular" in the Western case. Taylor's observation is certainly important, if only in drawing our attention to the problematic of intercultural translation. To call Chinese civilization "secular" does indeed create more confusion than clarity. The drawback of all these ultimately Weberian arguments, however, is that they essentialize civilizational units (the West, India, China) to make them comparable but do not sufficiently explore the highly fragmented and contradictory histories of these societies. These arguments also tend to underestimate the influence of thought that does not fit easily in the immanent-transcendent framework, such as all those religious movements in India and China that emphasize the unity of being and the denial of difference.

A step forward beyond these civilizational essentializations would be to compare historical processes of state formation in India and China. When one examines the empires that preceded the modern political formations of colonized India and republican China, it is remarkable that both were empires ruled by "outsiders" (to the Hindu or Han civilizations) and that the Mughals kept to Islam while the Manchu (Qing) assimilated to the Confucian worldview. There were ethnic tensions at the heart of these empires: Manchu-Han and Muslim-Hindu. The processes of unification show such tensions, resulting in distinctive ways of using concepts like "civilization" and "ritual." These distinctions are again transformed by different kinds of anticolonial nationalism under the influence of imperialist encounters that resulted in colonizing India and transforming China.

When one examines contemporary society one needs to avoid interpreting the Communist state as representing ancient ideas of state power in China, since doing so would understate the fragmentary nature of premodern empires as well as the importance of the "warlord" period of half a century between the fall of the Qing and the foundation of the Communist state. Similarly, to explain the weakness of the Indian state in terms of caste as the essence of Indian society underestimates the enormous transformations of caste under British rule and in postcolonial India under conditions of democratic rule.

Weber, despite all his subtlety and genuine insights, also offered a historical analysis of oriental deficiency or, in other words, what the East lacked to develop modernity, and in that way essentialized its differences with the modern West. Hegel and later Marx saw a historical role for Europe in transforming the East but understood this simply as an impetus from outside to create change. A history of the interactions between East and West has to open up the fragmentary and contradictory nature of imperial encounters as well as the ways they produce new formations at both sides of the interaction. This is not a plea to do away with "local histories" but a plea to understand "the local" in terms of an "interactional history" of modernity. One continues to have a need to engage with the traditions that are central to societies and the ways they have been interpreted to form the civilizational core of national history, but one needs, at the same time, to acknowledge the contradictory and fragmentary nature of these traditions.

In my view we need to avoid essentializations of civilizations, without denying the deep histories of especially religious traditions and processes of state formation that connect people over vast territories. Of great importance is to resist the temptation to narrativize unity. When we look at "tradition" we may want to use Talal Asad's definition. "A tradition consists essentially of discourses that seek to instruct practitioners regarding the correct form and purpose of a given practice that precisely because it is established, has a history. These discourses relate conceptually to a past (when the practice was instituted, and from which the knowledge of its point and proper performance has been transmitted) and a future (how the point of that practice can best be secured in the short or long term. Or why it should be modified or abandoned), through a present (how it is linked to other practices, institutions, and social conditions)."[12] Central to a tradition is therefore the debate about authenticity and transgression.[13] While Weber would not disagree with this, he would try to come to ideal-typical descriptions of these traditions rather than focusing on the points of friction and the nature of the debate.

Traditions project themselves as timeless, transcending history, and their discursive authority lies precisely in that claim. It is thus not so much that in the modern period traditions are cast away in a process of westernization, but that the debate about how indigenous traditions relate to the necessity to measure up against the modern power of the West becomes central. When we examine nationalism and modernity in India, China, and Europe we should not see this simply as a break with the traditional past but as a reworking and transformation of traditions that are now portrayed as constituting the essence of national identity or as its civilization. As Norbert Elias has pointed out, the term *civilisation* in French identifies the national characteristics of the French, while the German *Zivilisation* stands for outward, material civilization and is inferior to *Kultur*, which is purely spiritual (*rein geistig*) and much less connected to politics.[14] In the second half of the nineteenth century these concepts were made to stand for essential differences between the French and the Germans.

To sum up, the concept of civilization is used in the modern period to essentialize national unity both in western Europe and in civilizational states like India and China. In India the concept of civilization can be translated as "Sankriti," but this is an ideal of Perfection that is carried by Brahman groups, not a unity at all. From the sixteenth century, state formation was largely carried out by Muslim groups that formed the Mughal Empire and a number of sultanates. The idea of a Hindu civilization unifying India became the founding myth of Hindu nationalism and has been used not only to unify castes, linguistic groups, and religious movements over the territory governed by the British but also to keep the Muslims out, since they have been seen (and increasingly have seen themselves) as belonging to a foreign Islamic civilization.

Confucian morality and statecraft is an important element of what in China is seen as civilization, but again this is a set of ideals rather than a reality. What we have in the Confucian worldview is a cosmology that emphasizes heaven (*tian*) as a metaphysical force that is impersonal and directs universe and human society through its Mandate (*tianming* 天命). This conception of a morally positive universe directed by the Mandate of Heaven had important ritual and political consequences: the emperor was the chief executor of the heavenly mandate in his ritual role as Son of Heaven. He was the performer of the great sacrifices to Heaven and Earth, these being the apex of a ritual-political system that integrated the empire. This system was *zheng* (正), which one may translate as "orthodoxy" but is perhaps better translated as "legitimate rule." Everything that was not in accordance with this political cosmology was *xie* (邪 heterodox or illegitimate). Besides this political orthodoxy there has been an element of self-cultivation and therefore of spirituality in Confucianism that was probably influenced by Chan Buddhism but aimed at tranquility and equilibrium. Moreover, there is a denial of the transcendent-immanent dyad to the extent that the ultimate unity of the internal and the external, of mind and nature, of self and the world, of being and nonbeing is emphasized.[15]

Confucianism then can be seen at the level of the state as a political cosmology. If one accepted this cosmology one could fill in personal spiritual needs with Buddhist devotion or Taoist magic or any other spiritual doctrine, like the Jesuit Matteo Ricci's doctrine of the Lord of Heaven. This looks syncretistic and tolerant, but it is all under the condition that one accepts the political cosmology. The concept of civilization can be translated as *wenming*, which stands opposite to "the uncivilized" or barbarians. A cognate concept, *wenhua*, can be translated as the process of civilizing others, assimilating them into Chinese civilization (whether or not they wish to). The character *wen* (文) stands for language and especially writing, signifying the importance of script and the literary tradition in Chinese conceptions of civilization. The modern Western understanding of civilization may actually be quite similar, since the French chair for the study of "noncivilized peoples" that was founded in 1888 at the École des Hautes Études was redefined by Claude Lévi-Strauss in the 1950s as "people without writing." Since the sixteenth century Chinese state formation has largely been carried out by a Manchu (barbarian) dynasty that has taken over Confucian ideals of civilization and tried to implement them. It was only in the transition from the Qing Empire to the Republican period that a civilization, carried by the Han majority, was ideologically tied to a Confucian civil religion and national unity. This notion of civilization has been adopted by the Communist Party, which first sought to replace "feudal" Confucianism with Communism, while keeping the idea of Han civilization alive. Today the Party is trying to combine Communism and Confucianism, as in Deng Xiaoping's combination of "material civilization [wuzhi wenming] and spiritual civilization [jingshen wenming]."[16] While one cannot say that Chinese conceptions of civilization have as their main function to keep the Muslims out, there is a strong sense that Uyghur Muslims do not belong to Chinese civilization and that even Hui Muslims (who are Han) do not belong either. Whenever I asked during my stay in Shanghai whether Muslims would belong to the city after residing in it for several generations, the answer was invariably: of course not. While other minorities are more and more integrated in Chinese society and their cultures are seen as a charming folkloristic addition to Chinese civilization, Muslims (and especially the Muslims of the North-West Frontier) continue to be seen as threateningly Other. This is exacerbated by the geographical location of Xinjiang, which resembles that of Kashmir in India, at the edge of national territory, and the fact that the majority of the population are Muslims.

In Europe the references to the ancient civilizations of Athens and Rome have been in the past made by both European cosmopolitans and Italian and Greek nationalists. Today these references are also made in providing the founding myth of Europe's modernity (its liberty, ideals of citizenship, rationality, and so on). In the imperial and nation-building period Europe's civilizational modernity (as described in Charles Taylor's work) was mainly used to explain Europe's ascendancy as well as its right to rule and educate others who had backward civilizations. The idea of civilization has thus been used not only to create national unity and class hegemony but also to portray modern progress both as developing from European civilization and as a measuring rod to judge the development of other civilizations. In the 1960s when postcolonial cultural theorists coined the slogan *the Empire is striking back*, the main issue became what to do with the backward others who did not stay in their colonies but were flooding (as the British politician Enoch Powell described it in 1968 in his infamous "Rivers of Blood" speech) our cities.[17] This problematic of diversity has been gradually translated into rhetoric of keeping the Muslims out. It is interesting that Chinese and Vietnamese are seldom seen today as troublesome immigrants in Europe and the United States, although they are culturally and racially recognizably different. The reason seems to be that they are seen to share a core value of modern civilization, namely, mobility through education, and do not seem to demand much recognition of their culture from their host societies.

CIVILITY

Let me now turn to the concept of civility that is closely related to that of civilization. In Adam Smith's understanding of commercial society, a stranger is someone who is neither friend nor foe, and uninvolved, indifferent, and impartial. Commercial society depends on impartial interaction, which requires self-constraint and civility in public spaces.[18] Smith thought that the growth of such interactions would lead to a universal sociability.[19] This is, in my view, close to Norbert Elias's interpretation of the process of civilization. According to Elias, social differentiation and longer chains of interdependence would result in regulation of conduct. While Smith emphasized market society, Elias emphasized state formation that led to pacification and a monopoly of the state on physical force. Elias also emphasized the control of affects and the ritualization of behavior at the court. In the arguments by Smith and Elias we find a teleological causality that makes us all into strangers and requires that we can treat each other impartially and without violence. To use Albert Hirschman's classic interpretation: we lose our passions because of our interests.[20]

I find the idea that we all have to become strangers to be able to enter commercial society exciting. It is close to the idea in modernization theory that ethnic bonds have to be replaced by civic bonds, as Geertz has argued, for example, in his essay on old societies and new states.[21] However, the more fundamental question, already raised in Adam Smith's theory, is how we can know what others think and how we are able to judge others' intentions. This is, obviously, also a central problem in ethnography. Geertz describes the task of the ethnographer as follows: "We begin with our interpretations of what our informants are up to, or think they are up to, and then systematize those." Geertz called this *verstehende* approach "thick description."[22] But how do we know what our informants are up to or think they are up to? Elsewhere in his essay Geertz quotes Wittgenstein to point out an obvious difficulty: "We . . . say of some people that they are transparent to us. It is, however, important as regards this observation that one human being can be a complete enigma to another. We learn this when we come into a strange country with entirely strange traditions; and, what is more, even given a mastery of the country's language; we do not understand the people. (And not because of not knowing what they are saying to themselves). We cannot find our feet among them." Wittgenstein gives this description of an intercultural encounter to illustrate what can be seen as a more general problem that may also be inherent in encounters within a culture. In her recent *A Widow's Story: A Memoir*, the American novelist Joyce Carol Oates describes her sudden widowhood after having been married to her husband for forty-seven years and twenty-five days. After this long marriage (of almost a lifetime) she comes to the conclusion that "for a woman, the quintessential male is unknowable, elusive. In our marriage it was our practice not to share anything that was upsetting, depressing, demoralizing, tedious—unless it was unavoidable. A wife must respect the *otherness* of her husband—she must accept it, she will never know him fully."[23] Nor can the reader fully know the author of this memoir, since in the long description of that year of grief she fails to mention that she has met, dated, and remarried another man. So little do we know even within our own culture! Even the Greek injunction *Gnothi Seauton* (Know Thyself), is an injunction precisely because it is not self-evident.

Let us assume for a moment that full knowledge, absolute transparency, between people is not possible and also not required for social life. For example, it has always struck me that people can trade over long distances with people they hardly know and whose languages they can hardly speak without this being an insurmountable difficulty. For this essential element of social life, the exchange of goods, it seems that one does not need to know what people really think. As long as people pay the right price and deliver the right goods there is no problem. There may be misunderstandings, but to an extent they belong to bargaining and finding advantage on the basis of that crucial resource in economic behavior: information. So rather than wanting to find out what people really think, the trader needs information. To reduce risk in the context of asymmetric information one needs trust and obligation, contractual arrangements. Contract theory in economics uses concepts like moral hazard to describe the inability to have access to verification of an actor's actions and uses algorithms to optimize decisions. As one knows, the philosopher Rousseau extended the notion of contract to social contract to describe appropriate and binding relations between rulers and the people. And as Hume sharply pointed out in his essay "Of Civil Liberty," this notion of social contract needs a metaphysical foundation, either in God or in a notion of the People.[24]

Money is said to provide a measure to evaluate and exchange things of different kinds between people who do not know each other. The circulation of money and the ways it enhances the circulation of everything in society is crucial to social life and public culture. What money *really* is, however, is as elusive as what people *really* think. As Marcel Mauss has argued, it is in the exchange itself that the power of the object is created.[25] It is not possession as such that is at issue but imaginative value. Money is a perfect illustration of this, since it is a complete abstraction without any of the concrete characteristics of a commodity. The English expression *Put your money where your mouth is* refers to money as making possible the evaluation of the sincerity of speech, but it is precisely money that is often seen as a corrupting force that threatens the morality of society.

These metaphysical uncertainties that surround our exchanges of words and goods as well as the order of society in law and government are exactly that: metaphysical. What then is the metaphysics of a culture and society in which one wants to know what people really think, since it is not immediately apparent that this desire or need exists everywhere at all times in the same measure. What one could perhaps say is that there are different kinds of need and requirements in communication that are specific to spheres within society or in contact zones between societies, such as, in my earlier instance, commerce. And one could add that different cultural traditions may divide these spheres differently as well as developing different "language-games" that belong to them.

One tradition that seems to be troubled by uncertainty about what people really think is Protestantism. Like any other tradition this has many arguments and streams and currents, but the issue of sincerity seems to come up in a number of different ways. One current has been a prime subject of Weber's sociology, that of the seventeenth-century Puritans, who were averse to ritual, idolatry, and rhetorical extravagance. They promoted "plain and simple speech." Richard Bauman and Charles Briggs connect this to the contemporary scientists who founded the Royal Society and their preference for "a naked, natural way of speaking."[26] The Protestants are interesting because they are often seen as forerunners of imperial modernity and thus create realities that are also inescapable for non-Protestant outsiders. If we take Charles Taylor as our guide to understand the Western modern self, crucial features are individual agency and the valued capacity to change. According to Taylor, a new understanding of individual identity emerged at the end of the eighteenth century. "We might speak of an individualized identity, one that is particular to me, and that I discover in myself. This notion arises along with an ideal, that of being true to myself and my own particular way of being."[27] In Taylor's reconstruction of modernity's history, the earlier moral view, in which one was in touch with a transcendent source, is now located deep within the self, indicating a new interiority. Taylor refers to the aforementioned Rousseau and to Herder as articulating this new sense of a secular self. These references are relevant to an anthropological discussion, since these thinkers are often seen as forefathers of a discipline of anthropology that is rooted in this modern need for authenticity. For Taylor it is important to emphasize that we develop this modern self in dialogue with significant others. It is here where our modern problematic (and the problematic of anthropology) really emerges. It is not that identity and recognition by others did not exist earlier but rather that now the inwardly generated identity is deeply in need of a recognition that is based not on status and material goods but, as Webb Keane puts it, on "the character and condition identified with its own identity."[28]

While I do not doubt the importance of the cult of the individual in modern society, I am not convinced that this cult or this "ideology," as Louis Dumont called it, is as encompassing as it is claimed to be.[29] It may be a "metadiscourse" about the relations between words and interior states, but it is only one discourse among others. One only has to look at the collectivist dreams of nationalism, socialism, or communism to realize that transcendence (the nation, the working class as agents of history) is still there. The individual and the modern collective are, in fact, produced simultaneously. As Taylor argues, it is precisely in recognition, in dialogue, that interiority surfaces. If this is the case, our attention should be focused on what emerges in communication rather than on interior states as such.

According to Keane, sincerity is conveyed by "sincere speech" for the Sumbanese, who were converted by Dutch Calvinist missionaries. This is because Calvinist Protestants do not have any ritual except the sermon, the prayer, and the catechism. I think that that observation is correct but still does not pay enough attention to the fact that extralinguistic evidence about someone's sincerity continues to be an important element in Calvinist constant watchful observation of each other's adhering to Christian norms. The Netherlands has for a long time been a very controlled society precisely because of this surveillance. "Not by word alone" could be the Calvinist motto. And Calvinists are only one brand of Protestants. In Henry Abelove's engaging account of the Methodist John Wesley's popularity, it was precisely his extravagant and transgressive behavior that attracted many followers.[30] Not puritanical, not Calvinist, but something else altogether.

The Calvinist worldview closely resembles a legal one. The law ascribes agency to people; it takes them to be responsible for their actions; it is more interested in evidence of their guilt than in their sincerity and sees confession as an important element of the process of punishment and redemption. However, the Calvinist theory of predestination and original sin complicates matters of crime and punishment considerably. Calvinism contains an essential contradiction in asserting that human beings are born in sin and will be always sinful and in ascribing agency to subjects who are free to choose between sin and non-sin. This predicament, and essential uncertainty, mostly leads to following the collective opinion in the church community of what "living in sin" is and what it is not.

Other (non-Calvinist) Protestants, such as Evangelicals and Pentecostals, are even further away from the need to know what people really think as well as from the notion that one's words and actions do not have a transcendent source. Speaking in tongues is definitely authentic speech, but who is speaking? For Pentecostal Christians it is the Holy Ghost who is speaking while using human tongues. Evangelical preachers may look very insincere in their constant emphasis on money acquisition, but their followers do not seem to be bothered. The televangelist scandals involving Jimmy Swaggart and Jim and Tammy Bakker did little, in fact, to diminish Evangelicalism's appeal. Rather, the televised confessions of sin moved people because they showed the pastors to be mortal, sinful beings (like everyone else) who represented their flock in their fall and in the performance of their sinfulness.[31] One could probably see President Bill Clinton's confessions in the

Monica Lewinsky affair as following the same model, showing the extent to which it has become generalized in American culture.

In my view, both the transcendental and the magical are much more present in both Protestantism and Western modernity than is often assumed. Even in Protestantism there is a mix of speech acts and other acts, including ritual, that constitutes religious behavior. Of course, Protestant missionaries often expressed doubts about the sincerity of the native conversion. There is much in the missionary literature about "rice Christians," which refers to those who may have converted in order to feed their bellies, especially during famines. It is probably the case that both missionaries and converts have been engaged in trying to improve their situations by converting or by being converted. The motivations and their interpretation are varied and not immediately transparent. The missionaries were, for example, engaged in a number game with their sponsors at home. They had to show some success, and numbers are extremely useful in this. This interest in numbers continues today in the Pew Foundation's emphasis on quantitative studies of world Christianity and the Chinese government's fixation on numbers of Christians. What people do or do not believe is not what counts.

Weak ties or being strangers to one another was certainly an important element of commercial society even before modern times. When one cannot rely on family or ethnicity and has to trust complete strangers, one needs to have trust-inspiring codes of conduct. This need to deal with strangers increases with long-distance trade and with increasing complexity of society. In traditional Japanese society, civility and social trust are closely related, perhaps because it is a society in which homogeneity is stressed to an extraordinary extent.[32] In modern society throughout the world this is partly class based; it is what one learns in high school and at the university. However, there are different spheres of civility with cognoscenti and strangers. This resonates with what Robert Weller identifies as a crucial Chinese term for "civility": *li* (禮) is also "ritual" and especially "court ritual" and thus regulates proper behavior within and outside the family.[33] This reminds one of Norbert Elias's description of courtly society in France and its development of etiquette. In Confucian thought the patriarchal family and the relation between ruler and his people are modeled on each other and we find something similar in Europe in the notion of patrimony. Ultimately such ritualistic behavior and other forms of bodily discipline have to be understood as parts of state formation, as Norbert Elias has proposed in his work on "etiquette." They are rules that are enforced under conditions of power.

Students of China have pointed to the importance of *guanxi*, practices like gift-giving and banquets, to establish relations between strangers.[34] Since much of this involves eating pork and drinking alcohol, Muslims with food and drinking taboos have difficulty in participating in them. However, they may be able to create their own ethnic enclaves in the business community where civility is ethnicized and trust and solidarity grow out of the very fact of exclusion from wider commerce. Indians with their caste-based food taboos can relax them during business transactions. In buffet meals both meat and vegetarian dishes are served. However, again Muslims tend to be excluded, not so much because they eat meat but because they (are thought to) eat beef. At the same time, this exclusion may further some niche commercial activity. As in China, commercial activity can be ethnically specialized, and Muslims, by token of their ethnic-religious long-distance networks and their "nonbelonging" to local society are often traders in both India and China. Ismaili Muslim business groups (Bohras, Khojas) are among the most successful in India, reminding one of the success of Jewish business groups.

In Europe it is another aspect of civility, namely public appearance and behavior, that tends to exclude Muslims as strangers. It is in the anonymity of the city that, according to Simmel, we are all strangers.[35] Public civility is imposed on everyone so as to be able to be in one another's faces in public transport or shopping malls. Here civility is in an interesting way connected to indifference or ways of not seeing.[36] Strangers have to acquire these forms of conduct to be able to become invisible. It is here that dressing codes especially are crucial. In Europe the visibility of difference (especially of a gendered nature) of Muslims in the public sphere is one of the main issues in politics. I hardly have to mention the importance of covering one's head for modesty for debates about inclusion or exclusion of Muslims. Especially in France, Muslim modesty is interpreted as obscenity, as uncivil behavior that signifies the subjugation of women in modern society, in which equality, individuality, and liberty are supposed to be the guiding social values.[37]

Finally, connected to civilization and civility is the notion of civil society. This is generally understood as an aspect of modern civilization. In accounts by Norbert Elias and Roger Chartier, civility is the code of behavior that is required in the new, free spaces of communication of citizens, those who belong to the political community. As I have noted, it is also a requirement for commercial society. Civil society refers to voluntary associations outside state control and thus the possibility of the free exchange of ideas that constitutes the public sphere. Theorists like Habermas, Rawls, and Taylor have all attempted to describe the nature of civil society and to prescribe the nature of communication in it. Since the 1980s much of the critique of the twin concepts of civil society and public sphere has focused on who have been excluded from it—women, blacks, and so on. A major element of the arguments of Rawls and Habermas has been that the public sphere had to become completely secular to be neutrally accessible to all. These are arguments not about the content of the debate but about procedures of conducting a rational debate and creating an overlapping consensus, but still they depend on the secular as the frame of any debate. This is even true for later reformulations of their position. Rawls argues that religious arguments could have a place in the debate as long as they were translatable in secular terms. Habermas argues that they are permissible and can even be helpful as long as there is no direct appeal to a transcendent notion of ultimate truth. Taylor has responded to this by putting forward that Habermas's own demand of complete rationality is in fact a claim to a transcendent value.[38]

In Europe the practical political question is not whether religious arguments can be discussed in the public sphere or whether religious organizations can be part of civil society. In Germany and Holland, with their strong Christian Democratic traditions, there is no question about this, while in France, with all the emphasis on laïcité, one should not underestimate the strong presence of Catholicism in political life. In Britain the queen is head of the Anglican Church, and dissenting traditions have been important sources for the politics of the Labour Party. The practical political question in Europe today is whether Muslims can be allowed to be part of civil society as Muslims. To what extent can religious arguments based on interpretations of Islamic tradition be uttered and heard in European civil society? When one looks at the treatment of a Muslim intellectual like Tariq Ramadan, who tries to argue for a modern European Islam and for Muslim participation in democracy, listening to Islam-based arguments is still very precarious.

The mainstream theoretical debate about civil society does not look outside the West. I have already referred to Eiko Ikegami's argument that Japan in the Tokugawa period had civility without civil society. About

Communist China we can say that it has various spheres of civility, as for example in the art of creating relations, *guanxixue*, but no civil society. In response to a talk about civil society I gave some time ago at Renmin University in Beijing, students and faculty said that "civil society" was a typical Western concept that was imposed on China.[39] In their view, Chinese are able to find their own ways of creating relatively free spaces, especially in creating economic opportunity. What I think was not fully appreciated by my audience is that there is a Marxist understanding of civil society (taking the German term *bürgerliche Gesellschaft*) that argues that the bourgeoisie, as the social locus of civil society, should be destroyed in order to achieve an equal and just society. This locates all power and decision-making in the party-state. It was the path taken in Communist China until 1978. What we now have in China seems to be commercial civility and the rise of a bourgeoisie without civil society. Commercial activity depends on good contacts within the party-state. In China religious voluntary organizations are not allowed to play the role they have played in Europe (or in Taiwan, according to Richard Madsen) to shape civil society.[40] This is particularly true for those voluntary organizations that are placed outside the common civilization, namely Christian and Muslim ones. Kenneth Dean has argued in his work on Fujian that local temples and voluntary temple associations play an important role in creating relatively autonomous spaces in a region that is firmly connected to Southeast Asia and may thus have resources that are specific to this network.

In contrast to China, India has a robust civil society and public sphere in which religious organizations play a significant role. The civility of that civil society, however, is quite doubtful. Pogroms against Muslims and to a lesser extent Christians have been a major part of political democratization in India, with the doubtful result that in the 2014 Indian elections the chief minister of Gujarat, who did not prevent and probably actively instigated these pogroms against Muslims, became the prime minister of the country.

CONCLUSION

Muslims have come to be seen as the quintessential strangers in Europe and India. As a category they are defined as in many ways outside civilization, civility, and civil society. Assimilation into the mainstream society does not always work, as demonstrated by the assimilation into *Bildungsbürger* of German Jews before the Holocaust. In India one may be totally unrecognizable as Muslim, but in times of communal violence the ultimate check is whether one is circumcised or not. The male body marks who one really, truly is.

In China Muslims are seen as excluded from civilization, and to an extent from important forms of civility, while the question of civil society does not come up. A real political problem surfaced when the sovereignty of the state was challenged in Xinjiang. While the traditional states in India and China tried to absorb strangers and hierarchically include them in the civilization, modern states work much more through exclusion. Philosophers like Seyla Benhabib think that the problem of the stranger can be solved in a legal manner by inclusive citizenship rights, but Muslims in Europe, India, and China are citizens.[41] It is the application of cultural concepts like civilization and civility as the basis of national identity that identifies and excludes the stranger from civil society.

4 / THE AFTERLIFE OF IMAGES

In this chapter I want to compare one particular aspect of Indian and Chinese society that is of deep historical significance. The comparison can show us how processes and interventions that bear a great similarity have very different objectives and outcomes in India and China. My interest here is in visual regimes that govern the visible and the invisible. This topic can be approached in various ways, but often the focus is on media technologies and media forms. I take a different tack here by looking at what one might call iconicity, the icon and what it stands for. By doing so I do not address media per se, but I touch on mediation. My aim is to address the problematic of "seeing is believing" and "believing is seeing," which goes beyond new and old media into the more general problem of virtual presence (linked to the philosophical problematic of transcendence and immanence).

While much has been written about images, imagery, icons, and iconography in the historiography of China and India, iconoclasm—the deliberate destruction of sacred images or icons—may not have received the attention it deserves. In my view iconoclasm points at moments of crisis that highlight what is at stake in fundamental conflicts of a political and ideological nature. I do not want to get bogged down in definitional questions of what exactly is a sacred image or icon except to say that these are terms for "what is held sacred" and thus depend on shifting sets of relationships between objects and persons that are subject to ideological debate. Alfred Gell has argued that there are no universally applicable theories of the object or of representation.[1] Therefore, one deals with historically specific theologies or forms of secularism, carried by communities, political forces, and movements, that define objects and representations. As Talal Asad has argued in his discussion of symbol and meaning, "a symbol is not an object or event that serves to carry a meaning but a set of relationships between objects or events uniquely brought together as complexes or as concepts, having at once an intellectual, instrumental, and emotional significance."[2] Moreover, it is obvious that what is called sacred and nonsacred or religious and nonreligious is subject to definitional changes that are themselves part of the changing social configuration one wants to describe. It is this perspective on objects and events that will allow me to include sacred buildings like mosques and temples, as well as city planning and the destruction of parts of the city, in my discussion of icons and iconoclasm. To an extent this is what David Morgan defines as "visual culture," in which "seeing is an operation that relies on an apparatus of assumptions and inclinations, habits and routines, historical associations and cultural practices." However, I want to destabilize the distinction between the secular and the religious that is basic to his understanding of what he calls "the sacred gaze," "a religious act of seeing" that, in his terms, is "the manner in which a way of seeing invests an image, a viewer, or an act of viewing with spiritual significance."[3] As I have argued in my recent book *The Modern Spirit of Asia*, it was at the end of the nineteenth century that a syntagmatic chain of religious-secular-spiritual-magic emerged. These four terms are not simple essences, nor do they possess stable meanings independently from each other. They emerge historically together, imply one another, define one another, and function as nodes within a shifting field of discourse and power.

Here I want to focus on attempts to make the visible invisible by destroying it. This raises the question how virtual presence complicates the seemingly straightforward boundary between the visible and the invisible. I will first examine some important cases of religious iconoclasm in modern India and China. The prominent visibility of religion in India will not surprise anyone, but it can help us to highlight the ways it is made invisible in China. Second, I will examine the destruction of "the past" and the construction of "the new" (破旧立新 *po jiu li xin*, in Maoist language) in the building of modern cities and the visualization of "the modern" in India and China.

Both India and China have historically experienced campaigns of "icon-oclasm," which can be glossed as "violent destruction of sacred objects." Besides destruction of icons and objects one also finds complex narratives of subjugation, incorporation, and transformation of icons in rival visual regimes of signification. Such histories testify to the power of the icons and raise the question of the afterlife of images after destruction or transfor-mation. Destruction is often not total; traces remain, and what has been destroyed can be remade. This reminds us that visual regimes show a continuum between total visibility and total invisibility with a dynamic "in-between." In the modern period a major competitor for visual dominance is secular modernity, which aims to encompass the sacred icon and give it its limited space. These *longue durée* histories have therefore not ended with the coming of modernity. In fact, the sacred life of the image and its employment or destruction is today part of major cultural narratives and contestations in India and China.

India had a recent case of iconoclasm of great political significance. In 1992 a well-organized mob destroyed a mosque in the North Indian pilgrim-age center Ayodhya. The mosque was built by the Mughal emperor Babar in the sixteenth century. According to the attackers it was constructed on the site of the destroyed birthplace of Lord Rama, whose life story on earth was recorded in one of India's most important epics, the *Ramayana*. The attack was legitimated by arguing that almost fifty years after Independence and Partition the Hindu majority of India should not have to face the signs of its past humiliation (namely previous destruction of Hindu sacred objects) by Muslims anymore. The mosque was perceived as a material sign of that humiliation. The movement that aimed to destroy the mosque was called "a sacrifice to liberate Rama's birthplace." In the demonstrations I witnessed there was one monk who had dressed up as the god Rama and had bound himself in chains like a modern-day Houdini, without, however, being able to free himself. At the time I was doing fieldwork in Ayodhya, and I was puzzled by the fact that nobody seemed to think that Lord Rama could liberate himself, although he is theologically seen as *muktida*, giver of liberation, and Maryada Purushottam, the Lord of Self-Constraint, not as "the constrained Lord." Moreover, the most important image for wor-ship in Ayodhya and all over Northern India is that of Hanuman, Rama and Sita's prime servant and minister, depicted as endlessly strong and power-ful, as well as totally devoted to his masters. People go to pray to him for strength and endurance, but nobody I interviewed seemed to care that he had not been able to prevent the building of the mosque on Rama's birthplace. The youth wing of the Hindu nationalists that destroyed the mosque called itself Bajrang-Dal, the Party of Hanuman, and they were explicitly inspired by the strength of Hanuman, but still they had to do all the work of destruction with their own hands.

I do not want to sound too much like a Protestant iconoclast or Marxist antifetishist, but the question does come up: what do our informants think that images are up to? (This question is rather different from that raised by the image theorist Tom Mitchell: "what do pictures want?"[4]) And what happens when they, although considered to be very powerful, seem to be helpless in defending themselves against iconoclasts? What is the afterlife of images when they are discarded, destroyed, or displaced, thrown into the "dustbin of history," to use Trotsky's phrase? If things have a social life they may also have a social death. As I argued earlier, anthropologists and historians can only give contextual and no universal answers to such questions.

At one level the prehistory of the destruction of the Babar's mosque seems relatively straightforward. Islam proscribes the making of "likenesses or representations of God" and follows Judaism closely in this regard. Islam seems to demand from its followers the destruction of idols and the spread of the correct faith. This is, then, one would assume for lack of documentation, the reason why Ram's temple was destroyed by Babar's army. However, the story is not that straightforward, since not all temples were destroyed, and in fact we have evidence from various periods of Indian history that Muslim rulers patronized Hindu temples. The story of Muslims' destruction of an important Hindu temple was nevertheless the main legitimation for Hindu nationalists to retaliate and destroy the mosque. One would think perhaps that one cannot make an iconoclastic assault on Islam, since Muslims do not worship images. This particular proscription is important, but it should not be interpreted as implying that Muslims have no sacred objects, as we have seen recently in the furious Muslim responses to burnings of the Koran and destruction of mosques. The mosque is certainly a sacred place for the communal worship of God and thus a symbol of the Muslim community. During the Ayodhya campaign the Babar mosque had become the symbolic representation of the Indian Muslim community as a whole, and its destruction was felt as an attempt to wipe out the history of Islam in India and by that token the historical identity of the Muslim community. Muslims responded by rioting that resulted in a widespread Hindu backlash at the time, genocidal pogroms later, and a very unstable inimical relation between Hindus and Muslims today and in the foreseeable future.

That the mosque could be destroyed in 1992 depended on a political constellation in which Hindu nationalists had gained unprecedented power, not on some spontaneous upsurge of devotion for Rama. In fact, long before the destruction of the mosque in 1949, an image of Lord Rama had appeared in the temple. This image had been secretly planted by Hindu nationalists who had seen that the Partition had weakened the power and presence of the Muslim community in India. I knew the man who had done it, and he was privately (and later publicly) very proud of his action. Nehru's government thought it prudent (as indeed the British would have) not to have the image removed but to keep it in there, while prohibiting both communities from worshiping in the temple, except that a small committee of Hindus was allowed to worship the image of Rama once a year on the anniversary of its first appearance. The spontaneous appearance of images in India has an established historical significance in claims on land and sacred sovereignty. One can therefore say that there was power in the image in the sense that the Nehru government did not want to remove it and by that token create unrest among Hindu activists, but clearly the Parliament in Delhi and not Lord Rama was the sovereign power, although highly circumscribed and politically contextualized. Only half a century later the Bharatiya Janata Party claimed that there was no conflict between the sovereignty of Lord Rama and that of secular power, since India was in their claim a Hindu nation. This claim could only be successfully made at the emergence of a new political configuration.

However, the history of power and iconoclasm cannot be reduced to a relatively simple story of shifting political configurations. It is the cultural complexity of power that needs exploring. It is hard to understand the iconoclastic fury of Hindu nationalists in the 1990s when one ignores the deeper history of iconoclasm in the region. The best known iconoclast in Indian history (in a story repeated in any Indian history textbook used in schools) is Mahmud of Ghazni (971–1030), the destroyer of Somnath, an important Hindu temple in West India. It is said that he personally broke the gilded lingam, the symbol of the god Shiva. However, while Mahmud of Ghazni stands for the iconoclastic Islamic conquest of Hindustan, popular stories and forms of worship centering on his nephew Salar Masud Ghazi, or

Ghazi Miyan (Ghazi means "holy warrior" and Miyan means "Muslim"), in Bahraich, close to Ayodhya, tell a much more complicated story of power.

Both Hindus and Muslims worship the shrine of this martyred warrior-saint who came to conquer Hindustan and whose uncle was the terrible Mahmud. This is not unique in India, since one can find shrines for such saints all over the place and worshiped by all, even today. The historian Shahid Amin has studied the official Persian chronicles, which give the story of Ghazi Miyan as that of the martyrdom of this hero of Islam by the hands of the Hindus.[5] Amin contrasts this official narrative with vernacular ballads of local folklore in which the story is about his birth as the son of a barren untouchable woman who was blessed by a Muslim Sufi saint and his death as a virgin on his way to his marriage. Most curiously, he does not die in defense of Islam but in defense of cows and cowherds, which makes him in fact a perfect Hindu. Women who have been unable to bear children come to his shrine to get his blessings for offspring. The festival celebrating him is at the beginning of an agricultural cycle and has been immensely popular in North India. So the hero of war has become the god of fertility, but not entirely, since he is still a Muslim warrior-saint, a Ghazi.

Such popular reworkings and interpretations of a history of conquest and iconoclasm can be found everywhere. This is not to suggest that they are testimony to an easygoing, folksy syncretism, but that they are testimony to the complicated engagement of Islam with a largely non-Islamic culture. What we find in India is a history of iconoclasm that is largely tied up with Hindu-Muslim relations and ultimately with questions of sovereignty. Sacred power and profane power are directly connected, and the sacred object stands for the power of the ruler or, in democratic times, the community. As long as the community is not destroyed, its visual representation will be rebuilt and defended.

In China the historical configuration is quite different. There is a marginal (but not unimportant) Muslim presence in China, and the emphasis, historically, has been on the expansion of Han ethnic groups and of the imperial state, which may occasionally have led to destruction of sacred objects of non-Han ethnic groups but mainly has led to slow incorporation of diverse ethnic groups into the larger Han ethnicity, as well as the hierarchical incorporation of local gods into an imperial pantheon.[6] The imperial state also has persistently attempted to put Buddhist and Daoist groups under its control, sometimes by extensive destruction of Buddhist shrines, as when Emperor Wuzong in the Tang dynasty around 845 AD wanted to demolish what he called the "religion of idols." This is a large story, obviously, but the point I want to make is that while we cannot interpret iconoclasm in China by looking at the formation, as in India, of two large ethnoreligious groups that in the modern era have become increasingly antagonistic, sovereignty is central in China too.

Iconoclasm is very significant in China, perhaps even more significant than in India, despite the numerical insignificance of Muslims. What China offers is an interesting case of nearly total destruction of religious buildings and objects throughout the twentieth century, followed by very recent rebuilding. At the end of the nineteenth century the destruction of temples was part of a fervent desire among intellectuals and political leaders "to catch up with the world." "Smash temples, build schools" (毁庙办学 *huimiao, banxue*) is a particularly telling slogan that was used in a campaign against temple cults and religious specialists in reforms during the late Ching dynasty at the end of the nineteenth century. Before the Communist victory in 1949 a number of campaigns, first in late imperial China and afterward in the Republic, destroyed or "secularized" (in the medieval European sense of being taken out of the church and integrated in the world), according to one estimate, half of a million existing temples.[7] The twentieth century in China can well be regarded as the century of iconoclasm, since the nationalist campaigns against superstition were followed by a number of Communist campaigns, culminating in "smashing the four olds" (四旧 old ideas, old customs, old culture, old habits) as part of the Great Cultural Revolution. One may well wonder what was left standing, and I have been to famous Daoist sites where indeed not much was left. Nevertheless, there are many stories about how local believers have hidden images, and I myself heard a story in Xiamen from fishermen of how they had taken their Mazu (Mother Goddess) image to Taiwan and had returned it now to Xiamen. In some other cases the object of veneration has been destroyed, but its power still lingers, as in the following case.

In the summer of 2014 I visited Mianning County (Liangshan Yizu Autonomous Prefecture in Sichuan, Southwest China, only eighty kilometers outside Xichang, the capital of the prefecture). On a beautiful mountain called Lingshan (灵山 Magic Mountain) one finds a huge temple visited by tens of thousands of devotees during the pilgrimage season. To get to the temple one has to climb the mountain or travel on a mule. As is typical in China, during the climb one passes several temples in a row. The first displays a huge statue of the fat, laughing Budai; then there are several other

Buddhist temples, until one comes to the highest level, where there is only a simple shrine with a little statue and the portrait of a Daoist saint who lived there in the eighteenth century. This is Master Yang (杨祖师爷), who was born in 1748 and died in 1804, and whose body was once kept there in a mummified state until Red Guards removed and destroyed it during the Cultural Revolution in the 1960s. According to the abbot, Master Yang's ashes and bones are kept somewhere else, but it is unclear when they will be brought to the temple as relic. There is a huge investment in the temple, running into millions of dollars, which according to the abbot comes entirely from devotees. The remarkable thing, however, is that the investment is going into building a Buddhist temple, while devotees come only for the shrine of Master Yang, who will fulfill all wishes. They bring huge incense josh sticks and burn them in rows.

The temple is maintained by monks who have been trained in a Buddhist college run by the state. The Buddhist monastic order seems to be just an extension of the state. Master Yang seems more a Daoist master than a Buddhist monk and was probably an ascetic who combined elements of both religions in a popular cult around his power. The Buddhist monks are more focused on the huge building project that is going on than on the cult surrounding Master Yang, and they effectively stop people from getting possessed by Master Yang at the shrine.

The story of Master Yang, revolving around his kinship with animals (tigers, elks, and mules), is depicted on a large rock relief. The story of the Cultural Revolution, despite its significance for Master Yang's mummy's destruction, is not included. In the temple one is told the story of how the mummy was stolen by thieves who were not captured until after the mummy had already disintegrated. The abbot himself mentioned that the mummy had been taken to another place in order to save it from thieves, but it had started to rot in the heat. Slowly the story of the Cultural Revolution seems to be fading.

People come to pray in front of Master Yang's image for health, for children, for luck. Their prayer is the main activity, and their worship and belief has survived the antisuperstition campaigns of the Communist state. Devotees come to the shrine not for a "religious experience," but for results. When they have received results they return to thank Master Yang by lighting firecrackers. Prayer here cannot be studied separately from the other things that go on: devotees continue to embrace the traditional belief that there is magical power (*ling*) on this mountain; they maintain that this power endured even when Master Yang's body was destroyed. They do not seem to be bothered that the place is being taken over by Buddhist monks with clear support from the state. Many people know that Master Yang's body was destroyed by Red Guards, but the Communist Party itself has already declared this period to be a black page in history, and many people seem ready to turn the page and forget about it, although to establish this definitively would require more research. What counts, however, is the tradition of Master Yang's power, which transcends history.

The really interesting question this case raises, in my view, is about the history of iconoclasm and the capacity of people to continue to believe in religious power when secular power seems so overwhelming. And, of course, about the popular understanding of the nature of power that blurs the distinction between religious and secular. Not only is Communism in many ways a political religion but also to imagine an alternative way of understanding China, as in the novel *Lingshan* (translated as "Soul Mountain," but "Magic Mountain" would also have been possible, although perhaps too close to Thomas Mann's *Der Zauberberg*), by Nobel Prize–winner Gao Xingjian, religion seems to be of fundamental importance.

The twentieth-century orgy of destruction was not unprecedented in China. The Taiping Tianguo (太平天国) rebellion (1850–64), under the charismatic leadership of Hong Xiuquan, who thought of himself as the younger brother of Jesus, not only left 20 million people dead but also destroyed Buddhist and Daoist temples over a vast area. The millenarian fervor of this movement and its fanatic iconoclasm was inspired by Protestant Christianity, but one has to understand that Protestant Christianity attached itself to a strong existing tradition of Chinese millenarianism. What is remarkable then and now is the reconstruction of religious sites when the storm of iconoclasm has blown over. Most of the temples that were destroyed during the twentieth century are being rebuilt.[8] This makes one think that iconoclasm in Chinese culture is a form of what one might call "kalpa-ism" (from the Buddhist term *kalpa*, the end of a world-cycle; 劫 *jie* in Mandarin), that is, a periodic cleansing, and that the Cultural Revolution might be at least partly thought of as the most recent instance of this.

Why don't people stop believing in the sacred power of the icon when it is destroyed? It is remarkable how much both in India and in China the icon is a *representation* of a *virtual reality*. It is not that the icon is not seen as real or that it has not been ritually "given breath" (*prāṇa pratiṣṭha*) or consecrated, but that its destruction is not the destruction of the god. When the image is destroyed (or when the god's house, temple, or shrine is destroyed), it is often believed that this is because the believers have not been devoted enough or the end of a cycle in a cyclical worldview has come. As is usual with religion (and not only with religion, but also with psychoanalysis, for instance), all counterfactual evidence is seen as proving the case. While there is a strong sense of the weight of tradition, history (as a more or less accurate account of events) is seen as rather marginal to sacrality and efficacy. This might explain the (at least for contemporary Europeans, brought up in the tradition of nineteenth-century conservationism) rather careless attitude toward historical monuments that can be destroyed and rebuilt at will without such activity having an effect on what Mircea Eliade called "the hierophany" of the sacred place.[9] The failure to protect the image or to save the temple in bad times reflects on the agency of the person or the community but in the end does not affect the god or, better, the belief in the god as eternal. Only when that belief dies does the god die. Or, in more sociological terms, images can only be actants (material objects that can act), to use Latour's term but not his theory, if human actors make them work. Our informants can and often do attribute agency to objects, but it is still they who attribute it for their complex reasons. I do agree with Alfred Gell's "Maussian" theory that from an anthropological perspective, art objects are persons, and this is certainly true for sacred images of gods (even sometimes in a legal sense, as in India).[10] They are persons but not quite. Even in the study of "the thing itself" we will have to focus on the Geertzian question of "what do our informants think they are up to" and not on "what the image thinks that it is up to." Nevertheless, our informants may well think that the images are up to something, and that has to be taken as seriously as any other statement.

Both in the Indian and in the Chinese case, iconoclasm has to be understood as an issue of sovereign power. It is a part of state formation or of the maintenance of the sovereign power of the state.

THE MODERN URBAN

Let us now move from iconoclasm in the accepted sense of destruction and effacement of icons to a broader sense of destruction and effacement that one can find in urban renewal. The evocative title of Italo Calvino's novel *Invisible Cities* raises the question of visibility and invisibility, immanence and transcendence that motivates this chapter. Even Marxist theorists seem to feel that there is something elusive in "the urban" that cannot be entirely understood by the study of capitalism, as in this quotation from Lefebvre's book *The Urban Revolution* by the contemporary theorist Andrew Merrifeld: "The signs of the urban are signs of assembly: the things that promote assembly (streets, squares, spaces, surfaces, sidewalks and buildings) and the requirements for assembly (seats, lights). The urban is most forcefully evoked by the constellation of lights at night, especially when flying over a city—the dazzling impression of brilliance, neon, street signs, streetlights, incitements of various kinds, the simultaneous accumulation of wealth and signs." The urban, he adds, is:

> pure form: a place of encounter, assembly, simultaneity. This form has no specific content, but is a center of attraction and life. It is an abstraction, but unlike a metaphysical entity, the urban is a concrete abstraction, associated with practice. Living creatures, the products of industry, technology and wealth, works of culture, ways of living . . . Its contents (things, objects, people, situations) are mutually exclusive because they are diverse, but inclusive because they are brought together and imply their mutual presence. The urban is both form and receptacle, void and plenitude, super-object and non-object, supra-consciousness and the totality of consciousnesses.[11]

Lefebvre's evocative text recalls those of Baudelaire, Benjamin, and Simmel, which seems to indicate that there is something about the city that calls for more poetic accounts than materialism usually allows. Contemporary urban theorists, like Merrifeld, who are inspired by Lefebvre even go back to Spinoza for a metaphysics of the city, but despite this taste for Pantheism, what is lacking in all these theorists is an antenna for religious aspirations and understandings in the city.[12]

Urban planning is commonly seen as a secular process based on technical and financial expertise and arguments. It is portrayed as the heroic effort of engineers, architects, and construction workers combined with the machinations of city bureaucrats and project developers who plan urban renewal and urban expansion. With the gradual urbanization of human society over the last century and its acceleration in Asia over the last decades, urban planning is at the heart of social transformation. Whatever the theoretical difficulties with the generality of the notion of "modernization," it is here that it seems least problematic. The financial and political aspects can be understood from the perspective of political economy, while the technical aspects require a scientific mindset.

What anthropologists like Jim Holston have been pointing out, how-ever, is that the implementation of urban planning often meets all kinds of unexpected (unplanned) realities "on the ground," so to speak.[13] The clash between the vision of planners and the perspectives of those who are living in these visions is particularly striking in cases of radical modernist plan-ning, as for example Niemeyer's Brasília or Corbusier's Chandigarh. From this anthropological work it emerges that the rationality and functionalism of urban planning is in fact part of a visionary exercise that can be called utopian, metaphysical, even magical. The extent to which urban planners are able to ignore or dismiss social reality is an indication of the aspirational nature of their endeavors.

It is strikingly common how magical and religious is the nature of those "facts on the ground" that urban planners often have to encounter. This per-haps has something to do with the sacred nature of space. In other words, space is one of the elements of the sacred; urban planning has to deal with sacred spaces, such as cemeteries and religious places of worship. Because of the large amounts of money that are involved in urban planning and project development, the spoils are enormous. This is an arena of great speculation, in which information is a crucial asset. Given the inequality of access to information and the shifting nature of political decision-making, no one can be certain about where things are heading. This fundamental uncertainty can be addressed in a variety of ways, but one set of possible approaches can be called "religious" or "magical." There is in fact no distinc-tion between religion and magic in a formal sense, although it may play a role in internal debates in the society being studied. Participation in lot-teries, buying shares or land at the advice of religious specialists, practices of self-cultivation, prayer, ritual worship of deities, Ponzi schemes, invest-ment in houses, project development, all are parts of speculative practices that cannot be easily divided into secular versus religious. In Asia the open-ing up of markets previously highly regulated by state socialism has created a feverish atmosphere of opportunity, luck, and misfortune. Everyone, from high to low, is in some way participating in urban aspirations that are tied to urban planning.

The foregoing indicates that the process of urban planning, despite its image, cannot be separated from various forms of utopianism. Its image of engineering, overcoming technical obstacles, dealing with recalcitrant populations, all in the name of progress hides the magic of power. This is very clear from the history of "master plans" in South Asia, which shows an enormous confidence on the part of urban planners that their spatial interventions can create a "modern" society without caste and religion.[14] Planning is thus as magical as some of the obstacles, resistances, and "facts on the ground" that it encounters.

Cosmological symbols are important in cities that become national capitals. This is because every great capital must somehow be presented as a universal center, a paradigm for the rest of the world. In an article comparing the designs of Washington and Beijing, Meyer shows that while Washington at first glance appears to be an architectural expression of a secular government, it is on the contrary a capital steeped in many levels of religious symbolism, the least interesting being its numerous churches, synagogues, and mosques.[15] Although the original plan for Washington lacked the cosmic pretensions of Beijing, symbols have a way of straining toward what might be called their "natural fulfillment." Eventually Washington did acquire a kind of symbolic cosmic centering. By the mid-nineteenth century such drawings as the U.S. Geological Survey's "Compendius Chart" showed the Capitol as the center not just of the nation but of the entire world, echoing the 1787 prophecy of Congressman James Wilson of Pennsylvania that America's new federal government would "lay a foundation for erecting temples of Liberty in every part of the earth." The U.S. capital, if not a cosmic center in the archaic sense, would be seen as the moral center of the whole world.

China's capital, Beijing, has been for centuries the cosmic center of China, ruled from the Forbidden City, organized according to the feng shui principles of yin and yang. When the Communists took over, Mao Zedong personally decided to locate the government in the old city, making use of this ancient conception of the cosmic center, but at the same time destroying the old buildings. We see here a form of iconoclasm that is quite common, namely the appropriation of a sacred place, destroying the previous religion and appropriating its sacred power for the new religion. Tiananmen "had to be transformed from an insulated imperial quarter into an open space for political activity."[16] "Open," however, only in a spatial sense, not in the sense of Habermas's *Öffentlichkeit*. Tiananmen became not only the square where the Party showed its ideological centrality—in the architecture, in the huge portrait of Mao that dominates the square, and in the Party's regular manifestations, for example the Party Congress in the Great Hall of the People—but also the space for challenging that hegemony, as seen in 1989. With the transformation of Tiananmen into a huge public square (with the possibility of containing 600,000 people) Mao created a space for the demonstration of the Party's power, but occasionally the Party's power is misunderstood by the Chinese as the people's power. Today such mistakes continue to be bloodily repressed, but the Party lives in constant fear of the spread of a revolutionary fervor to its squares (as during the recent Jasmine Revolution in the Middle East, when the Chinese word for jasmine (*molihua* 茉莉花) was censored on the Internet).

At a high level of abstraction secular modernity aims at being an encompassing cultural frame in which religion receives its location. In China the creation of that modernity has focused on the elevation of moral teaching and the removal of a "blind belief" in the power of sacred objects. At the end of the nineteenth century there was an attempt by the same intellectuals who led the campaign of temple destruction to create a cult around Confucius. In the attempt to create some traditional foundation for modern nationalism, this was envisaged to be a civil religion similar to Shintoism. This project faltered because of the ritual deficit of the cult of Confucius. Besides the image of Confucius, one has tablets of revered teachers and ancestors, which can be worshiped at the local level, but the cult cannot deal with the plethora of beliefs in spirits, powers, misfortune, and illness that invade society. It is interesting to note that the Communists have long wanted to destroy the worship of Confucius since they took over power, because they saw it not only as the worship of ancestors but also as part of the feudal system that had to be removed in order to bring in the socialist era. The Party has put atheist visuality in its place, which shows itself most clearly in the faceless anonymity of the Party Congress but that finds its limit in the Mao cult (epitomized by the mausoleum and gigantic portrait of Mao in Tiananmen Square). However, today there is quite some confusion around Confucius. One can find new statues of Confucius everywhere (especially in universities) and often in places that before would have had statues of Mao. This confusion came recently to a head in Beijing. A Confucius statue thirty-one feet high was unveiled at the National Museum, opposite Mao's mausoleum, in the heart of the sacred cosmological center of the heavenly kingdom that, as I have noted, was not destroyed but annexed by the Communists, namely Tiananmen Square. The sculpture was revealed with quite some celebration in December 2011. Four months later the seventy-one-ton statue was unceremoniously removed under the protection of the night, and everyone, including the museum and the sculptor, declined to comment. It was rumored that opponents of the revival of Confucianism at the Central Party School in Beijing had been successful. The struggle over the visual representation of culture is very much part of a power struggle within the Communist Party.

India's capital, Delhi, had been for centuries the cosmic center of the Mughal Empire before it was succeeded by the British Empire. The Red Fort and the Jama Masjid, with the area surrounding it, came to be called Old Delhi when the British started to build the colonial capital southwest of it. New Delhi's governmental architecture and huge avenues produce colonial and postcolonial secular visuality, largely designed by the architect Edward Lutyens. The British moved their capital away from the old center of Mughal power but kept the old town alive. After Independence, postcolonial secularism continued to be expressed by colonial monumentality, but some references to India's glorious civilizational past were added. It is characteristic of Indian secularism, however, that Indian society is far from being secularized and that there is no political project to do that with force. The symbolism of India's leading political party, the secularist Congress Party, remains very much tied to religious imagery (for instance, Bharat Mata—Mother India), while the party's Hindu nationalist opponent, the Bharatiya Janata Party, openly flaunts religious images in its political campaigns. The political-religious imagery of extraparliamentary mobilization that was developed by Gandhi (a god-like mahatma) in the struggle for independence has become a brand for popular demands for clean politics, most recently employed by the populist leader Anna Hazare. The secular is located not in society but in the state and visually in the great culture heroes King Ashoka and King Akbar, both seen as symbolizing syncretism and tolerance. The symbols of the Indian state are the four lions of the Ashoka pillar and the Wheel of Buddhism, found in Sarnath, the place where the Buddha is supposed to have started his teaching of peace. Under the Ashoka pillar one finds the Sanskrit text *satyam eva jayate* ("Truth alone triumphs," which in my reading is not directly a message of peace but more a message of truth, with the understanding that one knows what that leads to).

In the 1980s the relative invisibility of Hindu culture in the capital of India began to bother Hindu nationalists. This happened at the same time the program to wipe out the Babar mosque started. When the Ayodhya mosque was destroyed, the building of the Prithviraj Chauhan Memorial (also called Qila Rai Pithora), commemorating the pre-Islamic capital of a Rajput king, was started.[17] The evidence for all of this is heavily contested, but the desire to show a pre-Islamic presence in Delhi is evident. There are several sites in Delhi that have also sprung up from a desire to assert a vigorous Hinduism. One of them is the Akshardham temple on the banks of the Yamuna in Delhi, inaugurated by the then president of India in the presence of a number of India's leading politicians in 2005. It is a huge temple complex of the powerful, transnationally organized Swaminarayan sect, whose base is in Gujarat, built in an area that was cleared of a large slum settlement and thus "beautified." Whereas the Prithviraj Memorial is looking toward a glorious past, the Akshardham temple is looking at a glorious present and future for a shining Indian middle-class religiosity, with a prominent application of new media and Disney-like entertainment technology. The Akshardham temple's footprint on Delhi's cityscape shows a Hinduism that is completely in tune with modern technology and modern consumption, while emphasizing that India as a nation is Hindu. Another instance of such Hindu assertiveness, but closer to the popular religiosity carried by a larger stratum of society, are the various huge statues of Hanuman that spring up in cities like Delhi, especially in new areas like Gurgaon.[18] In Delhi, with more than a millennium of Islamic history, this implies not so much an iconoclasm as a gradual effacing of that history and a renewed emphasis on strong Hinduism.

More than Delhi and Beijing, with their governmental monumentality, it is in the port cities Mumbai and Shanghai that one expects a cosmopolitan secular visuality to be dominant. Urbanity is often seen as secular or at least emancipated from rural, backward forms of religion. In China this kind of secular urbanity is the result not of a process of combined secularization and urbanization but of a Communist project. In megacities like Shanghai and Beijing, public manifestations of religion are not allowed or are heavily restricted. Processions (an important part of Chinese religion) are forbidden. Religious groups have to get permission to gather. Most of the foreign attention to this kind of repression is focused on the illegal or sometimes semilegal Christian house-churches where people gather in apartments to avoid the surveillance of the state. However, similar methods are used by Buddhist and Daoist groups in these cities but draw less foreign attention. The authorities in Shanghai have allowed some big temples and churches to continue in the heart of the city, but they are turned into tourist landmarks—for example, the huge Jing'An Temple in Shanghai (dating from 247 AD), which is renovated so as to include one wall that consists of a line of shops selling expensive foreign brands like Gucci and Vuitton. In that context rituals are being performed for and by believers, but quite literally encompassed by secular urbanity. It is real estate prices and the marginalization of religious groups that drive them into private apartments or to the outskirts of the city.[19]

In Shanghai the official modern is secular. That is the perspective not only of the authorities but also of major cultural theorists like Leo Ou-fan Lee, who in his classic cultural history of interwar Shanghai, *Shanghai Modern,* manages to omit any reference to the importance of Shanghai in Buddhist and Daoist modernism.[20] And this is not because of a strict separation of secular and religious spheres, as Zhang Zhen shows in her elegant analysis of the Shanghai "martial arts–magic spirit" (武侠神怪 *wuxia-shenguai*) movies of the late 1920s that were the precursor of the later Hong Kong martial arts movies, which are suffused with references to magical power and Buddhist monastic traditions (Shaolin). What brought the wuxia-shenguai genre to an end was the same force that repressed religion: the government forbade the showing of this popular genre that "fed on the superstition of the masses."[21] The neglect of religion and magic in cultural history is part of a common intellectual denigration of the religious as antiscientific and thus retrograde in China. In architectural terms Shanghai modern is largely colonial, with the Bund and the French Concession as its greatest historical landmarks. Shanghai nostalgia is focused on the 1930s. When the journal *Shanghai Literature* (上海文化) asked local novelists in the midst of the total remaking of Shanghai in the 1990s to write up their memories of particular lanes in Shanghai, the majority of the places described were in the French Concession.[22] While some contributions did depict the life in those parts of Shanghai where workers lived, there is very little sense of the huge destruction of temples and ancestral halls that were the centers of a vibrant religious life in the 1930s.

As the anthropologist Adam Chau has observed, urban modernity in China is accomplished by destruction (much more than in India).[23] More than earlier campaigns of modernization and development, it has been the property boom that started after the opening up of China's economy that has totally transformed China's major cities. Mao's campaigns of destroying old buildings (like the courtyard houses, *siheyuan*, in Beijing and the town-houses, *shikumen*, in Shanghai) led to the proliferation of the character *chai* 拆 (destroy) on the walls in old neighborhoods. The Beijing-based artist Wan Jinsong has gone around photographing buildings with the "destroy" sign on them and has made a successful montage of one hundred of them, which he has significantly numbered from 1900 to 1999.

China never had the resources to completely transform cities, but it began to have them in the 1990s, as seen in the building of the Pudong area in Shanghai in the 1990s and of Olympic Beijing in 2000–2010.

More recently, however, some fairly large renovation projects have also been carried out in Shanghai. The best known is Xintiandi (New Heaven and Earth), a neighborhood with traditional houses that was completely broken down and rebuilt in a "fake antique" fashion with lots of shops and cinemas and restaurants. It is a rather plastic renovation of this neighborhood that reminds one most of the entertainment- and consumption-oriented renovations of historic neighborhoods in the United States. Another one is Tianzifang (Artist Workshop District), which was a gradual renovation project of old houses inspired by the artist Chen Yifei and supported by local inhabitants, who used the project as an alternative to a big development plan that had envisaged razing the old neighborhood and replacing it with high rises as has been done in most places in Shanghai.

Mumbai is as different from Delhi as Shanghai is from Beijing. Mumbai is generally seen as India's most modern, most westernized city, a place to have fun, to enjoy romance, to be free of the bonds of caste and religious community. People often tell you that they are actually not much better off by moving to Mumbai from their village but that it is still much better to be in Mumbai. It is a happening place where one can go out dancing and drinking till deep into the night.

At the same time Mumbai's secularity is very circumscribed. Mumbai is a colonial city that was known as Bombay until 1995, when the state government of Maharashtra, where Mumbai is located, "indigenized" the name or, in fact, turned the vernacular pronunciation into the official name. The state government was then led by a Hindu fascist movement called the Shiv Sena or Army of Shivaji (a famous Maratha warrior of the eighteenth century). This movement, led by the late Bal Thackeray (who, ironically, did not change his anglicized name into a vernacular one), had made its political career as champion of the ethnic cause of the Maratha majority in Mumbai, first in language riots in the 1960s against Gujaratis over the control of Mumbai, later in antiimmigrant riots against Tamils over securing government jobs for the Marathas, and over the last twenty to thirty years in communal riots against Muslims. In the latter case the Shiv Sena at some point joined the communal bandwagon of the Hindu nationalist movement that became powerful all over India and was led by the Bharatiya Janata Party. While calling Bombay Mumbai can at one level be read as an anticolonial gesture, it is at another more important level a Hindu nationalist gesture.

Earlier in this chapter I discussed the national political developments that led to an increasing antagonism between the Hindu majority and the Muslim minority and culminated in 1992 in an attack on a mosque in the Hindu pilgrimage center Ayodhya. This resulted in nationwide rioting that also swept through Mumbai in 1992 and again in 2002 and left thousands, mostly Muslims, dead. The response to this massacre, which was allowed, supported, and in Mumbai often organized by the police and Shiv Sena politicians, has been a series of bomb attacks on major buildings in Mumbai. These terrorist attacks have been planned and executed by the major Muslim gang in Mumbai, led by a man called Dawood, who has fled Mumbai and, after living for a while in Dubai, seems to have more recently moved to Karachi. Such Muslim counterattacks have now become connected to the international enmity between India and Pakistan, as was most recently shown by the Laskar-e-Taiba attacks on the landmark hotels the Taj and the Oberoi, which have drawn international attention.

In Mumbai we find ethnoreligious divisions that crosscut class divisions, but we also find aspirations for the urban context that are derived from religious imaginaries carried by social movements as well as by the art scene and entertainment industry. We find urban politics and governance that is focused on space, services, and security and is mapped on communal divides but in which religious understandings of space and movement play a significant role. Besides the more obvious religious imaginaries produced in temples and shrines, there is Bollywood, the largest film industry in the world, in which "mythologicals" (movies based on religious stories) always play a significant role.

Religious processions through the city create arenas of interaction, since they cannot be confined to neighborhoods that are dominated by one community. They are loud and in your face and the expression of a right to be there. In the extraordinarily cramped housing and transport situation of Mumbai, processions are events of great significance. By far the most impressive festival in Mumbai is the Ganapati festival, celebrating the Hindu god Ganapati or Ganesha. Where in Delhi one has Hanuman, in Mumbai one has Ganesha.

The connection between the rise of Ganesha worship and Hindu nationalism at the end of the nineteenth century in Maharashtra has been well researched.[24] Today the interesting thing about the Ganapati festival and the growing popularity of the large Vinayak temple, where people start lining up for worship at 3 AM, is that they represent a form of Hindu collective assertion and of individual anxiety alleviation. Ganesha and Hanuman are gods understood to cater particularly to people who are taking a risk, trying their chances in the world. It is tempting to see this connected to the great opening of opportunities since the liberalization and globalization of the economy in the 1990s. Urban conditions are no less dependent on political patronage than before, but there are more opportunities to make it in the city. A common scapegoat for not making it in the city or for the abysmal conditions of virtual all public services are the Muslims, who are the least socially mobile. Despite these connections, one should still maintain that there are no direct causal relations between changes in the political economy and the rise of particular symbolic repertoires. I would rather argue for weak linkages between political economy and symbolism in the context of extreme religious nationalism that alter the understanding of these age-old gods.

In Nile Green's historical account, Bombay has been not only a colonial city in the past but also an Islamic city, although in a different way than Delhi.[25] Here the emphasis was on trading communities that kept the connections across and around the Indian Ocean going. Religion and trading were interwoven in what Green calls "a new nexus of production, interaction, and consumption" that emerged in the nineteenth century. One of the most important Muslim trading communities, with strong ties to the Middle East and Africa, has been the Shi'a Ismaili Bohras. One of their branches, the Dawoodi Bohras, has taken up its quarters in Bhendi Bazaar in South Mumbai. Bhendi Bazaar is a neighborhood of immense historic significance. Several market hubs of the city, such as Null Bazaar, Crawford Market, and Chor Bazaar, lie in its vicinity. The mausoleum of Syedna Taher Saifuddin, one of the spiritual leaders of the Bohras, constitutes the sacred center of the neighborhood and one of the most important religious sites of Mumbai. Several other mosques, shrines, and buildings of different Muslim groups in the wider Mohammad Ali Road area are also within the precincts of Bhendi Bazaar. Many of the buildings in this area are a century old, dating back to the early twentieth century, when this neighborhood was first set up by the British to decongest the Fort area. These buildings contain both residential spaces and commercial establishments. This commingling of the sacred, quotidian, and commercial has made Bhendi Bazaar one of the most vibrant and historically cosmopolitan neighborhoods of the city. Yet in popular imagination, fueled by its depictions in Bollywood movies, it tends to be associated with the darker side of the city, seen as a dingy, crumbling neighborhood.

One of the largest cluster redevelopment projects currently under way in Mumbai was initiated by the spiritual leader of the community, Syedna Mohammed Burhanuddin, who recently passed away. The project brings together modernist planning and development with the maintenance of spiritual values and practices. It will further contribute to the expression of the distinct cultural identity of the Daudi Bohras in the city. This can be seen not only in concrete form in distinctive architectural styles, as exemplified by the Saifee hospital built in 2005, but also in the attempt to balance a modern and scientific outlook with deep community bonds forged by the spiritual connection to the Syedna. Given the proposed completion date of the redevelopment project of 2014–15, the transformation of the neighborhood will be rapid. Samoon Rassiwala, architect of the project, said in an interview with DNA magazine on July 9, 2011: "Around 2,080 buildings will be restructured by constructing 20 buildings ranging from seven to 40 storeys. It will accommodate 25,000 people besides 2,000 shops. In this area, most of the buildings are old and in a dilapidated condition. It is one of the best projects in Asia and we want to materialize it. Residents will get 350 sq ft of usable area in the new project, while commercial establishments will be given same existing area. The buildings designed to cut air-conditioning costs, lawns on all terraces and water recycling."[26] By "restructuring," the architect means destruction. This is in fact a large-scale destruction of a historical neighborhood and its replacement by the icons of modern architecture, high rises. However, these are high rises surrounding the spiritual center of the Bohras, the saint's grave.

The Bohra project reminds one of nothing more than the outlook presented by the Akshardham temple in Delhi, created by a very similar upwardly mobile community from Gujarat, but Hindu. One sees here a new spiritual visuality that combines references to scientific modernity with "ancient" spirituality, as well as a social conservatism combined with modernist entrepreneurialism.

Besides modern cityscapes it is urban consumption patterns, boosted by advertising, that may show up urban modernity and secular visuality in shopping malls, cineplexes, and billboards. Owning a house, and a car, and modern amenities in the house, as well as spending money on the education of one's children, are all secular aims that create modern cityscapes. In all these pursuits, however, religious imagery is never far away. In India and China this can be seen in the growing popularity of astrology and numerology. The unpredictability of modern financial markets leads people to seek assurance in ancient forms of science that connect to sacred power. In China this focuses on numbers. There are auctions of license plate numbers that fetch huge amounts of money for a series of lucky numbers. People are willing to pay handsomely for money bills that show a sequence, like 1, 2, 3. Lotteries are immensely popular, and to predict the results one needs again to follow certain numerological principles. Most Western scientists would call this pseudoscience, but that requires a general belief in the authority of scientists as against other authorities. In fact, these are all forms of belief outside of the rarefied arena of scientific debate.

Secular time in both India and China, determined by a Western calendar that connects economic activities globally, is punctuated by a lunar calendar that regulates life cycle rituals and auspicious moments for starting a business, a journey, or any kind of endeavor. Astrologers and other specialists have a thriving business in predicting the future and controlling it. Good luck is a rare commodity that depends on controlling time and space. It is especially at the big festivals, such as that of the passing of the old year into the new, Divali in India and the Spring Festival in China, that consumption patterns are closely tied to ancient beliefs. The sacred calendar is made visible in Indian cities by massive processions, like Ganapati for Hindus and Muharram for Shia Muslims, while this is proscribed in Chinese megacities.

CONCLUSION

Religious regimes of visual and virtual presence are particularly productive sites for exploring modes of visibility and invisibility in India and China. The iconoclasm of Hindu nationalists in India today can be fruitfully compared with the iconoclasm of secularists in China over the last century. Legitimation of such violent destruction of what is sacred to a part of the population is found in a vision of national progress that is seen to be blocked by those who have the wrong beliefs and practices (either all religious believers or believers in the wrong religion). The iconoclasts' reasoning seems to be that if one only could remove those false beliefs by destroying their visual presence one would be able to attain national glory and power again (after the humiliation by imperial powers). These nationalist iconoclasms have quite different targets in India and China. In India it is the visibility of the powerful past of the Muslim minority that is an eyesore to Hindu nationalists, who want to purify national territory from foreign elements. The reestablishment of a Hindu sovereignty is seen by these nationalists as necessary for India to become equal with other powerful nations. In China one has had over the last century an all-encompassing project of destroying the past in order to build the new that affects everyone and everything. Both projects show a religious fervor that is obvious in the Hindu nationalist's case, while in the Maoist case it is denied but clearly visible if one examines the constant campaigns to mobilize the people that resemble nothing so much as the millenarianism of the past. Both projects are also ultimately unsuccessful. One can marginalize Muslims in India and religious practitioners in China, but by destroying their shrines one does not destroy or efface them by assimilation. The belief in the sacrality of the icon or of the shrine is a belief in the visualization of an invisible, virtual presence that is indestructible as long as the community of believers exists. Much of the fervor of iconoclasm, however, is produced by an open-ended and never fulfilled utopianism. It is similar to a religious project in that it is the "becoming" that demands constant attention and is perhaps more directed at motivating the iconoclasts than at destroying the idolaters.

I have argued that there is something metaphysical and transcendent about "the urban" and that it is useful to include urban renewal in a discussion of iconoclasm. I have compared the transformations of cities in India and China and their effect on the visibility of modern sovereign power and the sacred. Modernity is made visible in cities, especially in opposition to the backwardness of the countryside. The partly accidental iconoclasm of urban renewal seems to be much more thoroughgoing and successful than any motivated campaign. In China urban renewal, especially over the last few decades, has totally transformed cityscapes while retaining some important visual references to the continuity of central power in Beijing and to the "cosmopolitanism" of Shanghai. The urban landscape is cleansed from references to a religion, both in terms of shrines and temples and in terms of processions and public rituals. In India urban renewal has been much more limited.

The visual regime of Delhi is primarily showing the continuity of power in colonial monumentality. However, the glorious Muslim past is also visibly present in old Delhi, while new neighborhoods that are planned outside of these central areas show the confidence of aspiring Hindu groups in huge statues of Hanuman. Mumbai's cosmopolitanism is circumscribed by the recent history of Hindu and Muslim antagonism and violence, which also finds its way into city planning, not only, as can be expected, in the ghettoization of poor Muslim settlements but also in the assertion of a modernist architectural vision of a prosperous Muslim community.

PART III / COMPARING EXCLUSION

5 / LOST IN THE MOUNTAINS
NOTES ON DIVERSITY IN THE
SOUTHEAST ASIAN MAINLAND MASSIF

Between Yunnan and Bengal is a landmass dominated by mountains, known as the Southeast Asian mainland massif. These mountains are populated by a great variety of people, ranging from Yi, Miao, and Akha to Kachin, Shan, and Naga and dozens of other societies. This is a veritable anthropology-land, explored from the nineteenth century onward by Western missionaries, adventurers, colonial officers, traders, botanists, geologists, and anthropologists. When one crosses the mountains from Kunming toward Burma and India or toward Vietnam, Thailand, and Laos, one finds oneself in an extremely diverse ecological and human terrain, where people often do not speak each other's languages or recognize each other's cultures from one valley to another. There are trade routes through this area for exchanging silk, salt, cotton, tobacco, and other commodities. There is mining for iron, tin, jade, and gold. Parts of the area are famous for growing opium. Nowadays the hydroelectric potential of the huge rivers that traverse the area is of paramount strategic interest. However, it is a terrain that is much less studied than its oceanic counterpart, the Indian Ocean and the Chinese Sea, which was the monopoly of trading communities from Fujian, Guangdong, Tamil Nadu, and Kerala, from Yemen and Gujarat, before it came to be controlled in the sixteenth century by European maritime nations.

Centralized political control of this area has always been fragile and continues to be so today. On March 1, 2013, Naw Kham, a powerful warlord in the Golden Triangle of Thailand, Laos, and Burma, was paraded on Chinese television and then executed along with three other foreigners for the killing of thirteen Chinese fishermen on the Thai side of the border. Naw Kham had been an associate of Khun Sa (also known as Chang Chi-Fu, as he was the son of a Chinese father and a Shan mother), the drug-trafficking leader of the Shan United Army and the Mong Tai Army, who died of natural causes in Burma in 2007. Khun Sa had worked together with parts of the Kuomintang army who escaped after 1949 to the Wa area across the border from China. Because of the global ramifications of heroin trafficking, the Golden Triangle has received intense international attention, but in fact no part of the area, from Nagaland to the borders of China, is "pacified," that is, brought under central control. The political instability of the area has only been enhanced by its militarization in border wars between China and India in 1962; the American Vietnam War of 1961–75 with its deep impact on Thailand, Cambodia, and Laos; the China-Vietnam war of 1979, as well as the many "civil wars" in Assam, Burma, Laos, Tibet, and elsewhere. Long-distance trade in valuable commodities like opium, tea, gold, and jade is part of the attraction of this area for outsiders. The great rivers that traverse the area, the Mekong, the Irrawaddy, the Salween, and the Brahmaputra, have become potential resources for hydroelectric power, and their control is contested by many states, with China being the major player in water politics.

Anthropology has from the start been somewhat different from the other social sciences in its focus on the study of societies that were not nation-states or contained by nation-states, but gradually the emphasis has shifted from seeing them in isolation to seeing these societies in interaction. As such, they are important "to think with" in destabilizing notions of sovereignty, territory, and civilization that are foundational to nation-states and the social sciences that study them. The Southeast Asian massif forces us to engage some important questions about what Eric Wolf has called "the people without history," about historical knowledge, and about the sociology of knowledge (the question of power and knowledge). Wolf's book *Europe and the People without History* (1982) argued that the societies studied by anthropologists are less isolated than generally assumed and are in fact an important part of the story of the expansion of European capitalism over the globe. Wolf gives a Marxist world-system account but with more anthropological attention to Europe's Others than one finds in macro-sociological accounts like those of Immanuel Wallerstein or Andre Gunder Frank. Nevertheless, as Talal Asad observes, the story of "other societies" cannot be simply subsumed under the rubric of their transformation by world capitalism.[1] Wolf can only do so, as a Marxist, by way of a materialist reductionist assumption that these societies are all similar because they are determined by the same mode and relations of production. That perspective allows one to transcend the region, so to speak, and put these mountain societies in a comparative framework of small-scale societies of hunters and gatherers. In such an analysis a possible focus is the structural analysis of kinship, as exemplified in the famous dispute between Leach and Lévi-Strauss on the structural implications of matrilateral cross-cousin marriage, based on Kachin material.[2] Also in Marxist analyses the governing idea is that all these precapitalist societies are to be understood in terms of kinship as a mode or relation of production. However, there is no general key to the secret of noncapitalist societies, and kinship does not provide it.[3] Only in the case of capitalist societies may the concept of mode of production have a potential explanatory use, according to Asad. World capitalism is, to an extent, a unitary force that affects everyone everywhere and indeed shapes the conditions under which one makes one's historical choices, but it can only be understood as one element, however important, of the processes of political formation that affect differentially the Nagas, Kachin, Wa, Yi, and Miao as well as the Indians, Burmese, and Chinese. The story of political penetration into the mountains keeps unfolding in unpredictable ways.

Another guiding perspective in anthropological research in this mountainous area focuses on the relation between these societies and the civilizations that have become in the late nineteenth and early twentieth centuries the cultural core of nation-states in the area: Hinduism in India, Buddhism in Burma, Han culture in China. The *longue durée* expansion of civilizations involves those of Hinduism, Buddhism, and, on the Chinese side, Han civilization (with Buddhism, Daoism, and Confucianism as important elements besides the Chinese language).

In an article published in 1960 (and discussed at length in Stanley Tambiah's intellectual biography of Leach),[4] Edmund Leach proposes the following:

> The historically significant contrasts in present-day "Burma" are differences of ecology and differences of social organization. . . . The two sets of differences nearly coincide: roughly speaking the Hill People are patrilineal and hierarchical, the Valley People have a non-unilineal kinship organization linked with charismatic despotism. This coexistence is not a *necessary* one, if we are to explain why it exists then we

must seek an historical explanation. The explanation which I offer is that the Valley People took their social organization and their politics from India while the Hill People took their social organization along with their trade and kinship system from China. It is a possible explanation; I do not claim more than that.[5]

The concept of "charismatic despotism" requires some explanation. Leach points out that the Hindu-Buddhist polities of Burma and Thailand were relatively small, historically unstable ones, depending on the charismatic personality of a polygynous king and accompanied by violent succession struggles among the king's many progeny. Tambiah agrees with this general picture but adds an assertion of the ideological importance of the Buddhist model of the *dharmaraja-dharmapala* (righteous king and protector of the law), which makes the king into an incipient Buddha.[6] The latter is the subject of Tambiah's own work on Thai Buddhism, where he also develops the concept of "galactic states" with a sacred center and concentric circles of political and cultural influence.[7]

In Leach's view the model of the Chinese Empire was dynastic- and rule-oriented, guided by a nonhereditary, administrative class of literati. This model can be contrasted with the Indian model but was in fact not influential in the mountain areas. The Chinese were present in the higher mountains not for political control but to conduct trade. Ties of affinal kinship that spread widely over the hills were extremely useful for long-distance trade, and as Leach observes, girls in the hill culture "are married against a bride-price and the objects involved in bride-price transactions are the same sort of objects as are met in dealings with a Chinese trader" (66). . . . "Thus the ties of affinal kinship ramify widely, following trade routes and jumping across language frontiers and political boundaries."[8]

Answering questions about civilizational models and their penetration into the mountains is at least as difficult as traversing the mountains (and, as Leach admits, highly speculative in nature) since much of the history of the people of this area is of an oral nature. If there are written records they have to be read with much caution, since they are often themselves products of the civilizations that surround these societies. Today these societies are regarded as "nationalities" or "ethnic minorities" in China, India, and Burma, but one should realize that they have only become part of these nation-states by the vagaries of recent mapmaking, which has constructed national territories. This is a frontier area that has been divided into national territories, separated by lines on a map. The frontiers between Yunnan, Burma, and Vietnam have hardened only with colonial expansion, as can be seen in diplomatic exchanges between the British and the Qing as well as between the French and the Qing. An important aspect of the mapping of territories has been to determine the zones of influence of the French and the British in relation to the Qing Empire. The border disputes between India and China and between Vietnam and China, as well as the entire Tibet question, are part of this shifting landscape and its historical understanding.

In this chapter I will engage the question of the relation between civilization, political formation, and mountain people by examining James Scott's recent thesis on the nature of the relation between mountain people and the civilizational state. Since this thesis builds to an extent on Edmund Leach's *Political Systems of Highland Burma*, I will reflect on the nature of ethnography and the discussion of Leach's work. This will bring me to Francis Hsu's work from the 1940s on Dali in Yunnan and his theory of Chinese society, which he later uses for a comparative analysis of caste in India and clan in China. I will continue with a discussion of the contemporary predicament of the people in the mountains and the valleys. The argument I want to present is that the fragmentary nature of state formation in the area does not allow us to capture it in a model of state versus nonstate actors. This continues to be the case even today, despite the immensely increased potential of nation-states to execute their projects and the national imperative of turning frontiers into borders.

THE PEOPLES OF THE MOUNTAINS

High mountains are difficult to live and travel in. They are therefore often (but not always) sparsely populated, and their villages are relatively isolated. The geographical opposition of lowlands and highlands has social and cultural consequences. In the lowlands of South and Southeast Asia one finds wet-rice cultivation, which also allows the sustaining of larger populations and economic surpluses that can be used to build cities and organize kingdoms. The higher mountains only allow for small populations who depend on hunting and swidden (slash-and-burn) agriculture. Their cultures are therefore more narrowly bound to local communities. The geographical opposition of valley and mountain has also led to a stereotypical civilizational discourse on the opposition between the civilized and the barbarian.

The opposition between highlands and lowlands has been a general theme for thinking about Southeast Asian history and has recently been taken up by James Scott in a new and much-debated interpretation. In *The Art of Not Being Governed: An Anarchist History of Upland Southeast Asia* (2009) Scott has put forward the thesis that the highland-lowland opposition is at the same time the opposition between those who want to escape state dominance and those who want to impose state dominance.[9] This is in line with his previous work (*Seeing like a State, Domination and the Arts of Resistance,* and *The Moral Economy of the Peasant*),[10] which generally portrays the state as a negative political formation and common people as trying to escape from its clutches.[11] In this book the mountains provide a refuge for those who are under state persecution. To an extent this thesis is supported by the fact that people like the Miao have a narrative of escaping from Han domination, especially after rebellions. On the other hand people are rebelling and are being persecuted all the time and everywhere, and most of them do not flee into the mountains. To give just one example: Hui (Muslim) traders in Yunnan have started spectacular rebellions that were subsequently suppressed but whose participants have not fled into the mountains. In fact, they can be found in all the big cities in China. Moreover, the immense complexity and diversity of the peoples of the mountains cannot be explained by lumping them together in an undifferentiated category of "fugitives from the state." Scott's explanation of the fact that many of these societies do not use script is that they have made themselves "illegible" to the state by a deliberate strategy of language loss. This is unsupported by historical linguistics and in fact completely speculative. The question of language is, obviously, central to any attempt to understand any culture, but the difficulties in the mountains are immense. This can be illustrated by the example of an ethnographic study of two small villages in the 1960s in Tyrol by Eric Wolf and John Cole. Wolf, an Austrian Jew, spoke German as his mother tongue but could often not follow what the locals were saying. As the authors of this study put it, "we are not, after this fieldwork, too sanguine about our capacity to claim firm command of the informal content of communication among the people we studied."[12] Compared with the impenetrable Southeast Asian massif, Tyrol is like a well-integrated hill station ideally suited for vacationers from the plains. Our perhaps insurmountable problems with understanding what is going on in these societies are not served by generalized assumptions about strategies to refuse literacy.

Finally, the idea that people are "self-governing" when they escape "the state" may seem to correspond to a modern, anarchist fantasy, but in fact one needs to pay attention to the nature of kinship as a form of political control in so-called stateless societies. Obviously, Scott is right that the natural conditions of the mountains restrict possibilities of state formation that are economically based on rice farming. In that sense one does have a frontier situation, economically based on swidden agriculture (at least in some places), that explains limits on the penetration of state and civilizational structures. Even mapping these areas involves great difficulties, let alone controlling them. However, while mountains are good places for guerrilla warfare and difficult to control, they cannot be reduced to what Scott calls "outlaw corridors." Similarly, the general civilizational discourse about mountain peoples in terms of barbaric versus civilized cannot be critiqued by a romanticized discourse about "the untamed." It is ironic that ethnic groups who have an account of "fleeing" from Han domination, such as the Miao (whose case is emphasized in Scott's book) also have an account of their previous kingdom and their desire to restore it (which is not mentioned by Scott). Much of Miao millenarianism is focused on reuniting the Miao and restoring the kingdom.[13]

NOT A MOUNTAIN OF EVIDENCE

Scott's book both follows and departs from an anthropological classic: Edmund Leach's *Political Systems of Highland Burma*, published in 1954 and reprinted many times (and debated today). This book is about the social structure of the Kachin, a society in the Kachin Hills of Burma, adjacent to the Naga Hills of Assam, and located between India and China. The book has made several contributions to anthropological theory that became important, for example, in discussions of Lévi-Strauss's structuralism, but for my purpose here the most important contribution is that Leach refuses to consider "the Kachin" as a self-contained "tribe," as was at the time the common anthropological understanding of such an isolated mountain people. Instead, he argued that one has to understand the stateless Kachin in relation to their neighbors, the Shan, and the Shan's attempts at state formation. Leach proposes that there are three models of political organization at work here: Shan, *gumsa*, and *gumlao*. The Shan model has a hereditary chief and taxes, while the *gumlao* model is egalitarian and rejects all hereditary authority. Between these two models is the *gumsa* model, which hierarchically stratifies lineages of wife-givers and wife-takers. This model is unstable, with a tendency for heads of high-ranking lineages to move in the direction of the Shan model while lower-ranking lineages move in the direction of *gumlao*. Leach thus emphasizes the interactional and dynamic nature of this system in response to the (at the time) dominance of equilibrium theories.

The attraction of Leach's argument for Scott's thesis is obvious. However, the devil is in the details. Leach proposes in his foreword that "the facts of ethnography and of history can only *appear* to be ordered in a systematic way if we impose on these facts a figment of thought. We first devise for ourselves a set of verbal categories, and hey presto the facts are 'seen' to be systematically ordered! But in that case the *system* is a matter of the relation between concepts and not of relations 'actually existing' within the raw factual data."[14] Leach would have needed a thorough command of Kachin language to construct his interpretation of verbal categories. Eric Wolf's modesty in regard to his linguistic ability in understanding the Tyrolers, despite his being a native speaker of Austrian German, should make us cautious, and the discussion of Leach's work by those who have been able to do research in the area (which was for decades closed off by the Burmese army) indeed puts considerable doubt on Leach's understanding of these verbal categories. A more important observation to be made here, however, is that Leach does not provide any systematic references to the conditions of his fieldwork (war, loss of field notes, collapsing British rule). In spite of his emphasis on the dynamic nature of structural relations and his reliance on historical records, his book neglects the changing historical conditions in which his fieldwork took place.

What one gathers from ethnographic work on this entire area is a picture of ethnicities shading into each other, with language and cultural competences as markers of difference. There are processes of state formation that show both at the economic level of wet-rice cultivation and in the adherence to a world religion like Buddhism. However, it is important not to essentialize "the state" and its opposite "nonstate" but indeed to follow Leach's lead in looking at the dynamism of relations between various ethnicities and modes of production in the region. For example, from today's perspective the Yi of Sichuan and Yunnan are just one of the marginal ethnic minorities, but in the past there was a series of slaveholding and hierarchical Yi polities with their own language and script that controlled large parts of Sichuan and Yunnan. Attention to this kind of dynamic in history would also lead us to be much more focused on the nature of trade (especially opium growing and trading) as well as of warfare in the region than Leach was. That would allow a more flexible understanding of state formation. This has also been the thrust of a major critique of Leach's book by David Nugent (1982), who presents the daring thesis that the system described by Leach only originated at the end of the nineteenth century due to the destruction of an opium-based economy.[15] Yunnan and Upper Burma were major producers of opium (as Upper Burma continues to be today). In the last decades of the nineteenth century, major rebellions by Chinese Muslims in Yunnan (the dominant traders in the area) disrupted this trade (discussed later). When the British moved into Upper Burma they were successful in curtailing large-scale opium production and long-distance trade, which had been the main economic base of power in the Kachin Hills, thereby creating the conditions for *gumlao*.[16] Leach's response to this critique has been vehement, but the fact of the matter is that we do not know nearly enough about the changing political and economic conditions in the nineteenth century to come to a reliable picture, despite recent scholarship by Mandy Sadan and others.[17] This is also the major drawback of Jonathan Friedman's structural-Marxist approach to the development of kingship from kinship, and early state formation from chieftainship, through the development of exchange systems into the accumulation of wealth and surplus.[18] I find such mechanistic evolutionism theoretically not very attractive, but the main problem is still the lack of empirical evidence. Even someone like Magnus Fiskesjö, a student of the Wa, who embraces Friedman's theory, comes to the conclusion that in the case of the Wa this theory cannot account for many of the choices made by the Wa themselves.[19] Fiskesjö focuses on explaining the existence of a spirit of egalitarianism among the antistate Wa in relation to their control over a very important resource: mines. Political egalitarianism is found among a number of small-scale Southeast Asian societies in a great variety of circumstances, and sympathy for the anarchism that seems inherent in them can be found in the work not only of James Scott but of a number of authors.[20]

Leach's work on the Kachin has long been debated by theorists, for example, Nugent and Friedman, who have not done fieldwork in the area. Since the 1950s the Kachin have been involved in what would be called a civil war if a nation-state had been slowly built up in Burma instead of evolving out of post–World War II conditions. This is not particular to the

Kachin; in fact, the entire region has been constantly caught up in warfare, both regional and international. To reconstruct the longue durée history of the peoples involved is hardly feasible. That is why most of the attention for this study in the anthropological community seems to have gone into kinship theory and, more irrelevantly, into the relations between the various actors in the anthropological community, with special attention to Leach's "petulantly inconsistent" character as well as brilliance instead of to the empirical exploration of highland Burma. What remains is the large question of state formation in this mountainous region, which in the case of Yunnan can be partly traced from the comparatively well-preserved Chinese archives but much less from other archives.[21]

It is precisely the lack of integration in larger polities and thus the lack of state archives that creates a kind of continuity in the geographical region from India to China, with ethnicities shading into each other. It makes no sense historically to say something definite like "here India ends and China begins" or "here Thailand begins and Burma ends," although such are the issues wars are fought over, and borders do "harden" over time. The Naga Hills continue into the Kachin Hills and to the mountain ranges of Southwest China. Most of the societies here are Tibeto-Burmese speakers, but while that category suggests a kind of integration, in fact "Tibeto-Burman" is just a container concept for a huge range of mutually unintelligible languages.

One needs to disaggregate civilizations, too, as I have shown in chapter 3, and perhaps speak about elements, traits, and patterns that get solidified over long periods of time but also can get undone and disappear, for example, the clan structures that were so prominent in Chinese history and have been largely destroyed by Communist rule. The big rupture everywhere in the world, in my view, is the late nineteenth-century period of imperial expansion, which led, in the more recent period after World War II, to nation-state formation and, in the mountains, to the expansion of the global civilization of Christianity. Scott's perspective on the state projects the modern state back to the precolonial period and misunderstands the fragmented and discontinuous nature of power in that period.

THE PITFALLS OF CIVILIZATIONAL ANALYSIS IN SOUTHWEST CHINA

An ethnographic study of one of Yunnan's ethnic groups that later became recognized as one of China's officially recognized nationalities provides an excellent example of the pitfalls of a civilizational analysis. At the time of Leach's fieldwork (and military activities) in Burma, Francis Hsu was doing fieldwork in Yunnan. He had done his PhD under Malinowski at the London School of Economics in 1940. He was teaching at Yunnan University in Kunming together with Fei Xiaotong, whom he had met before in Malinowski's seminar at the London School of Economics (which was also attended by Edmund Leach) and who would play a major role in the establishment of the Chinese nationalities policy in the 1950s. It is not clear whether Fei, Hsu, and Leach met in 1942 when Leach escaped from the Kachin Hills via Kunming during the Japanese advance in Burma. Kunming was a very interesting place during the war, with the presence of many intellectuals who had been teaching at the evacuated Peking University (including the literary theorist I. A. Richards and his student William Empson). When Hsu published his book *Under the Ancestor's Shadow* in 1948, he had moved to the United States and had come under the influence of the American culture and personality school of anthropology, to whose development he devoted his distinguished career as chair of Northwestern University's Department of Anthropology and as president of the American Anthropological Association. Despite these distinctions, his semiautobiography is called *My Life as a Marginal Man*, and from it one gathers that he never felt sufficiently recognized. His descriptions of leading anthropologists like Evans-Pritchard are full of recriminations about their "colonial mentality" and convey his general feeling about the British that they were "stiff, correct, bleak, and cold."[22] His unease with Britain and British anthropologists may have led him to join the criticism of Malinowski's putative racism that followed the publication in 1967 of Malinowki's diary of his time among the Trobrianders (written in Polish). In an article he published in 1979, Hsu proposes a remarkable theory, namely that many societies know ethnocentrism but only the West has "positive ethnocentrism," which shows itself in proselytization: "Proselytization to let the only truth prevail everywhere was confined only to people with positive ethnocentrism. That is why all the world's missionaries and missionary movements were and are of Western, and secondarily Arab, origin. On the other hand, even when the Chinese Empire extended far and wide under Han, T'ang, and Ming, no Chinese court had ever attempted to spread Confucianism or any other form of Chinese beliefs or ethics, and no individual Chinese ever received a call from above to do the same."[23] In the rest of the article Hsu develops a remarkable argument about the advantages of studying one's own society. In his view, being Chinese made it possible for him to come to a deeper understanding of cultural patterns in China than his contemporary Western colleagues like Maurice Freedman and Arthur Wolf were able to arrive at.

In the preface to *Under the Ancestor's Shadow*, Hsu recorded his opinion that "the essential social structure of the community I have studied is typical of China as a whole." Hsu's study was of a semirural community that he called West Town, which is Xizhou, a village near Dali in Yunnan. In Hsu's view it was the clan organization that forms the basic unity of Chinese society, past and present. In his later comparative study *Clan, Caste, and Club* (1963), on India, China, and America, he argued that the clan structure created a situation-centered worldview in which "the individual is conditioned to seek mutual dependence. . . . The central core of Chinese ethics is filial piety." The American way of life is radically different in being individual-centered, that is, "characterized by temporary ties among closely related human beings. Having no permanent base in family and clan, the individual's basic orientation toward life and the environment is self-reliance." The Hindu supernatural-oriented world is in between these two extremes: "For example, in the supernatural-centered world ties among family and kin are more ephemeral than in the situation-centered world, while in other respects it is closer to the individual-centered world than to the situation-centered world."[24] Hsu's understanding of the Hindu system of values is almost opposite to Louis Dumont's understanding of it, which highlights the prominence of social ties and social situations while deemphasizing the more ephemeral reflection of those ties in the supernatural. Hsu's analysis of China is in fact closer to Dumont's analysis of India. Both Hsu and Dumont stress the importance of individualism in American society, but Dumont would see this as a general feature of "modern society" and thus not specific to America.

In a characteristically sarcastic review of Hsu's *Under the Ancestor's Shadow* in 1950 (which may well have been one of the causes of Hsu's unhappiness with British anthropology), Leach notices the essentializing nature of Hsu's analysis: "Dr Hsu appears to believe that geographical China, despite its vast size and linguistic diversity, possesses an essentially unified culture, so much so that all Chinese males can be docketed as possessing one or other of five 'personality configurations.' These Chinese universals are demonstrated by means of an analysis of family behavior in 'West Town' which the unwary might suppose to represent a 'typical' West China city. Careful reading plus a knowledge of local geography (Dr Hsu gives no map) show that West Town is in fact Hsi Chou, a Min Chia town-let near the north end of Lake Tali in Yunnan. This is about as typical of China as Londonderry is of England."[25]

Leach seems very certain that the so-called Min Chia are very different from the Han majority in the rest of China. He would have done better if he had applied his own theoretical perspective of dynamic interaction between categories and categorizations to this case. As Liang Yongjia shows in a recent article (2010), it was only in 1956 that the Minjia people of Dali were categorized officially as an ethnic minority called "Bai."[26] This official categorization led anthropologists to believe for decades that Leach was right and Hsu wrong. However, in the 1940s Hsu was quite right to see them as Han, since they themselves saw it that way and emphasized that their ancestors had migrated from central China to Yunnan. This simply underlines Leach's thesis of the dynamic nature of ethnic categorizations as well as (and more important) the crucial role of the new nation-state in trying to fixate them in stable "minorities" for which special policies could be devised. This is what Hsu completely misses in his culturalist approach of the essential characteristics of "Chinese society."

It is only the modern, intrusive state that is able to command the resources to do this classification of minorities and to make it attractive to ethnic minorities to insist on their difference. The "minjia" designation probably originated in a Ming household registration that made a distinction between army settlers (*junjia*) and local civilians (*minjia*). The garrisons were withdrawn during the Kangxi reign (seventeenth century), and the designation lost its significance.[27] During Hsu's fieldwork the only specificity of the local population would have been the local language (*bai hua*), but this could not be used as a boundary between Han and non-Han, since the Han themselves comprise very diverse (and mutually unintelligible) linguistic communities. The only socially relevant distinction linguistically is between those who (besides their local language) command Mandarin and those who do not.

Likewise, the Muslim Hui traders and farmers in the Dali area can, depending on the political context, emphasize their closeness to the Han or their distance from them. The Hui, with their wide-ranging trading connections, resisted Qing attempts to control them. A case in point is the Panthay rebellion (1856–73). Panthay seems to be a word derived from the Shan word *Pangshe*, which refers to Chinese traders coming to Burma.[28] This rebellion occurred in the same period as the Mutiny in India and the

Taiping Tianguo Rebellion in China and is separate from but connected to another widespread rebellion of Hui, the Dungan rebellion (1862–77). These political movements can perhaps best be understood as part of the entire landscape of imperial interactions that transformed political configurations drastically, with the demise of the Mughals and the decline of the Qing as important markers. It is interesting to note, for instance, that the leaders of the Panthay rebellion tried to get support from the British, while the Qing were successful in repressing the rebellion thanks to French artillery.

NATIONALITIES AND MINORITIES

It is clearly the modern state's ethnic classifications that matter most today in the entire region. Stevan Harrell is one of the leading ethnographers of the Yi; his answer to the question of who the Yi are is "Whoever the Nationalities Commission says they are" and to the question of how they got their identity is "Through the process of ethnic identification conducted in the 1990s, which employed Stalin's criteria of a nationality as having a common territory, language, economy, and psychological makeup expressed in a common culture."[29] Count, classify, culturalize, and control are elements of the state's ethnicity project, most pronounced in Communist China and Communist Vietnam but also present elsewhere. With "culturalize," I mean the attempt to make ethnic cultures into a harmless mosaic of folklorized elements of dance and arts contributing to the so-called unity in diversity of the nation-state. Since the mountains are border regions of new nation-states, the populations in them are under heavy control and surveillance. This only increases with border tensions and wars, such as the devastating U.S.-Vietnam War that has affected everyone in this area and the China-India border war as well as the China-Vietnam war of 1979. With their integration into the nation-state comes an increased interaction between majority people and minorities, which is enhanced by urbanization, with accompanying ethnic stereotyping and discrimination. While the mountains were previously relatively isolated from the lowlands and the capitals of states were at a distance, now everything has come into reach and everyone is on the move. Tourists come from the cities to the mountains, while people from the mountains go to the cities for work.

An important element of the ethnic minority project of the Chinese state (and the other states in the region, such as Vietnam, that follow similar policies) is that it furthers the exoticization and sexualization of the otherness of mountain people. The image of mountain women as beautiful, sexually free, exotic, and dressed in elaborate, colorful clothes has been available for a long time in Chinese poetry and folktales. The Han prince who is smitten with the face of a "barbarian" woman is a stock item in Chinese literature. One can already in the eighteenth century find "Miao albums," collections of paintings or block prints depicting different groups in a romanticized wilderness according to their description in the official Chinese gazetteers.[30] Often these are portraits of pretty, enticing women. Today in the age of photography this kind of erotic portrait is made into a mass product on the tourism market. Customs like the Miao "marriage-by-capture" or the matrilineal structure of the Naxi somehow add to the fantasy of a possible sexual adventure in the mountains. The state enhances the allure of diversity by organizing television shows with dance presentations by beautiful girls from the mountains. Places like Xishuangbanna in the Chinese border region with Thailand are especially known for prostitution involving "local girls" (in fact Chinese-speaking prostitutes who dress up like minority Dai). Places like Lijiang have become favorite honeymoon places for Han youth. The local Naxi population has been bought out by businessmen from elsewhere in China and now lives in modern housing outside town while their "authentic" (UNESCO-protected) houses are transformed into shops and lodges. One should not see this, however, as a wholesale fabrication producing a Han show with ethnic performers. In fact, large areas are not directly in touch with tourism, and the question is rather how these tourist spots and ethnic shows affect processes of ethnic identification together with the growing migration from the hills into the cities.

These processes take place all over this region, from India to China. Some are more peaceful than others. Mass tourism involves a massive transformation of the economy of entire regions and societies. It is perhaps most influential in the border region of Yunnan, Vietnam, Laos, and Thailand. In other areas tourism is not allowed because of massive militarization. In some of these areas one finds millenarian movements, as among the Hmong in Vietnam or independence movements, sometimes financially supported by opium trade, as in highland Burma. While China has successfully brought Yunnan under centralized state control since 1949, India is confronted with a very volatile separatist configuration in Assam and Nagaland.

The Nagas are Tibetan-Burmese speakers (a linguistic category that does not say much about ethnicity) occupying a contested buffer zone between India, Burma, and China. Before being made into a state in the Federal Republic of India, Nagaland had been part of Assam as the Naga Hills District. Assam had been taken over by the East India Company in 1826, and the Nagas seem at that time to have resumed their head-hunting, which they had stopped under an agreement with the previous Ahom rulers of Assam. The Ahom, or Tai-Ahom, are an offshoot of the Tai people (Shan in Burma, Dai in China). They probably came from Yunnan in the thirteenth century and established a kingdom that lasted for several centuries, until pressure from the Burmese led to the weakening of the Ahom state and invited the British in.[31] The Ahom kingdom bordered on the Cooch Bihar kingdom, which was a tributary state that the Mughals used as a frontier state. The Nagas have an unclear history of migration and trade that is related to their control over salt production. The relation of the Nagas to the Ahom seems structurally similar to the relation of the Kachin to the Shan as described by Leach. Not only that relation was important but also that between Nagas in the foothills, who had exchange and tributary relations with the Ahom and Nagas in the higher mountains who wanted to establish such connections.[32] This situation was continued in the colonial period, with the tea plantations in the foothills and plains and a line dividing this area from the higher mountains, where the people were left to their own devices unless they raided the lower ranges, as I will show later. This segregation of the hills from the plains is still the basis of Naga separatism. The plains are occupied more and more by Bengali settlers (Hindu and Muslim) today, and the Nagas and other Assamese groups see themselves pushed out into the hills (a different situation from fleeing state oppression).

Assam was given to tea planters, and from the 1840s onward the British were engaged in stopping Nagas from raiding the plantations. The armed struggles between the British and the Nagas, mainly involving British expeditions into the mountains to prevent head-hunting raids, continued until the 1930s. Christoph von Fürer-Haimendorf, trained as an ethnologist in Vienna, took part in one of these British expeditions in the 1930s and describes this adventure at length in his *The Naked Nagas*, a book otherwise partly devoted to somewhat romantic descriptions of the breasts of what he called the Naga *belles*. The expedition in hostile territory involved the freeing of slaves who were destined for human sacrifice and retrieving heads that had been taken from villages under British jurisdiction. When resistance was encountered, the villages of the headhunters were destroyed by fire. The British were not aiming at controlling the entire area directly but at containing the internal warfare between hostile Naga villages and preventing it from spilling over to the region where the tea plantations were located. Nagas in the parts that were under control refrained from head-hunting and slave-capturing. Two thousand of them went to France as part of the Labour Corps to work on infrastructure (roads, etc.) during World War I. Haimendorf reports that "to their deep disappointment they were not allowed to fight, but put to the more peaceful task of building roads: it was incomprehensible to them that they were even forbidden to cut off the heads of fallen foes. The only trophy that ever found its way into the Naga Hills was the spiked helmet of a Prussian grenadier—not a bad substitute for a head!"[33] The culture of head-hunting reminds us of the fiercely independent Wa headhunters. It reverses Scott's picture of people fleeing from the state. These warriors descended from the mountains to the plains to capture victims for their human sacrifice.

Haimendorf was an Austrian aristocrat who had come to India to work among "hill tribes" before World War II and was able to study the Nagas in the 1930s. He went on to become professor of anthropology at the School of Oriental and African Studies in London after the war and in many books continued to contribute to the ethnography of Hill peoples in South Asia. *The Naked Nagas* appeared in 1933, and in 1976 Haimendorf republished it with two added chapters about visits in the 1960s and 1970s. The republication is remarkable, since Malinowski's *Diary in the Strict Sense of the Term* that he wrote in Polish during his fieldwork among the Trobrianders had been published by his widow in 1967 and had drawn attention to his sexual loneliness and partly racist attitudes toward the people he studied (with its telling reference to Conrad's "exterminate the brutes"). Haimendorf's text is not a diary but an ethnography, and it is not considered a foundational text in anthropology, although it was successful enough to be reprinted. However, in the context of the uproar about Malinowski's writing, Haimendorf's text's explicit attention to the beauty of the breasts of young Naga women is quite astounding: "Climbing up the steep mountain with their high loads of fire-wood, their lithe, elastic bodies seemed immensely more beautiful than the figures on many a fashionable bathing-beach. I never saw a fat Konyak woman: even after innumerable pregnancies they preserve the slimness of youth in some miraculous way, and you are spared the sight of those pendular breasts which are so frequent among other races." "Among the girls is Ngapnun, I recognize her at once, for the last time I was in Long-khai I was struck by her graceful movements and perfect figure. Perhaps, for the first time in Nagaland, I almost regret the necessary reserve of the anthropologist, for to watch Ngapnun merely as a cool observer seems almost an insult to her beauty."[34] This goes on for pages, and one can only conclude that Haimendorf fancies himself to be a great connoisseur of physical beauty who tries to capture that beauty in the many photographs that adorn his ethnography. If anything, it reminds me of Leni Riefenstahl's obsessive interest in naked beauty, which led to her remarkable photos of the Nuba.[35] The exoticism and putative sexual freedom of mountain people beguile not only ancient Chinese poets and contemporary tourists but also professional anthropologists. That Haimendorf got away with it in a period of severe criticism of the "colonial gaze" is puzzling.

The personal (quite cheerful) tone of adventure and sexual innuendo of Haimendorf's text is almost completely opposite to that of Leach's text on the geographically adjacent Kachin. What both ethnographies have in common, though, is their neglect of the historical circumstances during their fieldwork. It is clear that their ethnography was only possible under the aegis of British expansion into the mountains of Assam and Burma that began in the second half of the nineteenth century, but these anthropologists do not problematize this heavy external impact. The Nagas are called on to participate in World War I, and one of the fiercest battles against the Japanese in the region was the 1944 battle of Kohima (a turning point in the war), fought in the heart of Nagaland. Nagas and Kachin could not escape from global warfare and were caught up not only in colonial schemes of control but also in nationalist projects for the future of postcolonial India and Burma. Another element that is mentioned (with some disapproval) in Haimendorf's text but overall neglected by both Haimendorf and Leach is the growing influence of Christianity, one of the most important social transformations affecting the Nagas and the Kachin in the area.

CHRISTIANITY IN THE MOUNTAINS

Christianity is as important as colonialism as an agent of transformation in the entire region and elsewhere. While Christianity (like anthropology) is dependent on colonial protection, it is not to be seen as a simple part of colonialism. In fact, as Haimendorf observes, "government officials and missionaries took unfortunately exactly opposite views on what was good for the Nagas,"[36] and it is clear that, as an anthropologist, he agreed with the government that one needed to protect "the Naga way of life," while at the same time getting rid of customs that would threaten colonial interests, like head-hunting and human sacrifice.

The anthropologist Vibha Joshi has recently given us a fuller account of the Christianization of the Nagas. From the 1830s onward the British started to develop tea interests in Assam. The colonial government invited the American Baptist missionaries to open a mission to educate the hill people in order to educate them to labor in the plantations. The Baptist Burma mission saw this as a possibility to move into the area to evangelize among the Shan in Burma and further onto southern China.[37] Missionaries in this area were doing the usual thing: bringing education and foremost literacy and bringing modern medicine, in short what can be called "conversion to modernity."[38] Gradually a large part of the population was converted to Christianity and to modern understandings of the world, for example, Naga nationalism. In the 1950s the American Baptists were thrown out of the country for their alleged sympathy for Naga separatism, but this only led to a further indigenization of Protestantism as well as diversification of Christianity. While the Baptists had enjoyed a monopoly on Christianity, now Catholics and a number of charismatic Protestants also came in. The charismatic revival movement has been especially successful since it is focused on healing, which is for all the Christian denominations a major aspect of religious practice.

Vibha Joshi has argued that the Nagas have become increasingly factionalized and that much of the violence that was earlier directed at the Indian army and Indian government is now part of factional strife.[39] Together with increased alcoholism and drug abuse, these may be the signs of a demoralized population, but they also remind one of the clan divisions that continue to dominate the Naga population, despite their attempts to achieve separatist autonomy. The blood feuds that characterize this factionalism resemble the old head-hunting raids without seemingly the belief in the magical power of captured heads.

The Nagas are not the only ones in the mountains who have in great numbers converted to Christianity. The Kachin have also been targeted since the mid-nineteenth century by missionaries, and the majority has converted. While India is a secular Hindu democracy, where the Christian minorities are protected to an extent, Burma declared itself a Buddhist state in 1960 and has been under military dictatorship since 1962. The extent to which Christianity is a religious marker of ethnic difference from the majority state for both Nagas and Kachin is an interesting question. In both cases there is a struggle for independence. The more successful one seems to be the independence movement fighting in the Kachin Hills against the Burmese army. The Kachin claim a homeland that comprises parts of China, Burma, and India but are now fighting not so much for independence as for autonomy within the Burmese state. Refugees from the violence flee to Thailand and China, lending an increasingly transnational element to the conflict. The Kachin Hills are rich in natural resources, including timber and jade, while a huge hydroelectric plant is being planned by the Chinese. Outside of the Kachin area there are other independence movements in the mountains, most notoriously in the opium-growing Golden Triangle in the Northern Shan state, which is dominated by the Wa independence movement, while Chinese Muslim merchants and miners (Panthay) are regionally prominent (and under threat as anti-Muslim sentiment grows in Burma today). This area has had a strong Chinese presence for a long time, partly because of Muslim traders, partly because of immigrants working in the mines, and partly because of the troops from the Kuomintang who escaped here after 1949 and who play a significant role in the area's politics. The Wa were headhunters like the Nagas, and their head-hunting, like that of the Nagas, seems to have been connected to a shifting political economy, in their case not dominated by tea plantations but by mines. Some of the Wa have been converted to Christianity but, according to Fiskesjö, in peripheral areas, not in the area where the Wa were in relative autonomous control of important mines until the 1930s.[40]

In Yunnan in the late eighteenth and early nineteenth centuries, Christian missionary activities were dominated by the British China Inland Mission and by the French Catholic Société des Missions Étrangères de Paris. As elsewhere, these missionaries operated as explorers who opened up the region for colonial penetration, although they were often outspoken about their differences with colonial authorities. They were the first to describe people like the Sani, a branch of the widespread Yi or Lolo set of societies in Yunnan, and give them an alphabet, a grammar, and a dictionary to write their language. The missionaries often (like James Scott) interpreted ethnic identity as a form of resistance against Han domination and their conversion to Christianity as a further boundary against assimilation.[41] By connecting the converts to the transnational Christian community they supported—perhaps unwittingly—a sense of separation from majority nationalism in the region and thus, in a number of instances, forms of separatism. Obviously, after the establishment of postcolonial states this kind of Christian-inspired separatism was interpreted by state officials as an imperialist ploy.[42] In China both indigenous culture and Christianity were targeted by Maoism—especially during the Cultural Revolution—as backward and treacherous. Since then, although there have been some attempts to turn indigenous culture into harmless folklore, the repression of Christian conversion has continued. My recent observations of church building by Jingpaw (Kachin) in Yunnan, however, seem to indicate a relaxation of this policy.

A special connection exists between Christianity and traditions of millenarianism among the Miao and other ethnicities in China and Vietnam. Christianity is, to an extent, a millenarian religion that can be interpreted in terms of indigenous millenarianism. The Miao believe that they had in the past their own kingdom, and they wait for the Miao king to unite all the Miao (who are spread over Guizhou, Yunnan, Vietnam, Laos, and Thailand) and reestablish the kingdom. Christianity (and especially some extreme millenarianists from the United States) easily finds a following among the Miao, despite strong government repression in all the states where they live. There are historical records of Miao uprisings against the Ming dynasty in the fifteenth century, continuing in regular revolts against the Qing and culminating in widespread rebellion in the 1850s. This tradition is only reinterpreted in conversion to Christianity in the late nineteenth century.

Like the Nagas, the Mizo, and other groups in India and Bangladesh, many of the Chinese ethnic minorities, such as the Yi and the Miao, have been "united" as a single "nationality," despite their dispersion over large areas and their linguistic and cultural heterogeneity. This kind of classification is primarily utilitarian, for governing purposes, but has real effects on the people involved, like any other social classification. Combined with forms of standardization of language—partly under missionary, partly under state influence—this leads to aspirations of unity that may go beyond what the central state sees as a desirable outcome of development.

Horses and mules can go over part of a mountainous terrain; the other part can only be traversed by human porters. Nevertheless, as we know, precious commodities have been carried over the mountains between India and China (and in all other directions). Maps of the boundaries of empire were made by the Ming and Qing and by the Mughals, followed in the nineteenth century by British military expeditions who surveyed the area as far as they could. All such expeditions were potential conquests, as exemplified in Francis Edward Younghusband's bloody expedition into Tibet in 1904. Of another kind were the botanist expeditions that looked for all kinds of plants unknown in the West, especially different species of rhododendron, and sent them to botanical gardens in the West.

Eric Mueggler has given us a vivid description of the life of porters in his book on Joseph Rock and other botanists in the early part of the twentieth century: "Carrying huge loads over the horrible roads of this thoroughfare was a way of life for thousands. Cotton yarn, produced in India, was the main product transported from Yunnan into Sichuan, where it was used in household cloth production. Porters walking the other way carried salt, noodles, kerosene lanterns, and slaughtered hogs. Their most common load, however, was tobacco." Mueggler cites Joseph Rock, the American botanist, writing in the 1920s: "The condition of the coolies we meet is pitiable. Their feet are bare or wrapped in palm fiber with toes protruding; their bodies are often much exposed through their torn and worn cotton garments. Every time they stop they sigh deeply. Their eyes are red and inflamed; their features haggard and drawn. Old and young are loaded down to the limit. The soldiers push them off the trail into the deep snow to let us pass."[43] Before one starts romanticizing the beauty of the landscape one realizes that one crucial element of life in the mountains was extreme poverty; another was constant violent conflict. In Joseph Rock's text we encounter slavery and slave raids in the Naga, Wa, and Yi areas, and they did not involve Hindu, Buddhist, or Han empires but immediate neighbors.

The history of life in the mountains is as fragmentary as the evidence we have of it. It cannot be unified by structural models, however dynamic, since social life cannot be explained by overriding structural oppositions between highland and lowland, mountain and valley. People are not in a settled and fixed habitat; they are on the move. One of the most important elements of the area, therefore, is trading. It is the values of people (sometimes as slave commodity), opium, tobacco, jade, and cotton yarn from India that create interactions that cannot be subsumed under a general history of capitalism or of civilizations.

Analytically speaking, political formations and connections of trade have to take precedence over the study of civilizational expansion. Buddhism may well have spread over a large part of the area, but Buddhism itself is part of statecraft. Today the modern nation-state (under Communist or military dictatorship) is the force that shapes much of the possibilities for livelihood in the mountains. It is, however, not so much the state as such that determines these possibilities but a variety of factors that are at the same time demographic (Hindu, Muslim, Burmese, Han settlers in the area) and economic (the scramble for scarce resources). The response by so-called minorities is not unified and cannot be reduced to a simple story of resistance against the state but might be understood as a perpetual struggle to better one's life under conditions not of one's own making. Ideological formations, like Christianity, or material conditions that favor the growing of specific crops, like opium, may be important instruments in these aspirations, which are part of local understanding of what a better life entails (which may well be further integration in the national body instead of "fleeing from the state"). Geography is part of the story, but one does not have to be in the mountains to mount a separatist movement. The fragmentary nature of social life in the mountains does not allow us to assume a civilizational unity or continuity of state power outside them. Leach's and Tambiah's speculations about the influence of an "Indic kingly model" or Hsu's speculations about the pervasiveness of Chinese civilization do not explain much of what is going on in this area. Scott's "anarchic model" similarly does not explain the variety of political formations and ambitions in the region. Leach's hunch about Chinese merchants and miners is, in my view, a good research direction for the Burmese side of things, while similarly the tea trade explains much about shifting relations in Assam and Nagaland. Colonial expansion (and its relation to world trade) is the historical pathway that sets the stage for the later violence of inclusion in a small number of nation-states and the violent response to that inclusion. The fact that these mountainous areas constitute the borders of newly formed nation-states explains the intensity of the conflicts. Mountain life is good to think with, but it may only very partially constitute a reality that is different from what lies beyond the mountains.

6 / WHO CARES?
CARE ARRANGEMENTS AND SANITATION
FOR THE POOR IN INDIA AND ELSEWHERE

Katherine Boo's much acclaimed novel *Behind the Beautiful Forevers: Life, Death and Hope in a Mumbai Undercity* (2012) pictures the terrible life of people in the filthy underside of the city. Despite being rather obviously a fictionalized account, claiming intimate knowledge of people's inner thoughts and feelings, its claim to be nonfiction is not entirely untrue, since Boo manages to give a faithful description of the precariousness of the life of scavengers and the brutality of the police, as well as the indifference of the judiciary toward them. It does away with any rosy picture of the entrepreneurialism and industriousness in the slums that some analysts and activists are spreading about Mumbai's slums. It also does away with any romanticization of the mutual solidarity of the poor. People who have to survive on very little have to be very competitive. What the novel does not do is analysis, and as such it can be only evaluated on the basis of its possible literary merit, much as the recent Hollywood movie about Mumbai, *Slumdog Millionaire*, has to be evaluated as a cinematic product. It is the task of the social sciences to come up with analysis.

The problem I want to address here is that of socially produced indifference in India toward the suffering of the urban poor and the consequences of this indifference. What I want to argue is that indifference is not typically Indian but in principle universal, and that in fact one needs to start explaining the opposite, namely taking care of the urban poor. I want to focus not on psychology, on emotions per se, but on sociology, on social arrangements and configurations. Emotions are connected to social arrangements, so I look at the sociogenesis of emotions, not at psychological explanations.

Finally, I want to examine the role of religion in addressing the plight of the poor in India. I will start with some observations about the history of care arrangements. Then I will discuss the reasons why Indian society seems to be an exception to that history. The Indian social science literature that I discuss focuses on Calcutta and Mumbai.

People all over the world broadly feel responsibility for their kin, and in cases when they don't, this is frowned on. Depending on the nature of their kinship systems, this can extend from the nuclear family out toward a wider circle of kindred. Fictive kinship—the inclusion of others in quasi-blood relations—can play a role in extending this feeling of responsibility. Forms of fictive kinship are based on common place of origin, ethnicity, or religion. However, the variety of forms of bonding is enormous, and the weakness or strength of ties beyond the family is relative. What one considers to be "us" and what one considers to be "others" varies and is dynamic to the extent that one cannot easily take natural or primordial ties for granted as the basis of caring for others. It is also not simply the case that human beings feel a universal, "natural" responsibility when they see the suffering of others. It is also not the case that "empathy" is required for social action to take place. Research in social psychology shows that "empathy," for example, in cases of sudden disaster like earthquakes, is short-lived, depends on specific framing of the narrative of suffering, and does not extend easily beyond individual cases with which one can "empathize."[1] In fact, people may feel all kinds of emotions, including a kind of elation that one is not suffering oneself or at least not to the extent that others are suffering. This shows that one cannot take universal emotions as the basis of an account of caring for others.

Caring for others outside the family is a product of collective social action. The attitudes toward the poor in a society are dynamic and change in relation to state formation and the ways poor and rich, established and outsiders, are connected to each other. In his book *In Care of the State* (1988) the Dutch sociologist Abram de Swaan illustrates the growing interdependence of rich and poor in nineteenth-century Europe as follows: "The outburst of mass epidemics like cholera was recognized in the nineteenth century as the consequence of living conditions among the urban poor. The better-off citizens could individually decide to move to healthier quarters, which they did in great numbers. As a—largely unintended—aggregate result of individual moves, urban space was partitioned into socially more homogeneous neighborhoods, ranging from residential areas to slums. But if the well-to-do wished to prevent epidemics from spreading beyond the poverty areas and paralyzing the city in its entirety, a collective effort at sanitation was still indispensable."[2] As was well known in the second half of the nineteenth century, both freshwater supply and an effective sewage system were necessary for this collective effort at sanitation. When this system was extended to slums *at public expense,* this became a true collective good.

In Europe and elsewhere a connection between poverty, vagrancy, and criminality led to the instituting of workhouses, where the poor were locked up and put to labor. After the Industrial Revolution the workhouses were replaced by more specialized institutions, like the prison, but the idea of disciplining the poor to labor continued to be of significance. Urbanization led to many poor people flocking into the cities, where they could not be avoided. They were seen as rats, as carriers of disease. However, more and more collective arrangements that included both rich and poor were created to change life in the city: "Illumination of the streets, construction of hard pavements (against mud and pools), supply of fresh drinking water, removal of human waste, collection of garbage and refuse from homes and streets, public transport systems, public schools for the poor and the not so poor, and later gas, electricity and telephone systems, and, most recently cable TV." After 1860 it was an established scientific fact that clean drinking water was an absolute necessity for public health. According to de Swaan, "the collective interest in public hygiene—the prevention of mass epidemics—set the ideological tone for much of these sanitary activities. . . . It was financed from compulsory rates, calculated independently of installation costs, either as flat rates or connected to volumes of use. Water and waste management had once and for all been transformed from a private concern to a public affair at the level of the city administration."[3] This is one way of narrating the collectivization of care arrangements in Europe. Although de Swaan's title is *In Care of the State,* his focus is not on the state as an independent actor (either a weak nor a strong state) or on the financial resources that the state has to its disposal but on collective interests, with a focus on interests and rational choice.

How can we narrate the failure in dealing with the urban poor in India? I want to look first at two arguments about waste management in Calcutta by prominent cultural historians. Before the reforms in the nineteenth century, European cities had their waste thrown all over public space, the stink of which has been well described by the historian Alain Corbin.[4] Nevertheless, according to Sudipta Kaviraj, we have to understand that in India the notion of the public is different from that notion in Europe. He begins his exploration of this difference by referring to a photograph of a common street scene in colonial Calcutta. It shows a municipal sign proscribing urination with the order "Commit no nuisance" and a row of unconcerned citizens right underneath engaged in this odious form of civil disobedience. In Kaviraj's view,

> the photograph is hilarious and evocative not only because it shows an act of modest, or unintended, defiance but also because it shows a dissonance at many levels between two ways of dealing with and acting upon the world—of the poor and the rich, of the powerful and the dominated, of those who own property and those who can only defile it, of legality and illegality, of obedience and furtive evasion of the rules. It shows in an everyday form the contest between a bourgeois order of the middle class and those who flout its rules. . . . Those who promulgated the notice had one conception of what public space meant, and those who defiled it had another.[5]

While this appears to be a class analysis, applicable to any class society with its emphasis on acts of defiance and resistance on the part of the lower classes (and with the usual neglect of the gender dimension that is quite important in urinating), Kaviraj goes on to give an interpretation that focuses on cultural difference.

According to Kaviraj, Indian notions of the public sphere are different from European ones. In Indian culture there is not an idea of universality of access, the idea that an activity is open to all, irrespective of their social attributes. The European concept of the public sphere tends toward universality, while in the Hindu social universe there is restricted inclusivity with clear distinctions of inside-outside. Kaviraj gives an example from his Calcutta experience. The inside of a Brahmin home would be immaculately clean to prepare it for *puja* (worship of the deities). But the garbage from this housecleaning would be dumped right in front of the house. One might imagine that these cultural traditions would be marginalized with the rise of communist politics in Calcutta, but according to Kaviraj, the predominantly *bhadralok* (high caste) leadership of the Communist Party was not interested in disciplining the poor, who now filled all public spaces. What he does not mention is a lack of Communist interest in disciplining the high-caste elites. In the end it is really indifference toward public space and collective goods that forms the difference with Europe.

Dipesh Chakrabarty, another cultural historian of Calcutta, has also addressed the question of public hygiene—in the colonial period.[6] He argues that the British representation of Indian public space as made of "cows, dirt and disease," to which the natives turned a blind eye, was a particularly colonial one. He interprets the rejection of the categories of public and private in India as a rejection of imperial modernism as well as of the nationalist bourgeois order. In Chakrabarty's view, state action to promote health and sanitation is felt by subalterns as an external imposition. He even suggests that bourgeois pursuits like long life and good health might not be universal and that subalterns may look at life differently. Like Kaviraj, he marks the opposition between inside and outside in Hindu culture, but he emphasizes the attractiveness of "the outside" as the space of a bazaar culture that might be full of dirt and danger but also of pleasure (which reminds one of Henry James's description of nineteenth-century London as a city of "dreadful delight").

In a critique of these interpretations of filth and garbage by Chakrabarty and Kaviraj, the political scientist Valerian Rodriguez points out that they entirely avoid even mentioning the ubiquity of the phenomenon of untouchability.[7] From the perspective of the anthropology of India, it is also surprising that both Kaviraj and Chakrabarty fail to comment on the fact that the category of "outside" in Indian rural life specifically designates the quarters of the untouchables who live outside the village and cannot use the village well. The other group who are seen as completely outside, living in their own quarters, are the Muslims. On the one hand, it is the phenomenon of untouchability and its relation to dirt, to impurity, that signifies the Hindu opposition of the inside and outside. On the other hand, it is the boundary between Muslims and Hindus. One needs to ask what happens with this opposition of "inside" and "outside" when one moves to the city. It is striking that Kaviraj and Chakrabarty limit their analysis to physical space. Despite Kaviraj's extended discussion of Habermas's notion of the public sphere in his article, there is no mention of the fact that the critique of that notion in social theory has centered on questions of social exclusion. In short, one needs to extend the categories of inside and outside to social space, to patterns of exclusion.

A recent interpretation of political life in Calcutta has been offered by the political scientist Partha Chatterjee.[8] Chatterjee confirms the importance of the opposition of inside-outside. In his earlier work on nationalism in the colonial period he already emphasized this opposition in claiming that Indians tried to be spiritually sovereign at home and leave the material outside world to be colonized. As I have pointed out elsewhere, this distinction is far too neat and fails to understand the extent to which the spiritual and the secular are parts of modernity that are entangled.[9] In recent work on "the politics of the governed" Chatterjee makes a distinction between civil society, which he understands as a closed association of modern elite groups who govern, and the popular life and politics of communities, of those who are governed. A related distinction is between citizens who have rights, constituting the sovereignty of the nation, and populations who are objects of policy, of surveillance, of pastoral care. In Chatterjee's theory this amounts to civil society in the Marxist sense of bourgeois society on the one hand and political society, those who are hardly citizens but subjected to governmentality, on the other. He focuses on the ways those who are in political society try to fend for themselves in struggles for housing and basic amenities.

This distinction of insiders and outsiders cannot do away with the fact that citizens who are in civil society cannot separate themselves entirely from the poor who live in political society. In fact, many of the problems that are troubling the poor are also troubling the relatively well-to-do, the foremost being the one of sanitation.[10] Like the symbolic opposition of outside versus inside, the theoretical opposition of civil society versus political society obscures more than it solves. The middle class resorts as often (and maybe more) to extraparliamentary action as do the poor, which makes "governance" a problematic notion. It is certainly not in electoral politics that people seek to participate in governance, despite the enthusiastic participation in it by poor and well-to-do alike.

The most spectacular manifestation of "civic anger" in civil (middle-class) society has been the "India against Corruption" movement, led by Anna Hazare, a self-styled "Gandhian" populist who, supported by the Indian media, captured the Indian political imaginary for a while in 2011. The role of the media in this has been of crucial importance. One may justifiably speak here of media activism, in which scandal and indignation fuel circulation and viewership. Especially the "sting operations" of the website Tehelka, in which politicians and military officials were recorded on tape while accepting bribes, have generalized an atmosphere of outrage that is not actually producing political change but mobilizes citizens against "politicians" and the "bureaucratic state." It is therefore not surprising that the media embraced Hazare's campaign "against corruption." The observation by scholars like Partha Chatterjee and Arjun Appadurai that the Anna Hazare movement mobilized primarily the middle class that itself was the main beneficiary of corruption may have led to the next step in escalating rhetorical virtuosity: the claim made by the highly regarded Indian social theorist Ashis Nandy at the 2013 Jaipur Literary Festival that it was the poor people of India who were the most corrupt (out of necessity, as he implied).[11] As usual in India, all this remains at the level of rhetoric, combined with some symbolic action, but does not lead to political change. What does emerge from it seems to be a generalized feeling among the middle class that while they are the main beneficiaries of the state, they cannot expect much from an inefficient state. Besides an activist media, an activist judiciary is foremost in championing claims (most of them from the middle class) that cannot be solved in the political process. So, in fact, the middle class is also part of political society. Except for Nandy's deliberately outrageous comments, none of the Indian theorists, including Chatterjee, addresses questions of caste, and especially untouchability, in relation to the question of corruption or, more neutrally formulated, unequal access to the state bureaucracy. Bureaucratic action is not arbitrary but in fact is slanted in terms of caste, class, and gender.[12] That poor people have not much chance to take part in state corruption may be the conclusion.

The European development of caring for others in order to take better care of oneself has not occurred in India in the colonial context or in the postcolonial context. According to the late Raj Chandravarkar's analysis of colonial Mumbai, "neither the Municipal Corporation, nor even the Development Department, were able to make a significant intellectual or practical contribution to the amelioration of social conditions. They failed to evolve any long-term strategy for the creation of a generally hygienic urban environment. They could not overcome their own institutional inertia or the massive complacence of the city's elites."[13]

The cultural arguments of the authors on Calcutta whom I have discussed do not analyze the problem that the outside always comes into the inside, as is graphically illustrated by the entrance of the untouchable sweeper (and other servants) inside the home. In postcolonial India neither the argument that India has been colonized nor that it is a poor society that cannot provide for its poor holds water after decades of political independence and economic growth. In fact, the extent to which Indian capital is channeled out of India is astounding, and according to all indicators, economic inequality is on the rise with economic growth. Since the conditions of the Indian urban poor have not been improved by a gradual extension of care arrangements from the middle class that would include them, they have to develop all kinds of survival strategies. In this they are helped by a number of NGOs and foreign developmental agencies, for example, the World Bank. These agencies require participation of the poor in, for example, rehabilitation schemes. This is sometimes called a "politics of inclusion." This kind of politics can be illustrated by an exceptionally well-described case in Mumbai.

The case I am looking at here is that of an NGO, the Society for the Promotion of Area Resource Centers (SPARC), which has been deeply involved in slum rehabilitation projects in the city. SPARC has developed a central tool of governmentality, namely surveying, mapping, and counting or statistics, into a tool of knowledge that the poor could use in their communications with outside agencies. Arjun Appadurai has called this "governmentality from below," something rather similar to Chatterjee's "political society."[14] But when SPARC represents the poor, the question remains how the poor themselves think about that representation. It is obvious that the category of the poor hides all kinds of class, ethnicity, kinship, and religion divisions that cannot be easily represented. It is equally obvious that SPARC represents not only the poor but also the World Bank and governmental agencies. SPARC in fact performs a role that is well described in anthropology, namely that of being a broker or middleman, a conspicuously ambivalent role that leads to its being distrusted by both sides, those who govern and those who are governed. Between "from below" and "from above" becomes "in the middle" and typically evolves systematically in patterns of patronage. In a careful study by Vinit Mukhija, we can find out not only how SPARC became part of a struggle between various stakeholders and used its ties in government agencies to further its own vision of property development but also how the process "induced SPARC to centralize its own internal operation, transform its mission from one of only advocacy to one of social investment in profitable enterprises, and seek a permanent seat in the centralized body created for conflict management. In other words, conflict with market institutions transformed SPARC such that it began to resemble market institutions. Similarly, conflict with government agencies induced SPARC to gain control over part of the government apparatus."[15] This is not necessarily bad, but studies of patronage systems in

India have shown a whole range of unhelpful practices such as graft, criminality, and exploitation that in the end does not deliver the care arrangements that were supposed to be put in place.

In my view, participation of the poor in political society cannot solve the problem with which I started my inquiry, namely that of the improvement of living conditions of the poor in order to prevent the spread of diseases. One also cannot assume that it is "resistance" against such improvements by the poor that explains the situation. Evidence from immunization programs is that the poor are generally quite willing to submit to vaccination like the more well-to-do members of society.[16] I would argue from historical experience that we need to look at those who are relatively well-off to see why they do not seem to care enough about the fact that the living conditions of the poor form a problem for the entire city population. To the extent that they care, middle-class citizens are primarily interested in removing slums (eyesores) and cleaning vagrants and hawkers from the streets of their own neighborhoods. People and garbage are both considered under the rubric of removal. Today much is written about the India middle class, but work on its relation to notions and practices of caste are hard to find, except when one cannot avoid them because of their obvious salience, as in electoral politics and marriage arrangements. For example, in Partha Chatterjee's book on *Lineages of Political Society* (2011), one finds a discussion of Tagore's ideas about caste, but nothing else. This is surprising, because Calcutta shows so clearly the transformation of a high caste *bhadralok* society into a middle-class society with many of the same characteristics.

It is not that caste and class has not been a theme in Indian sociology. One of India's leading sociologists, Andre Béteille, has published on it throughout his career. What Srinivas and Béteille found in the 1950s and 1960s was that some systemic elements of caste centering on purity and pollution, and emphasized in Louis Dumont's *Homo Hierarchicus*, have declined with urbanization, democracy, and new occupations. However, in a recent opinion piece Béteille now seems to argue for the growing irrelevance of caste in India, because "rapid economic growth and the expansion of the middle class are accompanied by new opportunities for individual mobility which further loosens the association between caste and occupation." This observation is contradicted by recent ethnographic work on the IT profession by Carol Upadhya that shows that this profession is in majority controlled by high castes, especially Brahmans.[17] Béteille in fact acknowledges the strong correlation between caste and occupation in another passage in his opinion piece: "There continues to be a general association between caste and occupation to the extent that the lowest castes are largely concentrated in the menial and low-paying jobs whereas the higher castes tend to be in the best-paid and most esteemed ones."[18]

In my view there is no escaping the fact that a continuing hierarchical mentality prevails in India that prevents care arrangements from being extended to the urban poor. We do not thereby return to a holistic view of an Indian caste system, as in Dumont's *Homo Hierarchicus*, because that would certainly be a wrong perspective on modern India. However, it does imply that turning our back on the significance of hierarchical values in Indian society by focusing on youth culture and media and other manifestations of an Indian cosmopolitanism does not make hierarchy go away.

While it is true that city planning in many parts of the Global South has produced quite unintended results of which the violent favelas of Rio de Janeiro and the urban chaos of Lagos are testimony, outside India there are hardly any examples of a general failure to bring basic services of sewage and drinking water to poor neighborhoods. To an extent one might argue that these services are not brought to the rest of the population as well (as electricity- and water-starved cities all over India may testify), but it is all a matter of degree, and the poor are obviously by far the worst off, and among them Muslims and Dalits are prominent. They are seen to be outside the fold and consistently set up against each other by politicians of higher caste in order to keep control over them. In cities like Ahmedabad, Muslims seem to have lost all access to patronage that would allow them to benefit from common goods.[19] In many cities they form the bulk of the poor people together with Dalits.

Because of the identification of caste with tradition and backwardness, it is a severely understudied topic in the study of urban India of the last couple of decades. What is much better studied is the middle class. It strikes me that there is very little middle-class activism for sanitation and extending care arrangements for the urban poor. The middle class is notoriously difficult to define, but in India there seems to be an interesting relation between higher caste community and middle-class habitus, centering on education and consumption. Housing societies in big cities are often based on caste-religious community. While only a few elite groups can afford to be totally exclusivist, others are mixing caste-religious community (including food habits like vegetarianism) and class. Since higher castes need servants, there is a coming and going of a servant class of lower caste that lives in the vicinity, as if in servants quarters. This is also the reason why there are always slums close to middle-class housing. It is this interdependence of masters and servants that does not allow for stricter spatial separation of the relatively well-to-do and the poor and raises again the question of proximity and sanitation.

In the Indian middle classes we find a continuation of a crucial distinction of high castes versus low castes, but the most important opposition is between pure castes and impure untouchables as well as between Hindus and Muslims. It is here that the opposition between inside and outside that has been observed by Kaviraj and Chakrabarty becomes salient. Outside is the place of garbage and human filth, "dirty people." The new forms of prosperity that characterize the Indian middle classes of today do not seem to alter the picture very much. While one often hears a morality tale about the growing indifference of the middle classes in their gated communities for the plight of others, there is in fact nothing new.

What role does religion play in attitudes toward the poor? In their analysis of religion Max Weber and Clifford Geertz have pointed out that the question of meaning and thus of suffering is foremost in many religions. This certainly also includes Indic religions, such as Hinduism and Buddhism. There is a wide variety of Hindu movements and communities, and here I can only examine one middle-class religious community that is quite prominent in India and abroad, the Gujarati Swaminarayanis. This is a Hindu religious community that is in principle open to all Hindus but in fact caters to a middle-class, higher caste Gujarati community. Swami Narayan was a nineteenth-century guru who was particularly successful among Gujaratis and especially among the peasant caste of Patils. This caste has over the years become a transnational community with strong business networks. In Gujarat the Patils have allied with Brahmans and Banias (a higher merchant caste) to create a middle-class bulwark that socially excludes lower castes but politically includes, through effective patronage, untouchables and tribals.[20] One can see here an alignment of business interests, marriage strategies, political influence, and religious conservatism. The political clout of the Swami Narayan community can be easily demonstrated by the fact that at its opening of the Akshardham Temple in Delhi in 2005, Man Mohan Singh, L. K. Advani, and the President of India Abdul Kalam were present. The president of India's speech contained a reference to the great work of Swaminarayani volunteers: "Akshardham has happened at the dawn of the twenty-first century with the commitment and dedication of one million volunteers. What has happened today at Akshardham inspires me and gives me the confidence that we can do it! The realization of developed India is certainly possible before 2020 with the millions of ignited minds like you."[21] This was an aspirational speech by a Muslim president who seemed to have no desire to look back at the recent pogrom against Muslims in Gujarat, the heartland of the Swami Narayan movement. In passing it can be remarked that volunteerism in India is often connected to communities and not to the wider public good. This is also true for various ways of using tax-free endowments for helping the poor of one's community.[22]

Dalits cannot be initiated into the ascetic order that is the nucleus of the community. According to Chris Fuller, the Swami Narayan community is a powerful and partially modernized organizational expression of hierarchical values. "The order demonstrates clearly how bhakti can be accommodated to institutionalized inequality in Hinduism and Indian society."[23] What we see in the Swami Narayan community is what we can also notice in other Hindu communities, namely the mixing of spirituality and business management. In her study of Akshardham, Christiane Brosius quotes a school principal who visits Akshardham: "This monument is like Infosys of Spirituality."[24] With these attitudes, there is not much to be expected from middle-class Hinduism in caring for the poor.

Untouchability can fruitfully be regarded as a form of bonded labor and slavery.[25] This raises the comparative question where the nineteenth-century Western movement to abolish slavery came from, on which there is a vast literature. There is hardly anyone in India who forthrightly defends the institution of untouchability, which is very similar to those toward slavery in the West in the period when slavery was practiced. What happened with slavery, however, was that it was transformed in the minds of people from a problematic and morally dubious institution into an evil and abominable one. Attitudes and sensibilities changed as part of a whole new perspective on how to deal with the poor and marginal that led also gradually in changes in housing and care arrangements. The historical evidence shows that it was not straightforward economic interests that impelled the abolitionists. The American historian Thomas Haskell has argued that the abolition of slavery cannot be explained by the interests of an emerging bourgeois class but might be explained by a new cognitive style and sensibility that was related to the rise of the capitalist market. These cognitive structures underlay both the reformers' novel sense of responsibility for others and their definition of their own interests.[26] How does the fact that people are suffering start to matter for other people? It depends, according to Haskell, on changing notions of causal involvement and of an awareness of new remedies. These changing notions give people confidence to intervene in society's future. To bring this idea into this discussion, in short, change comes from an awareness that the boundary between inside and outside is porous, that the inside can only be clean and protected by cleaning the outside. It is also an awareness that something can be done about it, which induces a sense of responsibility.

The comparison with changing attitudes and developments in the West will be seen by some as a typically orientalist way of showing the failures of "the East." To counter that objection and to show a quite different historical pathway from both the Indian and the European, I want to make a short excursion to the ways Communist China has tackled the problem of poverty, inequality, and care arrangements. Socioeconomic conditions were at a similar level in the late 1940s after both India and China created sovereign states. One striking difference between development in India and China in the 1950s was that India got rid of widespread famines, while in China the Mao-led government created a famine in the Great Leap Forward that may have cost the lives of more than thirty million people. Amartya Sen has attributed this difference to the fact that India has a democracy and can act as an "open society" with the inherent possibility of regime change.[27] Ideologically motivated mobilization campaigns in China, like the Cultural Revolution, likewise bore a heavy cost. The brutality of these campaigns and their heavy toll is the dark underside of a total transformation of social conditions in China.

A thoroughgoing land reform, especially, has taken the land from the ownership of relatively few and redistributed it to collectives of (in principle) individuals stripped of their ascribed status. There was discrimination, but it was against the former upper classes and their descendants, upsetting the traditional hierarchy. This implied also that the clan structure of Chinese society, with its land-based inequality, was abolished. The 1950s saw the building of an egalitarian education and health care system that was a great success in terms of universal literacy and higher life expectancy. The system was egalitarian not only in terms of class and clan but also in terms of gender, with a very high female participation in education and the economy. Special measures were also taken to integrate ethnic minorities living in the poor mountain areas into the mainstream of society, with all the contradictory consequences that I have highlighted in chapter 5. In

Maoism workers and peasants were the new masters of society, but obviously under the tight control of a new hierarchy created within the Party. Therefore, one should not have any illusion of an egalitarian paradise, as promised by Communism. Instead there is an extraordinary amount of arbitrary power and privilege in the hands of cadres whose ability to profit depends on their patronage skills and on broader political circumstances, such as the Cultural Revolution, as Richard Madsen depicted in an extraordinary ethnography.[28]

India on the other hand has never been able to abolish caste, which still dominates rural society, or to execute convincing egalitarian land redistribution. While India instituted in the 1950s a system of positive discrimination (reservation) measures to integrate so-called scheduled castes and tribes in society, this system has nowhere succeeded in diminishing the overall discrimination against these sections of the population or stimulate an overall upward mobility among them. In fact, the system has become ineffective as a policy since it was expanded to so-called Other Backward Castes (in some areas the majority of the Indian population) but is quite effective as in the service of electoral politics.

In the 1980s and 1990s both economies have "opened up" to the world market, resulting in astounding overall economic growth in China, with the proportion of people below the poverty line there dropping from 73.5 percent in 1981 to 8.1 percent in 2005.[29] Bardhan calls this "an unparalleled achievement in world history." In the Indian case, despite ten years of considerable economic growth, the proportion of people below the poverty line has dropped from 42.1 percent in 1981 to 24.3 percent in 2005. What is, however, very disturbing in the Indian data is that economic growth there has not resulted in better health care and especially infant care. The percentage of underweight children (younger than three) in India is 46 but only 8 in China. Just as disturbing is that educational inequality is abysmal in India, with the Gini coefficient of the distribution of adult schooling years in the population being 0.56 in India in 1998–2000 but 0.37 in China.

Despite a significant deterioration of medical services in China since the "opening up" of the economy, there can be no doubt that the poor in China are much better taken care of in terms of nutrition, health, education, and economic opportunity than the poor in India. In China you have fewer poor, and those who are poor are mostly better off than India's poor. Although income inequality is rising in both countries, this does not significantly affect the overall picture. Certainly, the idea of a socialist paradise where the workers would be in control has been entirely discarded in reality, especially since the disbanding of centralized production in state factories, though it is still very much present in the invocation of "the people" in Communist rhetoric, as Mun Young Cho shows in her recent ethnography of urban poverty in Harbin in Northeast China.[30] Not only is inequality in income and status increasing between "the successful" in the new economy and laid-off workers, but with the relaxation of *hukou* (residency registration) competition is also increasing between these laid-off urban workers and newly arrived rural migrant workers. The ecological consequences of rapidly increasing urbanization and industrialization in China are dire and are seriously threatening public health, but they affect everyone in quite similar ways. No inhabitant of Beijing can escape its heavily polluted air. India's much slower economic growth, however, has not resulted in a much better ecological picture. Delhi suffers perhaps even more from air pollution than Beijing.

One has to conclude that the Communist revolution in China has radically transformed a highly hierarchical society into first a society constantly mobilized around the lower categories of the previous hierarchy, namely peasants and workers, managed by Party hierarchy, and then since 1978 into one with much more opportunity for all (inevitably resulting in growing inequality), while India has not been able to effectively address the most important hierarchical arrangement in society, namely the systematic discrimination against former bonded laborers.

Turning from this general picture of differences in poverty alleviation between India and China—what about the specifics of the emergence of care arrangements? The Chinese case shows a revolutionary history of a straightforward attack on traditional social privilege and the extolment of the virtues of the working classes. Here we do not see a middle class acting out of self-interest to provide good care for proximate poor. Instead we see the violent destruction of the middle class. In the Marxist view, civil society expresses the interest of the bourgeois class that has to be removed from power. In China the care arrangements are available for each and every one; they are organized by work units (*danwei*) and ultimately controlled by the party-state. The urban situation is by the same token very different from the one in India. While in India the rural poor have been going to the cities since the 1960s in huge waves of migration, with an enormous pressure on housing, and thus resulting in the largest slums in the world, in China moving to the city (which is also happening with increasing speed) was in the early socialist period only possible when one had adequate housing and work (within the danwei). Today, with the "opening up" of the economy and the increasing possibility of setting up private enterprises, there is an unprecedented rural-urban migration in China. While the hukou system of urban residence permits is still in place, it no longer deters people from moving to the city without such a permit. This has resulted in a large urban "floating population" who do not have hukou or the privileges that come with it. That floating population can be as large as or even larger than the resident population, which has privileged access to health care and education. While this creates a new, typically urban inequality, it has not led (yet) to a permanently underpaid and discriminated underclass with very little opportunity for upward mobility, as one finds in Indian cities, or to the appallingly unhygienic circumstances in which that Indian underclass lives.

The comparison with China, a developing country that is in many ways comparable to India, has further highlighted the specific nature of the denial of basic services to the urban poor in India. One needs to ask, what are the consequences of ignoring the plight of the poor in India? There is no doubt that the institution of untouchability will not disappear through the abolition of the word *untouchability* by law or practice.[31] This was already realized by Ambedkar, who argued at the end of his life that another religious and moral sensibility than Hindu hierarchy had to emerge in India. His solution of conversion to Buddhism will not bring about that other sensibility if only his untouchable followers convert. One cannot expect that Hinduism will change into a religious liberating force that will change deeply ingrained habits of hierarchy. The consequence of this hierarchical indifference to the plight of the poor is, surprisingly, not more violence directed toward the relatively well-to-do. The poor are badly organized and relatively well contained by a more or less corrupt police force.

The violence one does find is primarily directed at other poor people, as one sees in many ghetto situations all over the world, but it does not make the rest of the city unsafe, as it does elsewhere in the world. While the Dalit population have been gaining more confidence over the last couple of decades, they remain relatively quiet and peaceful. It is only the Muslim poor who sometimes fight back from a self-assured sense of dignity, derived from being members of a global religion and from their powerful Indian past, and this resistance leads to a growing insecurity for the entire population. One can only expect that insecurity to become worse with the decline of Pakistan and the growing marginalization of Muslims in India. The other consequence is that the general conditions of health, sanitation, ability to work, and life expectancy of a large part of the population are terrible, posing grave challenges for not only them but also the rest of the population. In my view, social scientists studying India need to do more studies of the transformation of traditional hierarchical values into a middle-class habitus that leads the middle class to ignore the plight of the poor, with grave consequences for its own well-being. Again, it is not indifference to the poor per se that I find worth exploring but indifference to waste management and to the living conditions of the poor that threaten one's own well-being.

I have tried to keep here a tone of analytical distance without condemnation of moral attitudes, since I believe that the problems that face growing populations since the Industrial Revolution are everywhere quite similar and that self-interest might have been an important factor that has impelled people to do something about at least problems of hygiene. Where self-interest combined with growing knowledge of the causes of epidemic disease have failed to convince emergent middle classes and state authorities to provide basic public services for the poor, one needs to try to understand the cultural nature of such failure. Good health and a longer life, however understood culturally, can be found everywhere as human objectives, which makes their denial to large groups in the population not only a theoretical problem but also a political problem of considerable importance.

The main argument in this book is that the comparative project in anthropology and historical sociology needs to be revitalized, especially in the face of a growing generalism in sociology and the expanding influence of cognitive universalism in the social sciences in general. The original comparative project in the social sciences, as developed by Durkheim and Weber, was ultimately geared to understand Western modernity. The justified critique of the essentializations and ethnocentrism inherent in such a project have led to a decreasing interest in the comparison of entire societies, even in comparison in general. Sociologists have increasingly focused on the study of modern, Western society and have come to see the analysis of large data sets in order to construct general models as their main task. Anthropologists have abandoned the aim of comparison in pursuit of the analytical description of specificity and diversity. This book argues that anthropology is the discipline that has the empirical tools and theoretical insights to inform a comparative project that is post-Durkheimian and post-Weberian in its emphasis on translation and historical interaction. Its aim is not to come to a general model of human behavior, as for instance based on rational choice, but to further knowledge by comparative analysis. The anthropological lens focuses on the sociocultural fragment not so as to produce one "thick" description after another but so as to gain a holistic insight into how things (ideas, flows, objects) are configured in historically evolving, open configurations. Ethnography that depends on language acquisition as well as cultural knowledge and thus on the difficulties of translation enables an understanding of processes in society that are in interaction with outside forces. The clearest example of the interactive and reflexive nature of translation is that of the spread of the concept of "religion" over the world. This has led national elites everywhere to come up with translation of the concept and with translations of their traditions (practices, doctrines) in terms of the concept; a multisited, multidirectional translation under imperial conditions that have made religion into a "thing" that needs to be governed (defended, transformed, repressed) in order to attain a recognizable modernity in the mirror of imperial encounters. It is "religion" as a fragment of social life and its conceptualization that gives us a sense of what the importance of studying "a total social fact" is.[1]

In his lucid discussion of the comparative method in anthropology and sociology, Andre Béteille points out that Durkheim intended this method, which he saw as the essence of sociology, to provide generalizations by means of the classification and comparison of societies worldwide. The reader of this book will have seen that such generalization and classification is unfeasible in the light of the problems of reflexivity and translation.[2] However, Marcel Mauss's study of "gift-giving" as a "total social fact" that is simultaneously religious, economic, and spiritual or religious shows another road to follow. It is this elucidation of complex phenomena through comparison without "generalism" or modeling of "social systems" that allows one to steer clear of both universality and endless particularity.

In his discussion of Weber's comparative project Béteille points out that Weber exaggerated the differences between civilizations so as to be able to show the uniqueness and universal value of Western civilization. This book has focused on the problems with the concept of "civilization," which are those of ethnocentrism, in which one society is valued above others; of nationalism, in which one civilization is made into a general characteristic of a diverse society; and of essentialism, in which a complex set of traditions with their internal debates is reduced to unchanging essences. Anthropology's focus on the sociocultural fragment is able to avoid these unifying essences without denying their social power. It is especially the civilizational state and the nation as civilization that need to be studied through their fragments.

One cannot deny the importance of the nation-state as the dominant form of political and religious practice. Anthropologists also have to deal with the nation-state, both in terms of its everyday practices and in terms of its ideology, called nationalism. At the most practical level anthropologists have to get permission to do fieldwork on topics that are often deemed sensitive. They need passports and visas, if they are foreigners, and if they are citizens they need to be able to be critical of the state without endangering their own livelihoods or those of their families. Nation-states like India and China have become very wary of ethnographic research, since it is based on firsthand observation rather than on a second-level analysis of data provided by the state, and more often than not research permission is refused. This is becoming so troublesome that I see it as the greatest threat to the free inquiry that is the hallmark of anthropological research in India and China. Moreover, funding agencies are increasingly wary of funding research into sensitive topics and areas.

At the level of theory it is also hard for anthropologists to steer clear of nationalist ideology. How to avoid the majoritarianism implied in speaking about Hindu India or Communist China without denying the importance of Hinduism or Communism? How to avoid denying the importance of caste while emphasizing that Indian society cannot be essentialized as a caste system or avoid denying the importance of certain Confucian values and ideals while emphasizing that Chinese society cannot be essentialized as a Confucian society? It is important to see "the nation" as a specific political imagination that by its emphasis on "the people" distances itself from "the king" and makes a sharp distinction between "the new republic" and "the ancient regime." One thus always needs to ask: who are the people? And what is the difference between "the old" and "the new"? While the nation sees itself in the singular, it is always in the plural. The nation-form is globally spread as a societal formation, but it takes very different shapes, depending on the historical trajectories of the societies that have come to be shaped as nations. It is important to realize that the hyphen between "nation" and "state" indicates the conceptual difficulty of sharply distinguishing between nation and state, which results in very different arrangements of citizenship, cultural belonging, and rights regimes in different parts of the world.

Despite the fact that the nation-form is a global form for modern societies, nation-states are specific in their actual organization and functioning. In some societies the army plays an almost independent political role; in others there is only one party. Societies that forge their national imagination as a response to colonial interventions are a particular historical category. It would be wrong to see them as merely derivative, as Partha Chatterjee has argued in his early work, but they do emerge in an interactional space of imperialism.[3] Nationalism emerged in the nineteenth century, which was the period not only of nationalism but also of imperialism. Nationalism and the nation-state are not singular phenomena but have emerged during a process of European expansion and the creation of a world-system of economies and states.[4] Although sovereignty and self-determination are important elements of nationalism, they are conceptualized in a larger framework of international relations on a global scale. Similarly, so-called world religions, like Christianity, can never be entirely captured by individual nationalisms, since they have a global mission. Europe has been globalizing and has been globalized over many centuries, depending on which starting point in history one wants to take for which kind of globalization. Religions like Christianity and Islam are globalizing formations that take a conception of the world as their terrain, but regional religions, like Buddhism, Hinduism, and Daoism, are only regional because of certain limits to their ethnic bases and the extent of trading networks, not because of the fact that their cosmology is somehow not global. The globalizing religions, like Christianity and Islam, are among the powerful forces that open up the limits of national territories. It is the tensions that are inherent in the nation's conceptualization of "the inside" and the "outside" that form a major part of anthropology's topic and that legitimate its choice of "the fragment" instead of the "unified whole."

In this book I have compared India and China on the assumption that they are comparable. What I find important in this particular comparison is that it runs counter to the general, often unreflexive, comparison with the modern West. Such is true from Weber onward and also affects work done by Indian and Chinese social scientists, as witnessed, for instance, in the debate about secularism in India. This is not to imply, however, that one should first seek out the comparable. The incomparable is also of great significance in arguments against the universality of certain values and ideas.[5] The very fact that some society is incomparable to another is significant in itself. In that way the study of societies of the past and of the present that are examples of radical otherness are not to be seen as "marginal" because they are "not representative." Their extreme nonrepresentativeness is part of their importance for analytical understandings of problems that are posed by social science theory, as for instance the problem of individualism.

The study of large societies and their civilizations brings anthropology always into a creative tension with the discipline of history. It is the comparative angle that distinguishes the anthropological approach. Whether one works with ethnographic material or historical material, it is the theoretical engagement with comparison that sets anthropology apart. If historians want to avoid nationalism, a connection with anthropology is essential. Anthropology's focus on the fragment finds a common ground with especially the "micro-history" advocated by Carlo Ginzburg and others. In societies like India and China there is, obviously, no escape from the study of textual traditions and history. Anthropology offers a perspective in the study of historical change and cultural configurations that helps avoiding the homogenizing discourses that prevail in civilizations. As B. S. Cohn has shown in his work, the combination of anthropology and history is especially productive in illuminating colonialism and its forms of knowledge.[6]

Anthropology not only compares societies but also, especially, the social notions of collective civilization and of personhood. As Mauss made clear in an unfinished essay on "the nation," the individual and the collective are born in the same historical process.[7] Michel Foucault also points out that individualization and collectivization are intertwined processes. The birth of the modern state is at the same time the birth of the modern individual. The understanding of that individual as a *homo economicus*, a rational actor whose choices produce the common good, is an understanding that fits the ideology of the market economy but is nevertheless a figment of the collective imagination. It is true in its effects on social reality. The pervasive market ideology in the West and its spread to India and China has different effects in different places. The easy accommodations and mutual reinforcements of a "free market" and "opening up" to the world economy with Hindu (anti-Muslim) nationalism and with Communist authoritarianism may have confounded those who have a "systemic" view of the interconnections between the economy and freedom. This systemic view is often called "neoliberalism," after the economic reforms of President Ronald Reagan in the United States and Prime Minister Margaret Thatcher in Britain, but it is not a felicitous term for the social transformations that take place in India and China. It is unclear to me what is exactly "neoliberal" in India and China, except for the fact that at the governmental level one finds a global managerial language that is primarily produced in the United States. While management techniques are very popular among rising managerial classes in both the industry and the government (mostly trained in similar ways) the term *neoliberalism* only relates partially to the "facts on the ground" that can be accessed through fieldwork. Here it is caste (in the case of India) and family and friendship (in India and China) that are social facts that are hard to grasp in managerial terms. The recurrent campaigns against corruption in both India and China have a widespread popularity among the population but do not alter the pervasive inequalities that are based on social background. It is hard to understand caste politics in Uttar Pradesh or Tamil Nadu as "neoliberal" or the Chinese Communist Party's growing progressive blocking of access to Internet resources.

The global managerial language is accompanied by an interest in self-help psychology books, which also have an American provenance. In India and China they are only very partially translated into the vernacular and remain therefore limited to an English-reading middle class. Self-help psychology books confront understandings of personhood in India and China that are different from the modern notion of "the individual." A while ago McKim Marriott argued that the Indian conception could be better called "dividual." Dividual persons are not bounded; they absorb material influences and are altered by them. They also give particles of themselves to others—for example, body fluids—and alter these partners in transaction. McKim Marriott and his followers have tried to make this idea into a general theory of Indian society, but this suffers from the problem of generality that I have already discussed and rejected in this book. However, Marriott's attention to the problem of boundaries between the individual and the social body and his rejection of the Western notion of the individual as inadequate for Indian society is incisive. Findings like these are not limited to Indian society. Marilyn Strathern has likewise argued that the Melanesian person is "dividual."[8] Another Melanesianist, Kenelm Burridge, has argued in a philosophical essay not only that the modern European notion of the individual is, more often than not, inapplicable but, more generally, that the notion of a biologically bounded person, a single instance of the species, does not fit a reality in which people live "in an environment of dreams, thoughts, speech, images, emotions, stories, awarenesses, continuities and discontinuities, and explicit categories and articulate rules which govern interrelations and address to the world."[9] The environment Burridge speaks of varies across cultures. The role that dreams, ancestors, ghosts and spirits, and apparitions of gods and saints in the life of people in most parts of the world is extremely well documented in anthropology but almost totally ignored by those whose models are based on the bounded individual.

The ethnographic record fits a current interest in theories that seek to problematize the relation between persons and things, as in Bruno Latour's actor-network theory, and in theories of affects, as in Gilles Deleuze's proposition (without reference to anthropology) that the "individual" should be seen as "dividual."[10] Brian Massumi uses the latter argument in a recent book to launch an attack on the notion of the "rational actor" as the basis of economic action (see chapter 2 for a similar critique). Massumi shows how affectivity is in the heart of the notion of economic rationality. Self-interest in economic reasoning means "seeking satisfaction," but deferral of satisfaction and doubt and fundamental uncertainty about the future are very much part of economic action. Economic reasoning is not about calculation of risk but about uncertainty, and Massumi uses the concept of "dividual" to refer to everyone's swings between several moods that relate to the uncertain future. Rationality and affect are therefore intertwined, according to Massumi.[11] One has to conclude that what lies at the basis of much economic modeling and theories in macro-sociology, political science, and psychology is not so much Western "man," whose modernity is fundamentally different from that of people in other societies, but an ideology of the individual that is deeply unsatisfactory for understanding the modern West itself. Anthropology is the discipline that studies understandings of the world that differ from this ideology and by that token offers an ideological critique. Its radical comparative viewpoint allows us to come to a more fragmentary, but better, analysis of the societies that make up our contemporary world.

INTRODUCTION

1   Xiaotong Fei, "Plurality and Unity in the Configuration of the Chinese Nationality," Tanner Lecture, given in Hong Kong, November 15 and 17, 1988, http://tannerlectures.utah.edu/_documents/a-to-z/f/fei90.pdf, accessed March 29, 2015.

2   Fei, "Plurality and Unity in the Configuration of the Chinese Nationality," 186, 214, 219, 229.

3   Marcel Detienne, *Comparing the Incomparable* (Palo Alto, CA: Stanford University Press, 2008).

4   B. S. Cohn, *An Anthropologist among the Historians* (Delhi: Oxford University Press, 1987).

5   Ladislav Holy, introduction, *Comparative Anthropology* , edited by Ladislav Holy, 7 (London: Blackwell, 1987).

6   Holy, introduction, *Comparative Anthropology,* 8.

7   Harvey Whitehouse and Emma Cohen, "Seeking a Rapprochement between Anthropology and the Cognitive Sciences: A Problem-Driven Approach," *Topics in Cognitive Science* 4 (2012): 404–12.

8   Whitehouse and Cohen, "Seeking a Rapprochement between Anthropology and the Cognitive Sciences," 408.

9   Gilbert Herdt, *Guardians of the Flutes: Idioms of Masculinity* (New York: McGraw-Hill, 1981).

10 Marvin Harris, *Cannibals and Kings: The Origins of Cultures* (New York: Vintage, 1977).

11 Clifford Geertz, *The Interpretation of Culture* (New York: Basic Books, 1973), 39.

12 Philippe Descola, *Beyond Nature and Culture,* trans. Janet Lloyd (Chicago: University of Chicago Press, 2013).

13 G. E. R. Lloyd, *Being, Humanity, and Understanding* (Oxford: Oxford University Press, 2012), 23.

14 Edward Slingerland, "Body and Mind in Early China: An Integrated Humanities–Science Approach," *Journal of the American Academy of Religion* 81, no. 1 (2013): 6–55.

15 Slingerland, "Body and Mind in Early China," 8, 20.

16 One example being the work on "intentionality" by John Searle and the seemingly "intentional debate" between Searle and Derrida. John Searle, *Intentionality* (Cambridge: Cambridge University Press, 1983); Jacques Derrida, *Limited, Inc.* (Evanston, IL: Northwestern University Press, 1988).

17 See also Michael Herzfeld, "Performing Comparisons," *Journal of Anthropological Research* 57 (2001): 259–76.

18 Peter van der Veer, *Religious Nationalism, Hindus and Muslims in India* (Berkeley: University of California Press, 1994).

19 Partha Chatterjee, *The Nation and Its Fragments* (Princeton, NJ: Princeton University Press, 1993). See my critique of this dichotomy in Peter van der Veer, *Imperial Encounters* (Princeton, NJ: Princeton University Press, 2001).

20 Kenneth Dean and Zheng Zhenman, *Ritual Alliances of the Putian Plains*, vol. 1, *Historical Introduction to the Return of the Gods* (Leiden: Brill, 2009), and *Ritual Alliances of the Putian Plains*, vol. 2, *A Survey of Village Temples and Ritual Activities* (Leiden: Brill, 2010).

21 *Bored in Heaven* (2010), available at www.boredinheaven.com.

22 See, for instance, Sumit Guha, *Beyond Caste* (Leiden: Brill, 2013).

23 Marcel Detienne argues eloquently for the restoration of comparison in historical studies in *Comparing the Incomparable* (Palo Alto, CA: Stanford University Press, 2008).

24 Webb Keane, *Christian Moderns* (Berkeley: University of California Press, 2007).

25 Eric Klinenberg, *Heatwave: A Social Autopsy of Disaster in Chicago* (Chicago: University of Chicago Press, 2002).

26 Eric Mueggler, *The Age of Wild Ghosts: Memory, Violence, and Place in Southwest China* (Chicago: University of Chicago Press, 2001).

27 J. P. Parry, *Death in Banaras* (Cambridge: Cambridge University Press, 1994). For comparison see Maurice Bloch and Parry, eds., *Death and the Regeneration of Life* (Cambridge: Cambridge University Press, 1982).

28 Peter van der Veer, *Gods on Earth: The Management of Religious Experience in a North India Pilgrimage Centre*, LSE Monographs (London: Athlone, 1988).

29 Barend ter Haar, "Thee en Cup-a-Soup, Inaugural Address for the Chair in Sinology," Leiden University, October 2001. http://faculty.orinst.ox.ac.uk/terhaar/theeoratie.pdf, accessed August 24, 2015.

30 Sidney Mintz, *The Power of Sweetness: The Place of Sugar in Modern History* (London: Penguin, 1986).

31 W. H. Ukers, "All about Tea," *Tea and Coffee Trade Journal Company* (1953), cited in Mintz, *Power of Sweetness*, 112.

32 Peer de Vries, *Zur politischen Ökonomie des Tees* (Vienna: Böhnau, 1979), 43–44.

33 Available at http://www.fordham.edu/halsall/mod/1793qianlong.html, accessed August 22, 2015.

34 Hugh Tinker, *A New System of Slavery: The Export of Indian Labour Overseas, 1830–1920* (Oxford: Oxford University Press, 1974).

35 De Vries, *Zur politischen Ökonomie des Tees*, 97.

36 Amar Farooqui, *Opium City: The Making of Early Victorian Bombay* (Delhi: Three Essays Collective, 2005).

37 McKim Marrott, "The Feast of Love," in *Krishna, Myths, Rites and Attitudes*, ed. Milton Singer (Honolulu: East-West Center Press, 1966).

38 Frank Dikötter, "Patient Zero": China and the Myth of the 'Opium Plague,' " Inaugural Lecture at School of Oriental and African Studies, University of London, October 24, 2003. http://frankdikotter.com/publications/the-myth-of-opium .pdf, accessed October 24, 2014.

39 Dikötter, "Patient Zero," 5.

40 Shao-hua Liu, *Passage to Manhood: Youth Migration, Heroin, and AIDS in Southwest China* (Palo Alto, CA: Stanford University Press, 2010).

41 Eric Wolf, *Europe and the People without History* (Berkeley: University of California Press, 1982).

42 Marshall Sahlins, "Cosmologies of Capitalism: The Trans-Pacific Sector of 'The World-System,' " in *Culture/Power/History*, ed. Nicholas Dirks, Geoff Eley, and Sherry Ortner (Princeton, NJ: Princeton University Press, 1994).

43 Sahlins, "Cosmologies of Capitalism," 427–28.

44 James Hevia, *Cherishing Men from Afar: Qing Guest Ritual and the Macartney Embassy of 1793* (Durham, NC: Duke University Press, 1995).

45 Lydia Liu, *The Clash of Empires: The Invention of China in the Modern World* (Cambridge, MA: Harvard University Press, 2004).

1 / COMPARATIVE ADVANTAGE OF ANTHROPOLOGY

1 A recent example of the conceptual problems that occur when one designs a research program on such a phenomenon is the Templeton Foundation–funded SSRC program (2010–15) New Directions in the Study of Prayer, in which I participated as member of the steering committee. Despite these difficulties the program has produced a number of good ethnographic case studies, as for example in the special issue "Prayer and Politics," *Journal of Religious and Political Practice* 1 (2016).

2 Kenneth Dean, *Taoist Ritual and Popular Cults of Southeast China* (Princeton, NJ: Princeton University Press, 1995); C. J. Fuller, *The Renewal of the Priesthood: Modernity and Traditionalism in a South Indian Temple* (Princeton, NJ: Princeton University Press, 2003); Fredrik Barth, *Political Leadership among Swat Pathans* (London: Athlone, 1959); Fredrik Barth, *Sohar, Culture and Society in an Omani Town* (Baltimore: Johns Hopkins University Press, 1983); Fredrik Barth, *Ritual and Knowledge among the Baktaman of New Guinea* (Oslo: Universitetsforlaget, 1975); Fredrik Barth, *Cosmologies in the Making: A Generative Approach to Cultural Variation in Inner New Guinea* (Cambridge: Cambridge University Press, 1987); Fredrik Barth, *Balinese Worlds* (Chicago: University of Chicago Press, 1993);

Fredrik Barth and Unni Wikan, *Situation of Children in Bhutan: An Anthropological Perspective* (Thimphu: Centre for Bhutan Studies, 2011).

3   Marilyn Strathern, *Property, Substance and Effect* (London: Athlone, 1998), 1.

4   Clifford Geertz, *The Interpretation of Cultures* (New York: Basic Books, 1973), 15.

5   Clifford Geertz, *Islam Observed: Religious Development in Morocco and Indonesia* (Chicago: University of Chicago Press, 1971).

6   Clifford Geertz, "Religion as a Cultural System," in *The Interpretation of Cultures* (New York: Basic Books, 1973). Talal Asad has written a convincing critique of this definition as a typical modern Christian one in his *Genealogies of Religion* (Baltimore: Johns Hopkins University Press, 1993). Clifford Geertz, *The Religion of Java* (Chicago: University of Chicago Press, 1976). See John Pemberton's critical interpretation of "Javanism" in *On the Subject of Java* (Ithaca, NY: Cornell University Press, 1994).

7   Talcott Parsons, *Toward a General Theory of Action* (Cambridge, MA: Harvard University Press, 1951); Pierre Bourdieu, *Outline of a Theory of Practice* (Cambridge: Cambridge University Press, 1977).

8   Bruno Latour, *We Have Never Been Modern* (Cambridge, MA: Harvard University Press, 1993); Shmuel Eisenstadt, ed., *Multiple Modernities* (New Brunswick, NJ: Transaction, 2002).

9   Thomas Gibson, *Islamic Narrative and Authority in Southeast Asia from the Sixteenth to the Twenty-first Century* (New York: Palgrave Macmillan, 2007); Peter van der Veer, *Imperial Encounters* (Princeton, NJ: Princeton University Press, 2001).

10   Arvind Rajagopal, *Politics after Television: Hindu Nationalism and the Reshaping of the Public in India* (Cambridge: Cambridge University Press, 2001).

11   I argue this point at greater length in my *The Modern Spirit of Asia* (Princeton, NJ: Princeton University Press, 2014).

12   Clifford Geertz makes the "models of" and "models for" argument in *The Interpretation of Cultures*. For a critique of the role of the IMF in the "Asian Crisis," see Joseph E. Stiglitz, *Globalization and Its Discontents* (New York: W. W. Norton, 2002).

13   R. W. Connell, "Why Is Classical Theory Classical?," *American Journal of Sociology* 102, no. 6 (May 1997), 1511–57.

14   Thomas Piketty, *Capital in the Twenty-first Century* (Cambridge, MA: Harvard University Press, 2014).

15   Paul Krugman, "Hitting China's Wall," op-ed, *New York Times*, July 18, 2013.

16   Harry D. Harootunian, James Chandler, and Arnold I. Davidson, *Questions of Evidence: Proof, Practice, and Persuasion across the Disciplines* (Chicago: University of Chicago Press, 1994).

17   Ronald F. Inglehart and Pippa Norris, *Sacred and Secular: Reexamining the Secularization Thesis* (Cambridge: Cambridge University Press, 2004).

18   Samuel P. Huntington, *The Clash of Civilizations and the Remaking of World Order* (New York: Simon and Schuster, 2011); Peter Katzenstein, with Il Hyun Cho, "In the Service of State and Nation: Religion in East Asia," in *Religion and International Relations Theory*, ed. Jack Snyder (New York: Columbia University Press 2011), 168–99.

19 Available at http://www.pewforum.org/2012/03/08/religious-migration-preface/, accessed August 25, 2015.

20 Ruth Benedict, *Patterns of Culture* (New York: Houghton Mifflin, 1934); Ralph Linton, *The Cultural Background of Personality* (New York: Appleton-Century-Crofts, 1945); Abram Kardiner and Ralph Linton, *The Individual and His Society* (New York: Columbia University Press, 1939); Francis Hsu, *Psychological Anthropology: Approaches to Culture and Personality* (Homewood, IL: Dorsey Press, 1961).

21 Jack Goody, *The Theft of History* (Cambridge: Cambridge University Press, 2006).

22 James Scott, *Seeing Like a State: How Certain Schemes to Improve the Human Condition Have Failed* (New Haven, CT: Yale University Press, 1999).

23 Clifford Geertz, "Anti Anti-Relativism," *American Anthropologist*, new ser., 86, no. 2 (1984): 263–78.

24 Louis Dumont, *Homo Hierarchicus: The Caste System and Its Implications* (Chicago: University of Chicago Press, 1981).

25 Sanjay Subrahmanyam, Velcheru Narayana Rao, and David Shulman, *Textures of Time: Writing History in South India 1600–1800* (Ranikhet: Permanent Black, 2013).

26 Arjun Appadurai, "Is Homo Hierarchicus?," *American Ethnologist* 13, no. 4 (November 1986). Arjun Appadurai and Carol A. Breckenridge were the founders of the journal *Public Culture*, which played a role in shifting scholarly attention to these phenomena.

27 Murray Milner, *Status and Sacredness: A General Theory of Status Relations and an Analysis of Indian Culture* (Oxford: Oxford University Press, 1994).

28 Gerald D. Berremann, "Caste in India and the United States," *American Journal of Sociology* 66, no. 2 (September 1960): 120–27.

29 Robert Deliege, *The Untouchables of India* (Oxford: Berg, 1999), 69–70.

30 C. J. Fuller, "Caste, Race, and Hierarchy in the American South," *Journal of the Royal Anthropological Institute* 17, no. 3 (September 2011): 604–21.

31 Sanal Mohan, *Modernity of Slavery: Struggles against Caste Inequality in Colonial Kerala* (New Delhi: Oxford University Press, 2015).

32 Smita Narula, "Caste Discrimination," *Seminar* 508 (December 2001).

33 André Béteille, "Race and Caste," *Hindu*, March 10, 2001, www.hindu.com/2001/03/10; Dipankar Gupta, "Caste, Race, Politics," *Seminar* 508 (December 2001).

34 Andreas Wimmer, *Waves of War: Nationalism, State Formation, and Ethnic Exclusion in the Modern World* (Cambridge: Cambridge University Press, 2013).

35 Ernest Gellner, *Nations and Nationalism* (Ithaca, NY: Cornell University Press, 1983).

36 Peter van der Veer, *Religious Nationalism* (Berkeley: University of California Press, 1994).

37 Benedict Anderson, *Imagined Communities*, rev. ed. (London: Verso, 2006).

38 Wimmer, *Waves of War*, 78, 97, 90.

39 Talal Asad, "Ethnographic Representation, Statistics and Modern Power," *Social Research* 61, no. 1 (1994): 55–88.

40 Asad, "Ethnographic Representation, Statistics and Modern Power," 78.

41 Peter van der Veer, *Gods on Earth: The Management of Religious Experience in a North Indian Pilgrimage Centre*, LSE Monographs (London: Athlone, 1988).

42 Marcel Mauss, "Techniques of the Body," *Economy and Society* 2, no. 1 (1973): 70–88.

43 Marcel Mauss, *Sociology and Psychology: Essays* (London: Routledge and Kegan Paul, 1979), 122.

44 Bourdieu, *Outline of a Theory of Practice*.

45 This is a very small field, since there are only a few primate centers in the world where one can do this research, and Leipzig and Atlanta are the leading ones. Frans de Waal, *The Age of Empathy: Nature's Lessons for a Kinder Society* (New York: Harmony Books, 2009); Michael Tomasello, *Why We Cooperate* (Boston: Boston Review Books, 2009).

46 Tehila Kogut and Ehud Kogut, "Exploring the Relationship between Adult Attachment Style and the Identifiable Victim Effect in Helping Behavior," *Journal of Experimental Social Psychology* 1, no. 49 (2013): 651–60.

47 Maurice Bloch, *Anthropology and the Cognitive Challenge* (Cambridge: Cambridge University Press, 2012), 49.

48 Marshall Sahlins, *The Use and Abuse of Biology: An Anthropological Critique of Sociobiology* (Ann Arbor: University of Michigan Press, 1976), 101.

49 Herbert S. Terrace, *Nim, a Chimpanzee Who Learned Sign Language* (New York: Columbia University Press, 1987); Beatrix Gardner and Thomas Gardner, *Teaching Sign Language to Chimpanzees* (Albany: State University of New York Press, 1989).

50 Pascal Boyer, *Religion Explained* (New York: Random House, 2008), 114.

51 Rodney Needham, *Belief, Language and Experience* (Oxford: Blackwell, 1972).

52 Pascal Boyer, "Being Human: Religion: Bound to Believe?," *Nature* 455 (October 22, 2008): 1038–39.

53 Boyer, *Religion Explained*, 119, 123, 124.

54 Pierre Liénard and Pascal Boyer, "Whence Collective Rituals? A Cultural Selection Model of Ritualized Behavior," *American Anthropologist* 108, no. 4 (2006): 814–27.

55 T. M. Luhrmann, Howard Nusbaum, and Ronald Thisted, "The Absorption Hypothesis: Learning to Hear God in Evangelical Christianity," *American Anthropologist* 112, no. 1 (2010): 66–78.

56 Stewart Guthrie, *Faces in the Clouds* (Oxford: Oxford University Press, 1993).

57 Paul Radin, *Primitive Man as Philosopher* (New York: Appleton, 1927).

58 Alfred Kroeber, *Nature of Culture* (Chicago: University of Chicago Press, 1952).

59 Joseph Henrich, Steven Heine, and Ara Norenzayan, "The Weirdest People in the World," *Behavioral and Brain Sciences* 33, nos. 2–3 (June 2010): 61–83.

1   For example, Gary S. Becker, *The Economic Approach to Human Behavior* (Chicago: University of Chicago Press: 1976).

2   For example, Rodney Stark, "Economics of Religion," chapter 3 of *The Blackwell Companion to the Study of Religion* (Oxford: Blackwell, 2006), 47–67.

3   Smriti Srinivas, *In the Presence of Sai Baba: Body, City, and Memory in a Global Religious Movement* (Leiden: Brill, 2008); Tulasi Srinivas, *Winged Faith; Rethinking Globalization and Religious Pluralism through the Sathya Sai Movement* (New York: Columbia University Press, 2010); Peter van der Veer, ed., *Conversion to Modernities* (New York: Routledge, 1996).

4   Arend Lijphart, *The Politics of Accommodation: Pluralism and Democracy in the Netherlands* (Berkeley: University of California Press, 1968).

5   Jose Casanova, "Beyond European and American Exceptionalisms: Towards a Global Perspective," in *Predicting Religion*, ed. G. Davie, P. Heelas, and L. Woodhead (Aldershot, UK: Ashgate, 2003).

6   J. Stolz, "Salvation Goods and Religious Markets: Integrating Rational Choice and Weberian Perspectives," *Social Compass* 53, no. 1 (2006), 13–32; "Secularization Theory and Rational Choice: An Integration of Micro- and Macro-theories of Secularization Using the Example of Switzerland," in *The Role of Religion in Modern Societies*, ed. D. Pollack and D. V. A. Olson (New York: Routledge, 2008), 249–270; "Gods and Social Mechanisms: New Perspectives for an Explanatory Sociology of Religion," in *Raymond Boudon: A Life in Sociology*, ed. M. Cherkaoui and P. Hamilton (London: Bardwell Press, 2009).

7   Rodney Needham, *Belief, Language, and Experience* (Oxford: Blackwell, 1972).

8   Steven Lukes and Martin Hollis, eds., *Rationality and Relativism* (Oxford: Blackwell, 1982).

9   As argued in an earlier Lewis Henry Morgan Lecture by Stanley Tambiah; see his *Magic, Science and Religion and the Scope of Rationality* (Cambridge: Cambridge University Press, 1990).

10 Birgit Meyer and Peter Pels, *Magic and Modernity* (Palo Alto, CA: Stanford University Press, 2003).

11 Caitlin Zaloom, *Out of the Pits: Traders and Technology from Chicago to London* (Chicago: University of Chicago Press, 2006).

12 Mary Poovey, "Can Numbers Ensure Honesty? Unrealistic Expectations and the U.S. Accounting Scandal," Notices of the American Mathematical Society, January 2003, 27–35.

13 Fenggang Yang, "The Red, Black, and Gray Markets of Religion in China," *Sociological Quarterly* 47 (2006): 93–122.

14 David Palmer, *Qigong Fever: Body, Science, and Utopia in China* (New York: Columbia University Press, 2007).

15 Yoshiko Ashiwa and David L. Wank, eds., *Making Religion, Making the State: The Politics of Religion in Modern China* (Palo Alto, CA: Stanford University Press, 2009).

16   Nanlai Cao, *Constructing China's Jerusalem: Christians, Power, and Place in Contemporary Wenzhou* (Palo Alto, CA: Stanford University Press, 2010); Jie Kang, *From Peasant to Pastor* (New York: Palgrave, forthcoming).

17   Karen Tranberg Hansen, "Informal Sector," in *International Encyclopaedia of the Social and Behavioral Sciences* (Amsterdam: Elsevier, 2001), 7450–53.

18   Most extreme are Fenggang Yang's statistical predictions in April 2014, http://www .telegraph.co.uk/news/worldnews/asia/china/10776023/China-on-course-to -become-worlds-most-Christian-nation-within-15-years.html, accessed December 1, 2015.

19   Peter van der Veer, *The Modern Spirit of Asia* (Princeton, NJ: Princeton University Press, 2014).

20   F. N. Pieke, "Bureaucracy, Friends, and Money: The Growth of Capital Socialism in China," *Comparative Studies in Society and History* 37, no. 3 (1995): 494–518.

21   Arjun Appadurai and Carol Breckenridge, "The South Indian Temple: Authority, Honour and Redistribution," *Contributions to Indian Sociology* 10 (1976): 187–211.

22   Charles Taylor, *A Secular Age* (Cambridge, MA: Harvard University Press, 2007).

23   Jürgen Habermas, *The Structural Transformation of the Public Sphere* (Cambridge: Polity, 1989); Reinhart Koselleck, *Critique and Crisis: Enlightenment and the Pathogenesis of Modern Society* (Cambridge, MA: MIT Press, 1988).

24   William James, *The Varieties of Religious Experience: A Study in Human Nature* (Oxford: Oxford University Press, 2012).

25   Arjun Appadurai, "The Ghost in the Financial Machine," *Public Culture* 23, no. 3 (2011): 521.

26   Jens Beckert, *The Transcending Power of Goods: Imaginative Value in the Economy*, MPIfG Discussion Paper 10/4 (April 10, 2010).

27   Steven Kemper, *Buying and Believing* (Chicago: University of Chicago Press, 2001). See also Thomas Malaby, *Gambling Life: Dealing in Contingency in a Greek City* (Urbana-Champaign: University of Illinois Press, 2003).

3 / KEEPING THE MUSLIMS OUT

1   Steven Vertovec, *Routledge International Handbook of Diversity Studies* (London: Routledge, 2015).

2   Entwurf eines Integrations-und Diversitätskonzepts für die Stadt Frankfurt am Main , September 2009, http://www.frankfurt.de/sixcms/media.php/738/Inte grationskonzept.pdf, accessed August 26, 2015.

3   See Peter van der Veer, ed., *Handbook of Religion and the Asian City* (Berkeley: University of California Press, 2015).

4   Samuel Huntington, *The Clash of Civilizations and the Remaking of World Order* (New York: Simon and Schuster, 1996), 26–27.

5   Jawaharlal Nehru, *The Discovery of India* (Delhi: Oxford University Press, 1946).

6   A brilliant comparison of the debate about Spanish in the United States and Islam in Europe is in Aristide R. Zolberg and Long Litt Woon, "Why Islam Is Like Span-

ish: Cultural Incorporation in Europe and the United States," *Politics and Society* 27 (March 1999): 5–38.

7   Samuel Huntington: *The Clash of Civilizations* (New York: Simon and Schuster, 1996), and *Who Are We? The Challenges to American National Identity* (New York: Simon and Schuster, 2004).

8   Peter Katzenstein, "Civilizational States, Secularisms and Religions," in *Rethinking Secularism*, ed. Craig Calhoun, Mark Juergensmeyer, and Jonathan Van Antwerpen (New York: Oxford University, 2011), 145–65.

9   S. N. Eisenstadt, ed., *The Origins and Diversity of Axial Age Civilizations* (Albany: State University of New York Press, 1986).

10 Karl Jaspers, *Von Ursprug und Ziel der Geschichte* [About the origin and goal of history] (Frankfurt: Fischer, 1955), 14.

11 Charles Taylor, "Afterword: *Apologia pro Libro suo*," in *Varieties of Secularism in a Secular Age*, ed. Michael Warner, Jonathan Van Antwerpen, and Craig Calhoun (Cambridge, MA: Harvard University Press, 2010).

12 Talal Asad, *The Idea of an Anthropology of Islam*, occasional paper series (Washington, DC: Georgetown University Center for Contemporary Arab Studies, March 1986).

13 Peter van der Veer, "Playing or Praying: A Sufi Saint's Day in Surat," *Journal of Asian Studies* 51, no. 3 (August 1992): 545–64.

14 Norbert Elias, *Über den Prozess der Zivilisation* [The Civilizing Process], vol. 1. (Frankfurt am Main: Suhrkamp, 1993).

15 See Chung-Ying Cheng and Nicholas Bunnin, eds., *Contemporary Chinese Philosophy* (Oxford: Blackwell, 2002).

16 Deng Xiaoping, *Deng Xiaoping Wenxuan* [Selected Writings of Deng Xiaoping], vol. 3 (Beijing: Renmin Chubanshe, 1994), 27–28.

17 Full text of Enoch Powell's speech in the *Telegraph* is available at http://www.telegraph.co.uk/comment/3643826/Enoch-Powells-Rivers-of-Blood-speech.html, accessed August 26, 2015.

18 Maria Pia Paganelli, "The Moralizing Role of Distance in Adam Smith: *The Theory of Moral Sentiments* as Possible Praise of Commerce," *History of Political Economy* 42, no. 3 (2010): 425–41.

19 Adam Smith, *The Theory of Moral Sentiments* (1759).

20 Albert Hirschman, *The Passions and the Interests: Political Arguments for Capitalism before Its Triumph* (Princeton, NJ: Princeton University Press, 1977).

21 Clifford Geertz, *The Interpretation of Cultures* (New York: Basic Books, 1973).

22 Clifford Geertz, "Thick Description: Toward an Interpretive Theory of Culture," in *The Interpretation of Cultures* (New York: Basic Books, 1973), 15.

23 Joyce Carol Oates, *A Widow's Story: A Memoir* (New York: Ecco, 2011).

24 David Hume, *Essays, Moral, Political, and Literary* (Indianapolis: Liberty Fund, 1987).

25 Marcel Mauss, *The Gift: The Form and Reason for Exchange in Archaic Societies* (New York: W. W. Norton, 2000).

26 Richard Bauman and Charles L. Briggs, *Voices of Modernity: Language Ideologies and the Politics of Inequality* (Cambridge: Cambridge University Press, 2003).

27 Charles Taylor, *Multiculturalism: Examining the Politics of Recognition* (Princeton, NJ: Princeton University Press, 1994), 28.

28 Webb Keane, "Sincerity, 'Modernity,' and the Protestants," *Cultural Anthropology* 17, no. 1 (January 2008), 74.

29 Louis Dumont, *Homo Hierarchicus: The Caste System and Its Implications* (Chicago: University of Chicago Press, 1980).

30 Henry Abelove, *The Evangelist of Desire: John Wesley and the Methodists* (Palo Alto, CA: Stanford University Press, 1990.

31 Susan Harding, *The Book of Jerry Falwell* (Princeton, NJ: Princeton University Press, 2001).

32 Eiko Ikegami, *Bonds of Civility: Aesthetic Networks and the Political Origins of Japanese Culture* (Cambridge: Cambridge University Press, 2005), 29.

33 Robert Weller, *Alternate Civilities: Democracy and Culture in China and Taiwan* (Boulder, CO: Westview Press, 1999).

34 Mayfair Mei-hui Yang, *Gifts, Favors, and Banquets: The Art of Social Relationships in China* (Ithaca, NY: Cornell University Press, 1994).

35 Georg Simmel, "The Stranger," in *Georg Simmel: On Individuality and Social Forms,* ed. Donald Levine (Chicago: University of Chicago Press, 1971), 143–50.

36 Michael Herzfeld, *The Social Production of Indifference* (Chicago: University of Chicago Press, 1992).

37 Joan Scott, *The Politics of the Veil* (Princeton, NJ: Princeton University Press, 2010).

38 John Rawls, *Political Liberalism* (New York: Columbia University Press, 1993). Jürgen Habermas and Charles Taylor in conversation, http://blogs.ssrc.org/tif /2009/11/20/rethinking-secularism-jurgen-habermas-and-charles-taylor-in-conver sation/, accessed August 30, 2014.

39 Kenneth Dean has drawn my attention to the fact that "civil society" belongs to the "seven unspeakables" in Chinese Communist discourse, according to Document no. 9, issued by the Communist Party Central Committee General Office, April 2013.

40 Richard Madsen, *Buddha's Dharma* (Berkeley: University of California Press, 2007).

41 Seyla Benhabib, *The Rights of Others* (Cambridge: Cambridge University Press, 2004).

4 / THE AFTERLIFE OF IMAGES

1 Alfred Gell, *Art and Agency: An Anthropological Theory* (Oxford: Oxford University Press, 1998).

2 Talal Asad, *Genealogies of Religion: Discipline and Reasons of Power in Christianity and Islam* (Baltimore: Johns Hopkins University Press, 1993), 31.

3 David Morgan, *The Sacred Gaze: Religious Visual Culture in Theory and Practice* (Berkeley: University of California Press, 2005), 3.

4 W. Mitchell, *What Do Pictures Want? The Lives and Loves of Images* (Chicago: University of Chicago Press, 2004).

5 Shahid Amin, "Un saint guerrier: Sur la conquête de l'Inde du Nord par les Turcs au XIe siècle." Annales. *Histoire, Sciences Sociales* 2 (2005) (sixtieth anniversary issue): 265–92.

6 Stephan Feuchtwang, *The Imperial Metaphor* (London: Routledge, 1992).

7 Vincent Goossaert, "1898: The Beginning of the End for Chinese Religion?," *Journal of Asian Studies* 65, no. 2 (May 2006): 307–35.

8 Goossaert and Palmer cite a statistical study that shows that the number of shrines in China is back to what it was in the early twentieth century; Vincent Goossaert and David Palmer, *The Religious Question in Modern China* (Chicago: The University of Chicago Press, 2011), 244.

9 Mircea Eliade, *The Sacred and the Profane: The Nature of Religion*, trans. Willard R. Trask (New York: Harper, 1961).

10 Alfred Gell, *Art and Agency: An Anthropological Theory* (Oxford: Clarendon, 1998), 9.

11 Henri Lefebvre, *The Urban Revolution* (Minneapolis: University of Minnesota Press, 2003).

12 For the importance of religious aspirations in Asian cities, see Peter van der Veer, ed., *Handbook of Religion and the Asian City* (Berkeley: University of California Press, 2015).

13 James Holston, *The Modernist City: An Anthropological Critique of Brasília* (Chicago: University of Chicago Press, 1989), and *Insurgent Citizenship: Disjunctions of Democracy and Modernity in Brazil* (Princeton, NJ: Princeton University Press, 2008).

14 Matthew Hull, *Government of Paper: The Materiality of Bureaucracy in Urban Pakistan* (Berkeley: University of California Press, 2012), and "Communities of Place, Not Kind: American Technologies of Neighborhood in Post-colonial Delhi," *Comparative Studies in Society and History* 53, no. 4 (2011): 757–90; Ravi Sundaram, *Pirate Modernity: Delhi's Media Urbanism* (New York: Routledge, 2010).

15 Jeffrey F. Meyer, "The Eagle and the Dragon: Comparing the Designs of Washington and Beijing," *Washington History* 8, no. 2 (fall/winter 1996/97): 4–21.

16 Wu Hung, "Tiananmen Square: A Political History of Monuments," in "Monumental Histories," special issue, *Representation* 35 (summer 1991): 9.

17 Sushmita Pati, "Jagmohan: The Master Planner and the 'Rebuilding' of Delhi," *Economic and Political Weekly* 49 (2014): 36.

18 Philip Lutgendorf, "My Hanuman Is Bigger Than Yours," *History of Religions* 33, no. 3 (February 1994): 211–45.

19 Something similar is found in Singapore by Kenneth Dean, "What Is Missing in the Singapore Model?," in *Handbook of Religion and the Asian City*, ed. Peter van der Veer (Berkeley: University of California Press, 2015), 273–99.

20 Leo Ou-fan Lee, *Shanghai Modern* (Cambridge, MA: Harvard University Press, 1999).

21 Zhang Zhen, "Bodies in the Air: The Magic of Science and the Fate of the Early 'Martial Arts' Films in China," *Post Script* 20, nos. 2–3 (winter/spring–summer 2001): 43–60.

22 Lena Scheen, "Mapping Memories. Shanghai Stories," paper presented at the Max Planck Institute, Göttingen, August 9–12, 2009, http://www.mmg.mpg.de/events/archive-workshops-conferences/2009/global-cities-conference/.

23 Adam Chau, "An Awful Mark: Symbolic Violence and Urban Renewal in Reform-Era China," *Visual Studies* 23, no. 3 (2008): 195–210.

24 Richard Cashman, *The Myth of the Lokamanya: Tilak and Mass Politics in Maharashtra* (Berkeley: University of California Press, 1975).

25 Nile Green, *Bombay Islam: The Religious Economy of the West Indian Ocean, 1840–1915* (Cambridge: Cambridge University Press, 2011).

26 Available at http://www.dnaindia.com/mumbai/report-mumbais-bhendi-bazaar-set-for-a-rs2000-crore-makeover-1563884, accessed August 28, 2015.

5 / LOST IN THE MOUNTAINS

1 Talal Asad, "Are There Histories of Peoples without Europe? A Review Article on Wolf's Book," *Comparative Studies in Society and History* 29, no. 3 (July 1987): 594–607.

2 Edmund Leach, *Claude Lévi-Strauss* (Chicago: University of Chicago Press, 1989).

3 Asad, "Are There Histories of Peoples without Europe?," 603.

4 Stanley Tambiah, *Edmund Leach: An Anthropological Life* (Cambridge: Cambridge University Press, 2002).

5 Edmund Leach, "The Frontiers of Burma," *Comparative Studies in Society and History* 3, no. 1 (1960): 49–68.

6 Tambiah, *Edmund Leach*, 128.

7 Stanley Tambiah, "The Galactic Polity in Southeast Asia," in *Culture, Thought, and Social Action* (Cambridge, MA: Harvard University Press, 1973), 3–31.

8 Tambiah, *Edmund Leach*, 134.

9 James Scott, *The Art of Not Being Governed: An Anarchist History of Upland Southeast Asia* (New Haven, CT: Yale University Press, 2009).

10 James Scott, *Seeing Like a State: How Certain Schemes to Improve the Human Condition Have Failed* (New Haven, CT: Yale University Press, 1998); *Domination and the Arts of Resistance: Hidden Transcripts* (New Haven, CT: Yale University Press, 1990); and *The Moral Economy of the Peasant: Rebellion and Subsistence in Southeast Asia* (New Haven, CT: Yale University Press, 1979).

11 Some of this reminds one of anti-Washington discourses in the United States, which are also couched in the language of freedom from the state.

12 Eric Wolf and John Cole, *The Hidden Frontier: Ecology and Ethnicity in an Alpine Valley* (Berkeley: University of California Press, 1999), 12.

13 Tam Ngo, *The New Way: Protestantism and the Hmong in Vietnam* (Seattle: University of Washington Press, 2016).

14 Scott, *Art of Not Being Governed*, xii.

15 David Nugent, "Closed Systems and Contradictions: The Kachin In and Out of History," *Man* 17 (1982): 508–27; Edmund Leach, "Imaginary Kachins," reply to Nugent, *Man* 18, no. 1 (1983): 191–99; David Nugent, "Reply to Leach," *Man* 18, no. 1 (1983): 199–206.

16 Nugent's argument reminds me of Nicholas Dirks's critique of Dumont's conceptualization of the caste system, in which he argues that what Dumont sees as a Hindu system is in fact a product of colonial forces; Nicholas Dirks, *The Hollow*

Crown: Ethnohistory of an Indian Kingdom, reissue ed. (Cambridge: Cambridge University Press, 2007).

17 Mandy Sadan, *Being and Becoming Kachin: Histories beyond the State in the Borderworlds of Burma*, British Academy Postdoctoral Fellowships Monographs (Oxford: Oxford University Press, 2013); Mandy Sadan and François Robinne, eds., *Social Dynamics in the Highlands of South East Asia: Reconsidering "Political Systems of Highland Burma" by E. R. Leach*, Handbook of Oriental Studies, sec. 3, Southeast Asia (Leiden: Brill, 2007), 18.

18 Jonathan Friedman, *System, Structure, and Contradiction: The Evolution of "Asiatic" Social Formations* (Walnut Creek, CA: Alta Mira Press, 1998).

19 Magnus Fiskesjö, "Mining History and the Anti-state War: The Politics of Autonomy between Burma and China," *Journal of Global History* 5, no. 2 (July 2010): 241–64.

20 See Thomas Gibson and Kenneth Sillander, *Anarchic Solidarity: Autonomy, Equality and Fellowship in Southeast Asia*, Yale Southeast Asia Studies (New Haven, CT: Yale University Press, 2011).

21 Bin Yang, *Between Winds and Clouds* (New York: Columbia University Press, 2008).

22 Francis Hsu, *My Life as a Marginal Man* (Taipei: SMC Publishers, 2009), 135, 136.

23 Francis Hsu, "The Cultural Problem of the Anthropologist," *American Anthropologist* 81, no. 3 (1979): 522.

24 Francis Hsu, *Clan, Caste, and Club* (New York: Van Nostrand Reinhold, 1963), 1–3.

25 Edmund Leach, "Review of Francis Hsu: Under the Ancestor's Shadow," *Man* 50 (March 1950), 283, 36.

26 Yongjia Liang, "The 'Ethnic Error' in *Under the Ancestors' Shadow* and Dali Society in the Period of the Nationalist Government," *Chinese Sociology and Anthropology* 42, no. 4 (2010): 78–94.

27 Liang, " 'Ethnic Error,' " 82.

28 David Atwill, *The Chinese Sultanate: Islam, Ethnicity, and the Panthay Rebellion in Southwest China, 1856–1873* (Stanford, CA: Stanford University Press, 2005).

29 Stevan Harrell, *Cultural Encounters on China's Ethnic Frontiers* (Seattle: University of Washington Press, 1995), 66.

30 David Deal, Laura Hostetler, and Charles F. McKhann, *The Art of Ethnography: A Miao Album of Guizhou Province* (Seattle: University of Washington Press, 2005).

31 Sanjib Baruah, *India against Itself: Assam and the Politics of Nationality* (Philadelphia: University of Pennsylvania Press, 1999), 217.

32 Baruah, *India against Itself*, 30.

33 Christoph von Fürer-Haimendorf, *The Naked Nagas: Head-hunters of Assam in Peace and War* (Calcutta: Thacker Spink, 1946), 126.

34 Haimendorf, *Naked Nagas*, 42, 222.

35 Leni Riefenstahl, *The Last of the Nuba* (New York: St. Martin's Press, 1995).

36 Haimendorf, *Naked Nagas*, 56.

37 Vibha Joshi, *A Matter of Belief; Christian Conversion and Healing in North-East India* (Oxford: Berghahn, 2012), 160.

38 Peter van der Veer, *Conversion to Modernities: The Globalization of Christianity* (New York: Routledge, 1996).

39 Joshi, *A Matter of Belief,* 240.

40 Fiskesjö, "Mining History and the Anti-state War," 249.

41 This seems to be a more general tenor of missionary propaganda. In South India the missionaries emphasize that the tribal population is different from the Brahmans who "oppress them" and couch conversion to Christianity in terms of resistance against Brahmanical domination.

42 Tam Ngo, "Missionary Encounters at the China-Vietnam Border: The Case of the Hmong," *Encounters* 4 (2011): 113–31.

43 Eric Mueggler, *The Paper Road: Archive and Experience in the Botanical Exploration of West China and Tibet* (Berkeley: University of California Press, 2011), 217; quotation from Joseph Rock.

6 / WHO CARES?

1 Tehila Kogut and Ilana Ritov, "The 'Identified Victim' Effect: An Identified Group, or Just a Single Individual?," *Journal of Behavioral Decision Making* 18 (2005): 157–67.

2 Abram de Swaan, *In Care of the State* (Cambridge: Polity Press, 1988).

3 De Swaan, *In Care of the State.*

4 Alain Corbin, *The Foul and the Fragrant: Odor and the French Social Imagination* (Cambridge, MA: Harvard University Press, 1986).

5 Sudipta Kaviraj, "Filth and the Public Sphere: Concepts and Practices about Space in Calcutta," *Public Culture* 10, no. 1 (fall 1997): 84.

6 Dipesh Chakrabarty, "Open Space, Public Space: Garbage, Modernity and India," *South Asia* 14, no. 1 (1991): 15–31.

7 Valerian Rodrigues, "Untouchability, Filth and the Public Domain," in *Humiliation: Claims and Context,* ed. Gopal Guru (Delhi: Oxford University Press, 2011), 108–23.

8 Partha Chatterjee, *Lineages of Political Society* (New York: Columbia University Press, 2011).

9 Peter van der Veer, *Imperial Encounters* (Princeton, NJ: Princeton University Press, 2001).

10 On water supply, see Lisa Björkman and Nikhil Anand, "Pressure: The Polytechnics of Water Supply in Mumbai," *Cultural Anthropology* 26, no. 4 (2011): 542–63; Lisa Björkman, *Pipe Politics, Contested Waters: Embedded Infrastructures of Millennial Mumbai* (Durham, NC: Duke University Press, 2015).

11 Arjun Appadurai, "Our Corruption; Our Selves," http://kafila.org/2011/08/30/our-corruption-our-selves-arjun-appadurai/, accessed August 31, 2015; Partha Chatterjee, "Against Corruption=Against Politics," http://kafila.org/2011/08/28/against-corruption-against-politics-partha-chatterjee/, accessed August 31, 2015. Nandy's precise remarks were: "It is a fact that most of the corrupt come from the OBCs [other backward classes] and scheduled castes and now, increasingly,

the scheduled tribes." See more at *Indian Express*, http://www.indianexpress.com /news/controversial-sociologist-ashis-nandy-leaves-jaipur-lit-fest-police-seek -session-video/1065387/#sthash.jME3kWw6.dpuf, accessed August 31, 2015.

12 John Harriss and Craig Jeffrey, "Depoliticizing Injustice," *Economy and Society* 42, no. 3 (August 2013): 507–20.

13 Raj Chandavarkar, *History, Culture, and the Indian City* (Cambridge: Cambridge University Press, 2011), 58.

14 Arjun Appadurai, "Deep Democracy: Urban Governmentality and the Horizon of Politics," *Environment and Urbanization* 13, no. 2 (2001): 23.

15 Bishwapriya Sanyal and Vinit Mukhija, "Institutional Pluralism and Housing delivery. A Case of Unforeseen Conflicts in Mumbai, India," *World Development* 29, no. 12 (2001): 2043–57.

16 See Streefland, Chowdury, and Ramos-Jimenez, "Patterns of Vaccination Acceptance," *Social Science and Medicine* 49 (1999): 1705–16.

17 Carol Upadhya, "Rewriting the Code: Software Professionals and the Reconstitution of Indian Middle Class Identity," in *Patterns of Middle Class Consumption in India and China*, ed. Christophe Jaffrelot and Peter van der Veer (New Delhi: Sage, 2008), 55–87.

18 André Béteille, "India's Destiny Not Caste in Stone," op-ed, *Hindu*, February 21, 2012.

19 Ward Berenschot, *Riot Politics* (New York: Columbia University Press, 2011).

20 Ward Berenschot, "Political Fixers and the Rise of Hindu Nationalism in Gujarat, India: Lubricating a Patronage Democracy," *South Asia* 34, no. 3 (2011): 382–401.

21 Cited in Christiane Brosius, *India's Middle Class* (New Delhi: Routledge, 2012), 147.

22 See Leilah Vevaina, "Good Thoughts, Good Words, and Good (Trust) Deeds: Parsis, Risk, and Real Estate in Mumbai," in *Handbook of Religion in Asian Cities*, ed. Peter van der Veer (Berkeley: University of California Press, 2015), 152–68.

23 Chris Fuller, *The Camphor Flame* (Princeton, NJ: Princeton University Press, 1992), 174.

24 Brosius, *India's Middle Class*, 182.

25 Rupa Viswanath, "Spiritual Slavery, Material Malaise: Missionaries, 'Untouchables' and Religious Neutrality in Colonial South India," *Historical Research* 83 (2010): 124–45.

26 Thomas L. Haskell, "Capitalism and the Origins of the Humanitarian Sensibility," parts 1 and 2, *American Historical Review* 90 (1985): 342.

27 Amartya Sen, *Democracy as Freedom* (New York: Anchor, 1999).

28 Richard Madsen, *Morality and Power in a Chinese Village* (Berkeley: University of California Press, 1986).

29 Pranab Bardhan, *Awakening Giants, Feet of Clay: Assessing the Economic Rise of China and India* (Princeton, NJ: Princeton University Press, 2010), table 6.

30 Mun Young Cho, *The Specter of "the People": Urban Poverty in Northeast China* (Ithaca, NY: Cornell University Press, 2013).

31 Typically, there is an entire debate in India about the use of the term *Dalit* in textbooks.

CONCLUSION

1   Peter van der Veer, *The Modern Spirit of Asia: The Spiritual and the Secular in India and China* (Princeton, NJ: Princeton University Press, 2014).

2   André Béteille, *Sociology: Essays in Approach and Method* (Delhi: Oxford University Press, 2002).

3   Partha Chatterjee, *Nationalist Thought and the Colonial Word: A Derivative Discourse* (Minneapolis: University of Minnesota Press, 1993).

4   Peter van der Veer, *Imperial Encounters* (Princeton, NJ: Princeton University Press, 2001).

5   Marcel Detienne, *Comparing the Incomparable* (Palo Alto, CA: Stanford University Press, 2008).

6   Bernard Cohn, *Colonialism and Its Forms of Knowledge: The British in India* (Princeton, NJ: Princeton University Press, 1996).

7   Marcel Mauss, "La Nation," in *Oeuvres* 3: 573–639 (Paris: Les Editions de Minuit, 1969).

8   Marilyn Strathern, *The Gender of the Gift* (Berkeley: University of California Press, 1988).

9   Kenelm Burridge, *Someone, No One: An Essay on Individuality* (Princeton, NJ: Princeton University Press, 1979).

10 Gilles Deleuze, "Postscript on the Society of Control," in *Negotiations* (New York: Columbia University Press, 1995), 180.

11 Brian Massumi, *The Power at the End of the Economy* (Durham, NC: Duke University Press, 2014). See also Jocelyn Pixley, *Emotions in Finance: Distrust and Uncertainty in Global Markets* (Cambridge: Cambridge University Press, 2004).

Abelove, Henry. *The Evangelist of Desire: John Wesley and the Methodists*. Palo Alto, CA: Stanford University Press, 1990.

Amin, Shahid. "Un saint guerrier: Sur la conquête de l'Inde du Nord par les Turcs au XIe siècle." *Annales. Histoire, Sciences Sociales* 2 (2005; sixtieth anniversary issue): 265–92.

Anderson, Benedict. *Imagined Communities*. Rev. ed. London: Verso, 2006.

Appadurai, Arjun. "Deep Democracy: Urban Governmentality and the Horizon of Politics." *Environment and Urbanization* 13, no. 2 (2001): 23–43.

Appadurai, Arjun. "The Ghost in the Financial Machine." *Public Culture* 23, no. 3 (2011): 517–39.

Appadurai, Arjun. "Is Homo Hierarchicus?" *American Ethnologist* 13, no. 4 (November 1986): 745–61.

Appadurai, Arjun. "Our Corruption; Our Selves." Accessed July 19, 2014. http://kafila.org /2011/08/30/our-corruption-our-selves-arjun-appadurai/.

Appadurai, Arjun, and Carol Breckenridge. "The South Indian Temple: Authority, Honour and Redistribution." *Contributions to Indian Sociology* 10 (1976): 187–211.

Asad, Talal. "Are There Histories of Peoples without Europe? A Review Article." In *Comparative Studies in Society and History*, 594–607. Berkeley: University of California Press, 1982.

Asad, Talal. *Comparative Studies in Society and History* 29, no. 3 (July 1987): 594–607.

Asad, Talal. "Ethnographic Representation, Statistics and Modern Power." *Social Research* 61, no. 1 (1994): 55–88.

Asad, Talal. *Genealogies of Religion*. Baltimore: Johns Hopkins University Press, 1993.

Asad, Talal. *The Idea of an Anthropology of Islam*. Occasional paper series. Washington, DC: Georgetown University Center for Contemporary Arab Studies, March 1986.

Ashiwa, Yoshiko, and David L. Wank, eds. *Making Religion, Making the State: The Politics of Religion in Modern China*. Palo Alto, CA: Stanford University Press, 2009.

Atwill, David. *The Chinese Sultanate: Islam, Ethnicity, and the Panthay Rebellion in Southwest China, 1856–1873*. Palo Alto, CA: Stanford University Press, 2005.

Bardhan, Pranab. *Awakening Giants, Feet of Clay: Assessing the Economic Rise of China and India*. Princeton, NJ: Princeton University Press, 2010.

Barth, Fredrik. *Balinese Worlds*. Chicago: University of Chicago Press, 1993.

Barth, Fredrik. *Cosmologies in the Making: A Generative Approach to Cultural Variation in Inner New Guinea*. Cambridge: Cambridge University Press, 1987.

Barth, Fredrik. *Political Leadership among Swat Pathans*. London: Athlone Press, 1959.

Barth, Fredrik. *Ritual and Knowledge among the Baktaman of New Guinea*. Oslo: Universitetsforlaget, 1975.

Barth, Fredrik. *Sohar, Culture and Society in an Omani Town*. Baltimore: Johns Hopkins University Press, 1983.

Barth, Fredrik, and Unni Wikan. *Situation of Children in Bhutan: An Anthropological Perspective*. Thimphu: Centre for Bhutan Studies, 2011.

Baruah, Sanjib. *India against Itself: Assam and the Politics of Nationality*. Philadelphia: University of Pennsylvania Press, 1999.

Bauman, Richard, and Charles L. Briggs. *Voices of Modernity: Language Ideologies and the Politics of Inequality*. Cambridge: Cambridge University Press, 2003.

Becker, S. Gary. *The Economic Approach to Human Behavior*. Chicago: University of Chicago Press, 1976.

Beckert, Jens. *The Transcending Power of Goods: Imaginative Value in the Economy*. MPIfG discussion paper. Cologne, April 10, 2010.

Benedict, Ruth. *Patterns of Culture*. New York: Houghton Mifflin, 1934.

Benhabib, Seyla. *The Rights of Others*. Cambridge: Cambridge University Press, 2004.

Berenschot, Ward. "Political Fixers and the Rise of Hindu Nationalism in Gujarat, India: Lubricating a Patronage Democracy." *South Asia* 34, no. 3 (2011): 382–401.

Berenschot, Ward. *Riot Politics*. New York: Columbia University Press, 2011.

Berremann, Gerald D. "Caste in India and the United States." *American Journal of Sociology* 66, no. 2 (September 1960): 120–27.

Béteille, André. "India's Destiny Not Caste in Stone." Op-ed. *Hindu*, February 21, 2012.

Béteille, André. "Race and Caste." *Hindu*, March 10, 2001. Accessed September 2, 2015. www.hindu.com/2001/03/10,.http://www.thehindu.com/2001/03/10/stories/0510 2523.htm.

Béteille, André. *Sociology: Essays in Approach and Method*. Delhi: Oxford University Press, 2002.

Björkman, Lisa. *Pipe Politics, Contested Waters: Embedded Infrastructures of Millennial Mumbai*. Durham, NC: Duke University Press, 2015.

Björkman, Lisa, and Nikhil Anand. "Pressure: The Polytechnics of Water Supply in Mumbai." *Cultural Anthropology* 26, no. 4 (2011): 542–63.

Bloch, Maurice. *Anthropology and the Cognitive Challenge*. Cambridge: Cambridge University Press, 2012.

Bloch, Maurice, and Jonathan Parry, eds. *Death and the Regeneration of Life*. Cambridge: Cambridge University Press, 1982.

Boo, Katherine. *Behind the Beautiful Forevers; Life, Death and Hope in a Mumbai Undercity*. New York: Random House, 2012.

Bourdieu, Pierre. *Outline of a Theory of Practice*. Cambridge: Cambridge University Press, 1977.

Boyer, Pascal. "Being Human: Religion: Bound to Believe?" *Nature* 455 (October 23, 2008): 1038–39.

Boyer, Pascal. *Religion Explained*. New York: Random House, 2008.

Brosius, Christiane. *India's Middle Class*. New Delhi: Routledge, 2012.

Burridge, Kenelm. *Someone, No One: An Essay on Individuality*. Princeton, NJ: Princeton University Press, 1979.

Cao, Nanlai. *Constructing China's Jerusalem: Christians, Power, and Place in Contemporary Wenzhou*. Palo Alto, CA: Stanford University Press, 2010.

Casanova, Jose. "Beyond European and American Exceptionalisms: Towards a Global Perspective." In *Predicting Religion*, ed. G. Davie, P. Heelas, and L. Woodhead, 17–30. Aldershot, UK: Ashgate, 2003.

Cashman, Richard. *The Myth of the Lokamanya: Tilak and Mass Politics in Maharashtra*. Berkeley: University of California Press, 1975.

Chakrabarty, Dipesh. "Open Space, Public Space: Garbage, Modernity and India." *South Asia* 14, no. 1 (1991): 15–31.

Chandavarkar, Raj. *History, Culture, and the Indian City*. Cambridge: Cambridge University Press, 2011.

Chatterjee, Partha. "Against Corruption-Against Politics." http://kafila.org/2011/08/28/against-corruption-against-politics-partha-chatterjee/.

Chatterjee, Partha. *Lineages of Political Society*. New York: Columbia University Press, 2011.

Chatterjee, Partha. *Nationalist Thought and the Colonial Word: A Derivative Discourse*. Minneapolis: University of Minnesota Press, 1993.

Chatterjee, Partha. *The Nation and Its Fragments*. Princeton, NJ: Princeton University Press, 1993.

Chau, Adam. "An Awful Mark: Symbolic Violence and Urban Renewal in Reform-Era China." *Visual Studies* 23, no. 3 (2008): 195–210.

Cheng, Chung-Ying, and Nicholas Bunnin, eds. *Contemporary Chinese Philosophy*. Oxford: Blackwell, 2002.

Cho, Mun Young. *The Specter of "the People": Urban Poverty in Northeast China*. Ithaca, NY: Cornell University Press, 2013.

Cohn, B. S. *An Anthropologist among the Historians*. Delhi: Oxford University Press, 1987.

Cohn, Bernard. *Colonialism and Its Forms of Knowledge: The British in India*. Princeton, NJ: Princeton University Press, 1996.

Connell, R. W. "Why Is Classical Theory Classical?" *American Journal of Sociology* 102, no. 6 (May 1997): 1511–57.

Corbin, Alain. *The Foul and the Fragrant: Odor and the French Social Imagination*. Cambridge, MA: Harvard University Press, 1986.

Deal, David, Laura Hostetler, and Charles F. McKhann. *The Art of Ethnography: A Miao Album of Guizhou Province*. Seattle: University of Washington Press, 2005.

Dean, Kenneth. *Taoist Ritual and Popular Cults of Southeast China*. Princeton, NJ: Princeton University Press, 1995.

Dean, Kenneth, and Zheng Zhenman. *Ritual Alliances of the Putian Plains*. Vol. 1. *Historical Introduction to the Return of the Gods*. Leiden: Brill, 2009.

Dean, Kenneth, and Zheng Zhenman. *Ritual Alliances of the Putian Plains*. Vol. 2. *A Survey of Village Temples and Ritual Activities*. Leiden: Brill, 2010.

Deleuze, Gilles. "Postscript on the Societies of Control." *October* 59 (winter 1992): 3–7.

Deliege, Robert. *The Untouchables of India*. Oxford: Berg, 1999.

Deng Xiaoping. *Deng Xiaoping Wenxuan* [Selected Writings of Deng Xiaoping], vol. 3. Beijing: Renmin Chubanshe, 1994.

Derrida, Jacques. *Limited, Inc*. Evanston, IL: Northwestern University Press, 1988.

Descola, Philippe. *Beyond Nature and Culture*. Trans. Janet Lloyd. Chicago: University of Chicago Press, 2013.

de Swaan, Abram. *In Care of the State*. Cambridge: Polity Press, 1988.

Detienne, Marcel. *Comparing the Incomparable*. Palo Alto, CA: Stanford University Press, 2008.

de Vries, Peer. *Zur politischen Ökonomie des Tees*. Vienna: Böhnau, 1979.

de Waal, Frans. *The Age of Empathy: Nature's Lessons for a Kinder Society*. New York: Harmony Books, 2009.

Dikötter, Frank. " 'Patient Zero': China and the Myth of the Opium Plague." Inaugural Lecture at SOAS, University of London, 2003.

Dirks, Nicholas. *The Hollow Crown: Ethnohistory of an Indian Kingdom*. 1987. Cambridge: Cambridge University Press, 2007.

Dumont, Louis. *Homo Hierarchicus: The Caste System and Its Implications*. Chicago: University of Chicago Press, 1981.

Eisenstadt, S. N., ed. *The Origins and Diversity of Axial Age Civilizations*. Albany: State University of New York Press, 1986.

Eisenstadt, Shmuel, ed. *Multiple Modernities*. New Brunswick, NJ: Transaction, 2002.

Eliade, Mircea. *The Sacred and the Profane: The Nature of Religion*. Trans. Willard R. Trask. New York: Harper, 1961.

Elias, Norbert. *Über den Prozess der Zivilisation*. Vol. 1. [The Civilizing Process]. 1939. Frankfurt am Main: Suhrkamp, 1993.

Farooqui, Amar. *Opium City: The Making of Early Victorian Bombay*. Delhi: Three Essays Collective, 2005.

Fei, Xiaotong. "Plurality and Unity in the Configuration of the Chinese Nationality." Tanner Lecture. Hong Kong, 1988. Accessed March 29, 2015. http://tannerlectures.utah.edu/_documents/a-to-z/f/fei90.pdf.

Feuchtwang, Stephan. *The Imperial Metaphor*. London: Routledge, 1992.

Fiskesjö, Magnus. "Mining History and the Anti-state War: The Politics of Autonomy between Burma and China." *Journal of Global History* 5, no. 2 (July 2010), 241–64.

Friedman, Jonathan. *System, Structure, and Contradiction: The Evolution of "Asiatic" Social Formations*. Walnut Creek, CA: Alta Mira Press, 1998.

Fuller, C. J. *The Renewal of the Priesthood: Modernity and Traditionalism in a South Indian Temple*. Princeton, NJ: Princeton University Press, 2003.

Fuller, C. J. "Caste, Race, and Hierarchy in the American South." *Journal of the Royal Anthropological Institute* 17, no. 3 (September 2011): 604–21.

Fuller, Chris. *The Camphor Flame*. Princeton, NJ: Princeton University Press, 1992.

Gardner, Beatrix, and Thomas Gardner. *Teaching Sign Language to Chimpanzees*. Albany: State University of New York Press, 1989.

Geertz, Clifford. "Anti Anti-Relativism." *American Anthropologist*, new ser., 86, no. 2 (1984).

Geertz, Clifford. *The Interpretation of Cultures*. New York: Basic Books, 1973.

Geertz, Clifford. *Islam Observed: Religious Development in Morocco and Indonesia*. Chicago: University of Chicago Press, 1971.

Geertz, Clifford. *The Religion of Java*. Chicago: University of Chicago Press, 1976.

Gell, Alfred. *Art and Agency: An Anthropological Theory*. Oxford: Oxford University Press, 1998.

Gellner, Ernest. *Nations and Nationalism*. Ithaca, NY: Cornell University Press, 1983.

Gibson, Thomas. *Islamic Narrative and Authority in Southeast Asia from the Sixteenth to the Twenty-First Century*. New York: Palgrave Macmillan, 2007.

Gibson, Thomas, and Kenneth Sillander. *Anarchic Solidarity: Autonomy, Equality and Fellowship in Southeast Asia*. Yale Southeast Asia Studies. New Haven, CT: Yale University Press, 2011.

Goody, Jack. *The Theft of History*. Cambridge: Cambridge University Press, 2006.

Goossaert, Vincent. "1898: The Beginning of the End for Chinese Religion?" *Journal of Asian Studies* 65, no. 2 (May 2006): 307–35.

Goossaert, Vincent, and David Palmer. *The Religious Question in Modern China*. Chicago: University of Chicago Press, 2011.

Green, Nile. *Bombay Islam: The Religious Economy of the West Indian Ocean, 1840–1915*. Cambridge: Cambridge University Press, 2011.

Guha, Sumit. *Beyond Caste*. Leiden: Brill, 2013.

Gupta, Dipankar. "Caste, Race, Politics." *Seminar* 508 (December 2001).

Guthrie, Stewart. *Faces in the Clouds*. Oxford: Oxford University Press, 1993.

Habermas, Jürgen. *The Structural Transformation of the Public Sphere*. Cambridge: Polity, 1989.

Hansen, Karen Tranberg. "Informal Sector." In *International Encyclopaedia of the Social and Behavioral Sciences*, 7450–53. Amsterdam: Elsevier, 2001.

Harding, Susan. *The Book of Jerry Falwell*. Princeton, NJ: Princeton University Press, 2001.

Harootunian, D. Harry, James Chandler, and Arnold I. Davidson. *Questions of Evidence: Proof, Practice, and Persuasion across the Disciplines*. Chicago: University of Chicago Press, 1994.

Harrell, Stevan. *Cultural Encounters on China's Ethnic Frontiers*. Seattle: University of Washington Press, 1995.

Harris, Marvin. *Cannibals and Kings: The Origins of Cultures*. New York: Vintage, 1977.

Harriss, John, and Craig Jeffrey. "Depoliticizing Injustice." *Economy and Society* 42, no. 3 (August 2013): 507–20.

Haskell, L. Thomas. "Capitalism and the Origins of the Humanitarian Sensibility." Parts 1 and 2. *American Historical Review* 90 (1985): 342.

Herdt, Gilbert. *Guardians of the Flutes: Idioms of Masculinity*. New York: McGraw-Hill, 1981.

Herzfeld, Michael. *The Social Production of Indifference*. Chicago: University of Chicago Press, 1992.

Hevia, James. *Cherishing Men from Afar: Qing Guest Ritual and the Macartney Embassy of 1793*. Durham, NC: Duke University Press, 1995.

Hirschman, Albert. *The Passions and the Interests: Political Arguments for Capitalism before Its Triumph*. Princeton, NJ: Princeton University Press, 1977.

Holston, Jim. *The Modernist City: An Anthropological Critique of Brasília*. Chicago: University of Chicago Press, 1989.

Holston, Jim. *Insurgent Citizenship: Disjunctions of Democracy and Modernity in Brazil*. Princeton, NJ: Princeton University Press, 2008.

Holy, Ladislav. Introduction to *Comparative Anthropology*, ed. Ladislav Holy, 7. London: Blackwell, 1987.

Hsu, Francis. *Clan, Caste, and Club*. New York: Van Nostrand Reinhold, 1963.

Hsu, Francis. "The Cultural Problem of the Anthropologist." *American Anthropologist* 81, no. 3 (1979): 517–32.

Hsu, Francis. *My Life as a Marginal Man*, 136, 135. Taipei: SMC Publishers, 2009.

Hsu, Francis. *Psychological Anthropology: Approaches to Culture and Personality*. Homewood, IL: Dorsey Press, 1961.

Hull, Matthew. "Communities of Place, Not Kind: American Technologies of Neighborhood in Post-colonial Delhi." *Comparative Studies in Society and History* 53, no. 4 (2011): 757–90.

Hull, Matthew. *Government of Paper: The Materiality of Bureaucracy in Urban Pakistan*. Berkeley: University of California Press, 2012.

Hume, David. *Essays, Moral, Political, and Literary*. Indianapolis: Liberty Fund, 1987.

Hung, Wu. "Tiananmen Square: A Political History of Monuments." In "Monumental Histories." Special issue, *Representation* 35 (summer 1991): 84–117.

Huntington, Samuel. *The Clash of Civilizations*. New York: Simon and Schuster, 1996.

Huntington, Samuel. *Who Are We? The Challenges to American National Identity*. New York: Simon and Schuster, 2004.

Huntington, P. Samuel. *The Clash of Civilizations and the Remaking of World Order*. New York: Simon and Schuster, 2011.

Ikegami, Eiko. *Bonds of Civility: Aesthetic Networks and the Political Origins of Japanese Culture*. Cambridge: Cambridge University Press, 2005.

Inglehart, F. Ronald, and Pippa Norris. *Sacred and Secular: Reexamining the Secularization Thesis*. Cambridge: Cambridge University Press, 2004.

James, William. *The Varieties of Religious Experience: A Study in Human Nature*. 1902. Oxford: Oxford University Press, 2012.

Jaspers, Karl. *Vom Ursprug und Ziel der Geschichte* [About the origin and goal of history]. Frankfurt: Fischer, 1955.

Joshi, Vibha. *Christian and Non-Christian Angami Nagas with Special Reference to Traditional Healing Practices*. Oxford: Oxford University Press, 2001.

Kang, Jie. *From Peasant to Pastor*. New York: Palgrave, forthcoming.

Kardiner, Abram, and Ralph Linton. *The Individual and His Society*. New York: Columbia University Press, 1939.

Katzenstein, Peter. "Civilizational States, Secularisms and Religions." In *Rethinking Secularism*, ed. Craig Calhoun, Mark Juergensmeyer, and Jonathan VanAntwerpen, 145–65. New York: Oxford University Press, 2011.

Katzenstein, Peter, with Il Hyun Cho. "In the Service of State and Nation: Religion in East Asia." In *Religion and International Relations Theory*, ed. Jack Snyder, ed., 168–99. New York: Columbia University Press, 2011.

Kaviraj, Sudipta. "Filth and the Public Sphere: Concepts and Practices about Space in Calcutta." *Public Culture* 10, no. 1 (fall 1997): 83–113.

Keane, Webb. *Christian Moderns*. Berkeley: University of California Press, 2007.

Keane, Webb. "Sincerity, 'Modernity,' and the Protestants." *Cultural Anthropology* 17, no. 1 (January 2008): 74.

Kemper, Steven. *Buying and Believing*. Chicago: University of Chicago Press, 2001.

Klinenberg, Eric. *Heatwave: A Social Autopsy of Disaster in Chicago*. Chicago: University of Chicago Press, 2002.

Kogut, Tehila, and Ehud Kogut. "Exploring the Relationship between Adult Attachment Style and the Identifiable Victim Effect in Helping Behavior." *Journal of Experimental Social Psychology* 49 (January 2013): 651–60.

Kogut, Tehila, and Ilana Ritov. "The 'Identified Victim' Effect: An Identified Group, or Just a Single Individual?" *Journal of Behavioral Decision Making* 18 (2005): 157–67.

Koselleck, Reinhart. *Critique and Crisis: Enlightenment and the Pathogenesis of Modern Society*. Cambridge, MA: MIT Press, 1988.

Kroeber, Alfred. *Nature of Culture*. Chicago: University of Chicago Press, 1952.

Krugman, Paul. "Hitting China's Wall." Op-ed. *New York Times*, July 18, 2013.

Latour, Bruno. *We Have Never Been Modern*. Cambridge, MA: Harvard University Press, 1993.

Leach, Edmund. *Claude Lévi-Strauss*. Chicago: University of Chicago Press, 1989.

Leach, Edmund. "The Frontiers of Burma." *Comparative Studies in Society and History* 3, no. 1 (1960): 49–68.

Leach, Edmund. "Imaginary Kachins." Reply to Nugent. *Man* 18, no. 1 (1983), 191–99.

Leach, Edmund. "Review of Francis Hsu: Under the Ancestor's Shadow." *Man* 50 (March 1950): 36.

Lee, Leo Ou-fan. *Shanghai Modern*. Cambridge, MA: Harvard University Press, 1999.

Lefebvre, Henri. *The Urban Revolution*, trans. Robert Bononno. Minneapolis: University of Minnesota Press, 2003.

Liang, Yongjia. "The 'Ethnic Error' in *Under the Ancestors' Shadow* and Dali Society in the Period of the Nationalist Government." *Chinese Sociology and Anthropology* 42, no. 4 (2010): 78–94.

Liénard, Pierre, and Pascal Boyer. "Whence Collective Rituals? A Cultural Selection Model of Ritualized Behavior." *American Anthropologist* 108, no. 4 (2006): 814–27.

Lijphart, Arend. *The Politics of Accommodation: Pluralism and Democracy in the Netherlands*. Berkeley: University of California Press, 1968.

Linton, Ralph. *The Cultural Background of Personality*. New York: Appleton-Century-Crofts, 1945.

Liu, Lydia. *The Clash of Empires: The Invention of China in the Modern World*. Cambridge, MA: Harvard University Press, 2004.

Liu, Shao-hua. *Passage to Manhood: Youth Migration, Heroin, and AIDS in Southwest China*. Palo Alto, CA: Stanford University Press, 2010.

Lloyd, G. E. R. *Being, Humanity, and Understanding*. Oxford: Oxford University Press, 2012.

Luhrmann, T. M., Howard Nusbaum, and Ronald Thisted. "The Absorption Hypothesis: Learning to Hear God in Evangelical Christianity." *American Anthropologist* 112, no. 1 (2010): 66–78.

Lukes, Steven, and Martin Hollis, eds. *Rationality and Relativism*. Oxford: Blackwell, 1982.

Lutgendorf, Philip. "My Hanuman Is Bigger Than Yours." *History of Religions* 33, no. 3 (February 1994): 211–45.

Madsen, Richard. *Morality and Power in a Chinese Village*. Berkeley: University of California Press, 1986.

Madsen, Richard. *Democracy's Dharma: Religious Renaissance and Political Development in Taiwan*. Berkeley: University of California Press, 2007.

Malaby, Thomas. *Gambling Life: Dealing in Contingency in a Greek City*. Urbana-Champaign: University of Illinois Press, 2003.

Marrott, McKim. "The Feast of Love." In *Krishna, Myths, Rites and Attitudes*, ed. Milton Singer. Honolulu: East-West Center Press, 1966.

Massumi, Brian. *The Power at the end of the Economy*. Durham, NC: Duke University Press, 2014.

Mauss, Marcel. *The Gift: The Form and Reason for Exchange in Archaic Societies*. New York: W. W. Norton, 2000.

Mauss, Marcel. "La Nation," In *Oeuvres*, 3: 573–639. Paris: Les Editions de Minuit, 1969.

Mauss, Marcel. *Sociology and Psychology: Essays*. London: Routledge and Kegan Paul, 1979.

Mauss, Marcel. "Techniques of the Body." *Economy and Society* 2, no. 1 (1973 [1935]): 70–88.

Meyer, Birgit, and Peter Pels. *Magic and Modernity*. Palo Alto, CA: Stanford University Press, 2003.

Meyer, Jeffrey F. "The Eagle and the Dragon: Comparing the Designs of Washington and Beijing." *Washington History* 8, no. 2 (fall/winter 1996–97): 4–21.

Milner, Murray. *Status and Sacredness: A General Theory of Status Relations and an Analysis of Indian Culture*. Oxford: Oxford University Press, 1994.

Mintz, Sidney. *The Power of Sweetness: The Place of Sugar in Modern History*. London: Penguin, 1986.

Mitchell, W. *What Do Pictures Want? The Lives and Loves of Images*. Chicago: University of Chicago Press, 2004.

Mohan, Sanal. *Modernity of Slavery: Struggles against Caste Inequality in Colonial Kerala*. Oxford: Oxford University Press, 2015.

Morgan, David. *The Sacred Gaze: Religious Visual Culture in Theory and Practice.* Berkeley: University of California Press, 2005.

Mueggler, Eric. *The Age of Wild Ghosts: Memory, Violence, and Place in Southwest China.* Chicago: University of Chicago Press, 2001.

Mueggler, Eric. *The Paper Road: Archive and Experience in the Botanical Exploration of West China and Tibet.* Berkeley: University of California Press, 2011.

Nandy, Ashis. *Indian Express,* January 28, 2013. Accessed December 14, 2015. http://www.indianexpress.com/news/controversial-sociologist-ashis-nandy-leaves-jaipur-lit-fest-police-seek-session-video/1065387/#sthash.jME3kWw6.dpuf.

Narula, Smita. "Caste Discrimination." *Seminar* 508 (December 2011).

Needham, Rodney. *Belief, Language, and Experience.* Oxford: Blackwell, 1972.

Nehru, Jawaharlal. *The Discovery of India.* Delhi: Oxford University Press, 1946.

Ngo, Tam. "Missionary Encounters at the China-Vietnam Border: The Case of the Hmong." *Encounters* 4 (2011): 113–31.

Ngo, Tam T. T. *The New Way: Protestantism and the Hmong in Contemporary Vietnam.* Seattle: University of Washington Press, 2016.

Nugent, David. "Closed Systems and Contradictions: The Kachin In and Out of History." *Man* 17 (1982): 508–27.

Nugent, David. "Reply to Leach." *Man* 18, no. 1 (1983), 199–206.

Oates, Joyce Carol. *A Widow's Story: A Memoir.* New York: Ecco, 2011.

Paganelli, Maria Pia. "The Moralizing Role of Distance in Adam Smith: *The Theory of Moral Sentiments* as Possible Praise of Commerce." *History of Political Economy* 42, no. 3 (2010): 425–41.

Palmer, David. *Qigong Fever: Body, Science, and Utopia in China.* New York: Columbia University Press, 2007.

Parry, J. P. *Death in Banares.* Cambridge: Cambridge University Press, 1994.

Parsons, Talcott. *Toward a General Theory of Action.* Cambridge, MA: Harvard University Press, 1951.

Pati, Sushmita. "Jagmohan: The Master Planner and the 'Rebuilding' of Delhi." *Economic and Political Weekly* 49, no. 36 (2014).

Pemberton, John. *On the Subject of Java.* Ithaca, NY: Cornell University Press, 1994.

Pieke, F. N. *Bureaucracy, Friends, and Money: The Growth of Capital Socialism in China.*

Piketty, Thomas. *Capital in the Twenty-First Century.* Cambridge, MA: Harvard University Press, 2014.

Pixley, Jocelyn. *Emotions in Finance: Distrust and Uncertainty in Global Markets.* Cambridge: Cambridge University Press, 2004.

Poovey, Mary. "Can Numbers Ensure Honesty? Unrealistic Expectations and the U.S. Accounting Scandal." Notices of the American Mathematical Society, January 2003, 27–35. *Comparative Studies in Society and History* 37, no. 3 (1995), 494–518.

Radin, Paul. *Primitive Man as Philosopher.* New York: Appleton, 1927.

Rajagopal, Arvind. *Politics after Television: Hindu Nationalism and the Reshaping of the Public in India.* Cambridge: Cambridge University Press, 2001.

Rawls, John. *Political Liberalism.* New York: Columbia University Press, 1993.

Riefenstahl, Leni. *The Last of the Nuba.* New York: St. Martin's, 1995.

Rodrigues, Valerian. "Untouchability, Filth and the Public Domain." In *Humiliation: Claims and Context*, ed. Gopal Guru, 108–23. Delhi: Oxford University Press, 2011.

Sadan, Mandy. *Being and Becoming Kachin: Histories beyond the State in the Borderworlds of Burma*. Oxford: Oxford University Press, 2013.

Sadan, Mandy, and Francois Robinne, eds. *Social Dynamics in the Highlands of South East Asia: Reconsidering "Political Systems of Highland Burma" by E. R. Leach*. Handbook of Oriental Studies, sec. 3, Southeast Asia. Leiden: Brill, 2007.

Sahlins, Marshall. *The Use and Abuse of Biology: An Anthropological Critique of Sociobiology*. Ann Arbor: University of Michigan Press, 1976.

Sahlins, Marshall. "Cosmologies of Capitalism: The Trans-Pacific Sector of the World-System." In *Culture/Power/History*, ed. Nicholas Dirks, G. Eley, and S. B. Ortner. Princeton, NJ: Princeton University Press, 1994.

Sanyal, Bishwapriya, and Vinit Mukhija. "Institutional Pluralism and Housing Delivery: A Case of Unforeseen Conflicts in Mumbai, India." *World Development* 29, no. 12 (2001): 2043–57.

Scheen, Lena. "Mapping Memories: Shanghai Stories." Paper presented at the Max Planck Institute, Göttingen, 2009.

Scott, James. *The Art of Not Being Governed: An Anarchist History of Upland Southeast Asia*. New Haven, CT: Yale University Press, 2009.

Scott, James. *Domination and the Arts of Resistance: Hidden Transcripts*. New Haven, CT: Yale University Press, 1990.

Scott, James. *The Moral Economy of the Peasant: Rebellion and Subsistence in Southeast Asia*. New Haven, CT: Yale University Press, 1979.

Scott, James. *Seeing like a State: How Certain Schemes to Improve the Human Condition Have Failed*. New Haven, CT: Yale University Press, 1999.

Scott, Joan. *The Politics of the Veil*. Princeton, NJ: Princeton University Press, 2010.

Searle, John. *Intentionality*. Cambridge: Cambridge University Press, 1983.

Sen, Amartya. *Democracy as Freedom*. New York: Anchor, 1999.

Simmel, George. "The Stranger." In *Georg Simmel: On Individuality and Social Forms*, ed. Donald Levine, 143–50. Chicago: University of Chicago Press, 1971.

Slingerland, Edward. "Body and Mind in Early China: An Integrated Humanities–Science Approach." *Journal of the American Academy of Religion* 81, no. 1 (2013): 6–55.

Smith, Adam. *The Theory of Moral Sentiments*. 1759.

Srinivas, Smriti. *In the Presence of Sai Baba: Body, City, and Memory in a Global Religious Movement*. Leiden: Brill, 2008.

Srinivas, Tulasi. *Winged Faith: Rethinking Globalization and Religious Pluralism through the Sathya Sai Movement*. New York: Columbia University Press, 2010.

Stark, Rodney. "Economics of Religion." In *The Blackwell Companion to the Study of Religion*, 47–67. Oxford: Blackwell, 2006.

Stiglitz, Joseph E. *Globalization and Its Discontents*. New York: W. W. Norton, 2002.

Stolz, J. "Gods and Social Mechanisms: New Perspectives for an Explanatory Sociology of Religion." In *Raymond Boudon: A Life in Sociology*, ed. M. Cherkaoui and P. Hamilton. London: Bardwell Press, 2009.

Stolz, J. "Salvation Goods and Religious Markets: Integrating Rational Choice and Weberian Perspectives." *Social Compass* 53, no. 1 (2006): 13–32.

Stolz, J. "Secularization Theory and Rational Choice: An Integration of Micro- and Macro-theories of Secularization Using the Example of Switzerland." In *The Role of Religion in Modern Societies*, ed. D. Pollack and D. V. A. Olson, 249–70. New York: Routledge, 2008.

Strathern, Marilyn. *Property, Substance and Effect*. London: Athlone, 1998.

Streefland, P., A. M. Chowdury, and P. Ramos-Jimenez. "Patterns of Vaccination Acceptance." *Social Science and Medicine* 49 (1999): 1705–16.

Subrahmanyam, Sanjay, Velcheru Narayana Rao, and David Shulman. *Textures of Time: Writing History in South India 1600–1800*. Ranikhet: Permanent Black, 2013.

Sundaram, Ravi. *Pirate Modernity: Delhi's Media Urbanism*. Oxford: Routledge, 2010.

Tambiah, Stanley. *Edmund Leach: An Anthropological Life*. Cambridge: Cambridge University Press, 2002.

Tambiah, Stanley. "The Galactic Polity in Southeast Asia." In *Culture, Thought, and Social Action*. Cambridge, MA: Harvard University Press, 1973.

Tambiah, Stanley. *Magic, Science and Religion and the Scope of Rationality*. Cambridge: Cambridge University Press, 1990.

Taylor, Charles. *Multiculturalism: Examining the Politics of Recognition*. Princeton, NJ: Princeton University Press, 1994.

Taylor, Charles. *A Secular Age*. Cambridge, MA: Harvard University Press, 2007.

ter Haar, Barend. " 'Thee en Cup-a-Soup,' Inaugural Address for the Chair in Sinology," Leiden University, October 2001.

Terrace, S. Herbert. *Nim, a Chimpanzee Who Learned Sign Language*. New York: Columbia University Press, 1987.

Tinker, Hugh. *A New System of Slavery: The Export of Indian Labour Overseas, 1830–1920*. London: Oxford University Press, 1974.

Tomasello, Michael. *Why We Cooperate*. Boston: Boston Review of Books, 2009.

Upadhya, Carol. "Rewriting the Code: Software Professionals and the Reconstitution of Indian Middle Class Identity." In *Patterns of Middle-Class Consumption in India and China*, ed. Christophe Jaffrelot and Peter van der Veer, 55–87. New Delhi: Sage, 2008.

van der Veer, Peter. *Gods on Earth: The Management of Religious Experience in a North India Pilgrimage Centre*. London School of Economics Monographs. London: Athlone, 1988.

van der Veer, Peter. "Playing or Praying: A Sufi Saint's Day in Surat." *Journal of Asian Studies* 51, no. 3 (August 1992): 545–64.

van der Veer, Peter. *Religious Nationalism, Hindus and Muslims in India*. Berkeley: University of California Press, 1994.

van der Veer, Peter, ed. *Conversion to Modernities*. New York: Routledge, 1996.

van der Veer, Peter. *Imperial Encounters*. Princeton, NJ: Princeton University Press, 2001.

van der Veer, Peter. *The Modern Spirit of Asia*. Princeton, NJ: Princeton University Press, 2014.

van der Veer, Peter, ed. *Handbook of Religion and the Asian City*. Berkeley: University of California Press, 2015.

Vertovec, Steven. *Routledge International Handbook of Diversity Studies*. London: Routledge, 2015.

Viswanath, Rupa. "Spiritual Slavery, Material Malaise: Missionaries, 'Untouchables' and Religious Neutrality in Colonial South India." *Historical Research* 83, 219 (2010): 124–45.

von Fürer-Haimendorf, Christoph. *The Naked Nagas: Head-Hunters of Assam in Peace and War*. Calcutta: Thacker Spink, 1946.

Warner, Michael, Jonathan Van Antweren, and Craig Calhoun, eds. *Varieties of Secularism in a Secular Age*. Cambridge, MA: Harvard University Press, 2010.

Weller, Robert. *Alternate Civilities: Democracy and Culture in China and Taiwan*. Boulder, CO: Westview Press, 1999.

Whitehouse, Harvey, and Emma Cohen. "Seeking a Rapprochement between Anthropology and the Cognitive Sciences: A Problem-Driven Approach." *Topics in Cognitive Science* 4 (2012): 404–12.

Wimmer, Andreas. *Waves of War: Nationalism, State Formation, and Ethnic Exclusion in the Modern World*. Cambridge: Cambridge University Press, 2013.

Wolf, Eric. *Europe and the People without History*. Berkeley: University of California Press, 1982.

Wolf, Eric, and John Cole. *The Hidden Frontier: Ecology and Ethnicity in an Alpine Valley*. Berkeley: University of California Press, 1999.

Yang, Bin. *Between Winds and Clouds*. New York: Columbia University Press, 2008.

Yang, Fenggang. "The Red, Black, and Gray Markets of Religion in China." *Sociological Quarterly* 47 (2006): 93–122.

Yang, Fenggang. "China on Course to Become 'World's Most Christian Nation' within 15 Years." *Daily Telegraph*, April 19, 2014. Accessed December 14, 2015. http://www.telegraph.co.uk/news/worldnews/asia/china/10776023/China-on-course-to-become-worlds-most-Christian-nation-within-15-years.html.

Yang, Mayfair Mei-hui. *Gifts, Favors, and Banquets: The Art of Social Relationships in China*. Ithaca, NY: Cornell University Press, 1994.

Zaloom, Caitlin. *Out of the Pits: Traders and Technology from Chicago to London*. Chicago: University of Chicago Press, 2006.

Zhang Zhen. "Bodies in the Air: The Magic of Science and the Fate of the Early 'Martial Arts' Films in China." *Post Script* 20, nos. 2–3 (winter/spring-summer 2001): 43–60.

Zolberg, R. Aristide, and Long Litt Woon. "Why Islam Is Like Spanish: Cultural Incorporation in Europe and the United States." *Politics and Society* 27 (March 1999): 5–38.

Christianity: Chinese repression of, 127; class and caste in U.S. and India and, 37; colonialism and, 124; millenarianism and, 127; missionaries, 75, 125–27, 168n41; in Southeast Asian mountain borderlands, 124–27. *See also* Protestantism
citizenship, wagers as acts of, 57
civility, 70–78
civilization and civilizational analysis: al-Qaeda and, 64; Chinese concept of *wenming*, 68–69; civil society and, 76–78; Confucianism in China and, 68–69; European concept of, 69–70; Hindu narratives, 63, 68; historical essentialization vs. historical comparative analysis, 64–67; Huntington's *The Clash of Civilizations*, 63–64; Indian concept of Sankriti, 67–68; individualization and collective civilization, 151; mountainous areas and, 109–11, 112, 116–20; stranger problematic and, 63–70
civil society, 76–78, 135–36, 164n39
clan structure, Hsu on, 118
The Clash of Civilizations (Huntington), 63–64
class and the poor, 135–36, 139–40, 142–43
Clinton, Bill, 74–75
cognitive science, 42, 47
Cohn, Bernard, 2, 151
Cole, John, 112
collective good, 132
Collins, Randall, 64
commerce and trade: mountain peoples and, 108, 128–29; stranger problematic and, 70, 75–76; tea and opium commodities in India and China, 11–19; uncertainty of what others think and, 71–72
communication: civil society and, 77; local-global opposition and, 47; Protestant plain or sincere speech, 73–74; uncertainty in knowing what others think, 72
comparison: as geared for Western modernity, 147–48; of historical state-formation processes in India and China, 66–67; the incomparable and, 150;

meaning of, 11; in political science with large data sets, 30–31. *See also* anthropology, comparative advantage of
confession, 74–75
Confucianism, 63, 68–69, 93–94
Congress Party, India, 63, 94
consumption, 57–58, 101. *See also* market theories
contract theory, 72
Corbin, Alain, 132
corruption, movement against, 135–36
costly signal hypothesis, 43

Dalits, 36, 37, 139, 141, 145. *See also* untouchability and the poor
Daoguang emperor, 15
Dawood, 98
Dawoodi Bohras, 100
Dean, Kenneth, 26, 78, 164n39
Deleuze, Gilles, 152–53
Delhi: Akshardham Temple, 95, 101, 140–41; iconicity and iconoclasm in, 94–95
Deliège, Robert, 36
Deng Xiaoping, 69
Derrida, Jacques, 156n16
description, 2–3, 71
"Description and Comparison in Cultural Anthropology" (Goodenough), 2–3
description in anthropology, 26–27
de Swaan, Abram, 131–32
Detienne, Marcel, 156n23
de Waal, Frans, 42
dharmaraja-dharmapala (righteous king and protector of the law), 110
Dikötter, Frank, 16–17
Dirks, Nicholas, 166n16
diversity as social interaction issue, 61. *See also* stranger, problematic of
"dividual" persons, 152–53
drink taboos, 76
Dumézil, Georges, 2
Dumont, Louis, 34–36, 73, 118, 138–39, 166n16
Dungan rebellion, 120
Durkheim, Émile, 9–10, 38, 41, 57, 147, 148

East India Company, 13–14, 122
economic growth in China and India, 143

economic modeling: contract theory, 72; *homo economicus*, 151; rational choice in, 48, 153; universal, 29. *See also* market theories

economy: "formal" vs. "informal," 30, 48–49; money, transcendental value of, 53–58; "traditional" vs. "modern," 53–54; visibility and invisibility in, 54

Eisenstadt, S. N., 65

Elias, Norbert, 67, 70, 75–76, 76–77

Empson, William, 117

Engels, Friedrich, 1

Entzauberung (demystification), 56

essentialism: "civilization" and, 19, 64–67; comparative project and, 147, 148; cultural difference and, 5; Leach on Hsu and, 118; nationalist ideologies and, 149; "state" vs. "nonstate," 114; Western ethnocentrism and, 46. *See also* civilization and civilizational analysis

ethnic classifications, state-based, 119, 120, 127

ethnicity in mountainous areas. *See* mountain peoples of the Southeast Asian Mainland Massif

ethnocentrism: Hsu's theory of "positive ethnocentrism," 117; in social sciences, 28, 45–46. *See also* civilization and civilizational analysis; universal modeling

ethnographic method, 25, 33

Europe: civility of public appearance and behavior in, 76; civilization concept and, 63, 69–70; collectivization of care arrangements in, 131–32; immigration into, 61–62; Muslim exclusion in, 70, 78–79; public sphere, concept of, 133; religion and public sphere in, 77; secularization theory, 49–50

Europe and the People Without History (Wolf), 17–18

Evans-Pritchard, E. E., 50, 51, 117

evolutionary anthropology: biological interpretation of human society, 42–43; Chinese, 1–2; cognitive science and, 42; discrediting of, 2; religion and, 43–46

exoticization of mountain people, 121–24

Fei Xiaotong, 1–2, 117

fictive kinship, 131

fieldwork, 26

First Opium War, 15

Fiskesjö, Magnus, 115

food taboos, 76

Foucault, Michel, 151

fragmentary approach: conceptual interpretation and, 27; tea and opium in India and China, example of, 11–19; value of, 9, 25–27

Frank, Andre Gunder, 108

Freedman, Maurice, 118

Freud, Sigmund, 44–45

Friedman, Jonathan, 115

Fuller, Chris, 26, 141

Gandhi, Mohandas, 94

Ganesha worship, 99

Geertz, Clifford, 18, 26–27, 33–34, 70–71, 158n12

Gell, Alfred, 80

Gellner, Ernest, 38, 39, 50

generalism, 31, 34, 148

George III of the United Kingdom, 14

Ginzburg, Carlo, 151

globalization and area studies, 46–47

globalizing religions, 150

global managerial language, 151–52

Golden Triangle, 107–8, 126

Goodenough, Ward, 2–3

Goody, Jack, 32–33

"governmentality from below," 137

Granet, Marcel, 2

Green, Nile, 99

guanxi practices, 76

Gujarati Swaminarayanis, 140–41

gumlao model, 112–13

gumsa model, 113

Gupta, Dipankar, 38

Guthrie, Stewart, 45

Habermas, Jürgen, 55–56, 77, 140

habitus, theory of, 41–42

hallucination, 45–46

Han ethnicity: Bai minority and, 119; civilization and, 69, 109; evolutionary thinking and, 1; history of, 1–2; Hui

Muslims and, 69, 119; iconoclasm and, 85; the Miao and, 112, 113, 121; missionaries and, 126–27; mountain tourism and, 121; Putianese and, 7

Hanuman, 82, 83, 95, 99, 103

Harrell, Stevan, 120

Haskell, Thomas, 141–42

Hazare, Anna, 94, 135–36

Hegel, Georg Wilhelm, 36, 66

Heine, Steven, 45

Henrich, Joseph, 45

Herder, Johann Gottfried, 73

Hevia, James, 18

Hinduism: Akshardham Temple, Delhi, 95, 101, 140–41; anthropology, majoritarianism, and, 149; civilizational essentialism and, 66, 109; Ganesha worship, 99; Gujarati Swaminarayanis, 140–41; Hsu on, 118; inside-outside distinctions and, 133, 134; untouchability and, 145. *See also* India

Hindu nationalism: Ayodhya Mosque, destruction of, 40–41, 82–84; civilizational thinking in, 68; Delhi and, 95; Ganesha worship and, 99; Parry on, 11; Shiv Sena (Army of Shivaji), 98

Hirschkind, Charles, 45

Hirschman, Albert, 70

holism, anthropological, 9–10, 25, 27, 31, 33

Hollis, Martin, 50

Homo hierarchicus, 138–39

honors (*mariyatai*), circulation of, 53, 58

Hsu, Francis, 111, 117–19

Hui Muslims, 69, 119–20

Hume, David, 72

Huntington, Samuel, 30–31, 63–64

Iceland, 54

iconicity and iconoclasm: Ayodhya mosque destruction (North India) and, 82–84; in capitals of Beijing and Delhi, 92–95; Chazi Miyan as martyred warrior-saint and, 84–85; Chinese destruction campaigns, 85–88; comparison of India and China, 102; Master Yang relics (China) and, 87–88; representation of virtual reality and capacity for continued belief, 88–89; secular vs.

religious and, 81; "seeing is believing," "believing is seeing," and, 80; Shanghai, Mumbai, secular urbanity, and, 95–101; significance of, 80–81; urban planning and, 89–92; visibility, invisibility, and, 102

Ikegami, Eiko, 77–78

imaginative value of money, 57, 72

indentured labor. *See* slavery and indentured labor

India: Ayodhya Mosque, destruction of, 40–41, 82–84; Calcutta, waste management arguments in, 132–34; caste, class, and race, differences between, 34–38; Christian missionaries and ethnic identity in South India, 168n41; civil society and civility in, 78; consumer-citizens and circulation of money in, 57–58; Delhi, iconicity and iconoclasm in, 94–95; Dumont on, 34–36; economic growth in, 143; historical state-formation processes in China vs., 66–67; honors (*mariyatai*), circulation of, in South Asian temples, 53, 58; lunar calendar and astrology in, 101; market theory of religion and, 48; Muslim exclusion in, 63, 76, 78–79; public sphere, concept of, 133; separatism in Assam and Nagaland, 121–22; tea and opium in, 12, 15–16; urbanization in, 61–62, 144. *See also* Hinduism; Mumbai; poverty, sanitation, and care for the poor in India

"India against Corruption" movement, 135–36

individual identity, 73, 151–53

inequality, social and economic: American South, black-white opposition in, 36; egalitarianism in China contrasted with India, 142–43; India, caste, race, and class in, 34–38; rising, in China and India, 143–44; social sciences, critical distance, and, 33–34. *See also* poverty, sanitation, and care for the poor in India

Inglehart, Ronald, 30

inside-outside opposition, 133, 134–35, 140

Institute for Evolutionary Anthropology, Max Planck Society, Leipzig, 42

interactions, cultural, among and within societies, 27–28
international relations, civilizational theory in, 64
Ireland, 54

James, Henry, 134
Jamieson, R. A., 16
Jan Sangh, 41. *See also* Bharatiya Janata Party
Jardine, William, 15, 16
Jaspers, Karl, 65
Jeejeebhoy, Jamsethjee, 16
Jing'An Temple, Shanghai, 96
Joshi, Vibha, 125
journalism vs. anthropology, 10

the Kachin, 112–16, 125–26, 127
Kalam, Abdul, 140–41
Katzenstein, Peter, 31, 64
Kaviraj, Sudipta, 132–34, 140
Keane, Webb, 10, 73–74
Kemper, Steven, 57
Khun Sa (Chang Chi-Fu), 108
kinship, 110, 112, 131
Klinenberg, Eric, 10
Kohima, battle of, 124
Kosselleck, Reinhart, 55
Krugman, Paul, 30

language and mountain areas, 112, 113. *See also* translation
Latour, Bruno, 27, 89, 152
Leach, Edmund, 109–19, 122, 124, 129
Lee, Leo Ou-fan, 96
Lévi-Strauss, Claude, 69, 109, 112
Liang Yongjia, 119
Liénard, Pierre, 44–45
Liu, Lydia, 18
local-global opposition, 47
Luhrmann, Tanya, 45–46
Lukes, Steven, 50
lunar calendar, 101
Lutyens, Edward, 94

Macartney, Lord, 17–18
Madsen, Richard, 78, 143
magic, 75, 81, 101

Malinowski, Bronislaw, 117, 123
managerial language, global, 151–52
Mandate of Heaven, 68
Mao Zedong, 92–94, 97
market theories: Chinese religions and, 48, 52–53; discourse, interplay of visible and invisible in, 55–56; Durkheim's sociology of religion and, 57; enchanted capitalism, new forms of, 51–52; modernity and backwardness assumptions, 51–52; Poovey's "culture of finance," 51; rational choice theory and religion, 48–51; red, black, and gray markets, 48; transcendental value of money, 53–58; the wager and, 57–58
Marriott, McKim, 16, 152
Marx, Karl, 1, 57, 66
Marxism: on civil society, 78, 135; local-global opposition and, 47; Morgan and, 1; Other analysis, 108–9; the urban and, 90–91
Masonic Lodges, 55
Massumi, Brian, 153
Mauss, Marcel, 2, 10, 41–42, 45, 72, 148, 151
Max Planck Institute for Evolutionary Anthropology, Leipzig, 42
metaphysical nature of state and money, 54–55
methodological nationalism, 32
Meyer, Jeffrey F., 92
the Miao, 112, 121, 127
middleman role, 137
migration, internal vs. external, 61–62
millenarianism, 112, 127
Milner, Murray, 35
the Minjia (or Bai), 119
minorities. *See* mountain peoples of the Southeast Asian Mainland Massif
Mintz, Sidney, 13, 17
missionaries, 75, 125–27, 168n41
models, universal. *See* universal modeling
modernity: Chinese iconoclasm and, 93, 97; individual identity and, 73; religion, rationality assumptions, and, 51–52. *See also* Western modernity
money: imaginative value of, 57, 72; transcendental value of, 53–58. *See also* market theories

poverty, sanitation, and care for the poor in India: Boo's *Behind the Beautiful Forevers* and, 130; caste, class, and, 133, 138–40, 143; Chinese poverty alleviation compared to, 142–45; civil society vs. political society and, 135–36; European attitudes, 131–32; inside-outside opposition and, 133, 134–35, 140; Muslims and, 139, 145; participation of the poor in political society and, 136–38; public sphere and collective goods, 131–34; religion and, 140–41; responsibility, kinship, and emotion, 131; socially produced indifference, 130–31; untouchability and, 134, 141, 145; waste management in Calcutta, arguments on, 132–34; Western abolition of slavery compared to, 141–42

Powell, Enoch, 70

Prithviraj Chauhan Memorial (Qila Rai Pithora), 95

proselytization, Hsu on, 51

prostitution, 121

Protestant ethic, 56

Protestantism: Calvinist, 74–75; missionaries, 75, 125–27, 168n41; sincerity and uncertainty of what others think and, 72–75; transcendental and magical in, 75

Public Culture, 159n26

public sphere, 77, 131–34

Qianlong, Emperor, 14

Qi Gong, 48

Qila Rai Pithora (Prithviraj Chauhan Memorial), 95

quantitative analysis: administrative practices and, 39; nationalism and, 38–40; Poovey's "culture of finance" and, 51; of religion, 53; survey data set validity, critique of, 29–31, 39. *See also* universal modeling

race, 35–38

Radin, Paul, 45

Ramadan, Tariq, 77

Rao, Narayana, 34–35

Rappaport, Roy, 44

Rassiwala, Samoon, 100

rational choice theory, 47–51, 151, 153. *See also* market theories

Rawls, John, 77

Reagan, Ronald, 151

regional religions, 150

relativism, 33–34

religion: attitudes toward the poor and, 140–41; Boyer's standard cognitive model of, 43–44; Chinese religions and market theory, 48, 52–53; class and caste in India and United States and, 37; concept and translation of, 148; evolutionary anthropology and, 41–46; Geertz's definition of, 27; globalizing vs. regional, 150; historical essentialization of, 64–66; Huntington's *The Clash of Civilizations* and, 64; iconoclasm, religious, 82–89, 92–95; Luhrmann on experiences of God, 45–46; nationalism and "world religions," 150; in Netherlands, 49; rational choice, market theory, and, 48–51; sacred/nonsacred and religious/nonreligious, 81; Shanghai, restrictions in, 95–96; social emphasis in study of, 41; Washington, religious symbolism in, 92. *See also* Buddhism; Christianity; Hinduism; Muslims, exclusion of; Protestantism

"resistance," 36

"resource structuralism," 35

Ricci, Matteo, 68

Richards, I. A., 117

Riefenstahl, Leni, 124

ritual, 18, 44–45, 75

Rock, Joseph, 128

Rodriguez, Valerian, 134

Rousseau, Jean-Jacques, 72, 73

Sadan, Mandy, 115

Sahlins, Marshall, 17–18, 43

the Sani, 126

sanitation. *See* poverty, sanitation, and care for the poor in India

Sankriti (civilization), 67–68

Sarnath, 94

Sassoon, David, 15

Savarkar, V. D., 63

Scott, James, 33, 111, 112–16, 123, 126, 129

Searle, John, 156n16

www.ingramcontent.com/pod-product-compliance
Lightning Source LLC
Chambersburg PA
CBHW070330270326
41926CB00017B/3833

* 9 7 8 0 8 2 2 3 6 1 5 8 9 *